OFF THE BEATEN PATH® SERIES

T0007366

ELEVENTH EDITION

TENNESSEE

OFF THE BEATEN PATH®

DISCOVER YOUR FUN

JACKIE SHECKLER FINCH

Globe
Pequot

Guilford, Connecticut

All the information in this guidebook is subject to change. We recommend that you call ahead to obtain current information before traveling.

Globe Pequot

An imprint of The Rowman & Littlefield Publishing Group, Inc.
4501 Forbes Blvd., Ste. 200
Lanham, MD 20706
www.rowman.com

Distributed by NATIONAL BOOK NETWORK

British Library Cataloguing in Publication Information available

ISSN 1539-8102
ISBN 978-1-4930-4426-9 (paper : alk. paper)
ISBN 978-1-4930-4427-6 (electronic)

∞™ The paper used in this publication meets the minimum requirements of American National Standard for Information Sciences—Permanence of Paper for Printed Library Materials, ANSI/NISO Z39.48-1992.

To my parents, Jack and Margaret Poynter,
for instilling in me the desire to travel.
And to my first traveling buddies—my sisters:
Elaine Emmich, Jennifer Boyer, Juliette Maples, and Jeanine Clifford;
and my brothers: Jim Poynter and Joe Poynter.

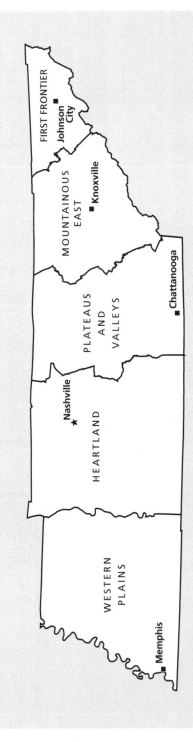

TENNESSEE

FIRST FRONTIER
Johnson
City ■

MOUNTAINOUS
EAST
Knoxville ■

PLATEAUS
AND
VALLEYS
Chattanooga ■

HEARTLAND
Nashville ★

WESTERN
PLAINS
Memphis ■

Contents

Acknowledgments

Many thanks to Tennessee residents, public relations officials, and business owners who took the time to help me update this book. Thanks especially to the folks at Tennessee Tourism who shared little nooks and crannies in this wonderfully diverse state. I'm grateful to my editor Sarah Parke, production editor Meredith Dias, and the friendly and professional staff at Globe Pequot.

My gratitude to my family for their encouragement: Kelly Rose; Sean Rose; Stefanie, Will, Trey, and Arianna Scott; and Logan Peters. And a special remembrance to my husband, Bill Finch, who taught me to value every day on this earth.

—Jackie Sheckler Finch

About the Author

An award-winning journalist, **Jackie Sheckler Finch** has covered a wide array of topics—from birth to death, with all the joy and sorrow in between. She has written for numerous publications and has been named the Mark Twain Travel Writer of the Year by the Midwest Travel Journalists Association a record five times, in 1998, 2001, 2003, 2007, and 2012. She has also won many photography awards. One of her greatest joys is taking to the road to find the fascinating people and places that wait over the hill and around the next bend.

Introduction

The word "Tennessee" conjures up many different images. To the lover of country music, Nashville comes to mind when Tennessee is mentioned. To the blues aficionado or the Elvis fan, it's Memphis. To whitewater buffs, it's more than likely the Ocoee River. To conservationists and outdoors lovers, it's probably the Great Smoky Mountains or West Tennessee's Reelfoot Lake. To football fans, it's definitely the University of Tennessee's Volunteers.

As with any state, Tennessee is many things to many people. It's a fun and funky state to explore. From the mountainous east to the delta plains of the Mississippi River in the west, the variety of natural and man-made wonders and attractions the state has to offer is awesome.

Once you drive along the back roads of this long and narrow state, you'll never again think of it in the same way. I'm here to help you do just that. In reality, it would take volumes to detail all that can be done and seen in Tennessee. However, in the book you now hold in your hands, I have narrowed your choices considerably by taking you off the interstates and onto the side roads, where the unique character of the state truly shines through.

My philosophy is important to understand here because I stayed true to it while writing this book. First of all, to me off the beaten path is more of an attitude than a place. I can enjoy something that's offbeat, funky, and unusual and consider it off the beaten path—even if it's on a major highway or in the middle of the city. Even though I may view it as off the beaten path, you may not. Don't worry; I'm sure we'll agree on something else.

Second, there are two types of people who will use this book: tourists and explorers. The tourists will bring home souvenirs; the explorers will bring home experiences. I'm an explorer, so don't expect too many stops at gift shops.

The state has a great highway system that is easy to follow, and while I won't be taking you down too many of the major highways, it is reassuring to know that they are usually nearby—in case you need to make a quick escape back to civilization.

As you drive along, look for signs that sport the image of the mockingbird, the state's official bird. They are mounted directly above the state highway designation numbers and signify that you are on a stretch of the 2,300 miles of the Tennessee Scenic Parkway System. Consisting primarily of two-lane roads, it connects the state's parks, major lakes, and historical sites, as well as this book's lesser-known attractions.

Along the way you'll definitely meet whittlers and collectors, and you might meet Dolly Parton. You'll meet ladies with hair higher than a church steeple. By the time you finish your journey, I'll have you floating on a lake 300 feet below the Earth's surface, playing miniature golf on the side of a mountain, cruising on a lake created by the strongest earthquake on record, and eating the world's sweetest-tasting, vilest-smelling vegetable.

Don't overlook some of the state's better-known tourist traps. Sometimes our trip down the less-traveled paths of Tennessee will intersect with the well-worn trails in order to highlight an event, an attraction, or a person worth visiting. I have found that sometimes it's worth fighting a crowd to see or do something that you'll probably never get a chance to see or do again.

Music is a big attraction as well as a big industry in Tennessee. From the birthplace of the blues in Memphis to the birthplace of the Grand Ole Opry in Nashville to the songs of the Appalachian mountain folk in East Tennessee, music is an important part of the heritage of our state.

Our tour will touch on much of that heritage and the people who have contributed to it. We'll visit the commercial monuments that honor Elvis Presley, Carl Perkins, Dolly Parton, and Loretta Lynn, among others. We'll also take a hike back into the woods to see the monument erected where Patsy Cline lost her life in a plane crash. We'll visit a museum honoring the best soul singers of the 1950s and 1960s, and we'll sit back and enjoy Sunday services at a Cowboy Church that passes a Stetson hat instead of the plate.

Southern hospitality is more than a myth in Tennessee, and our people may well be the state's friendliest attraction. There is one thing you'll never have to worry about as you travel through the state: You'll never truly be lost. Knock on any door or stop by any store, and chances are you'll get the directions you need, plus a whole lot more. Just when you think you've met the world's most colorful person, you'll meet one just a bit more fun. That's the way it is in Tennessee.

The state is full of crossroad communities with colorful and descriptive names. Usually the community has little more to offer than a gas station–general store combination, but here's where you'll usually find the most intriguing characters of the area.

In the summer these folks will be sitting on the porch of that store solving the world's problems. In the winter you'll find them sitting around the potbellied stove. There are more than 100 such communities with colorful names around the state, including Fly, New Flys Village, Defeated Creek, Ugly Creek, Pretty Creek, Dull, Soddy Daisy, Bell Buckle, Gilt Edge, Finger, Frogjump, Nutbush, Bucksnort, Only, Who'd A Thought It, and Skullbone.

This book has been broken down into five major areas:

The First Frontier. More than 200 years ago, this part of the state was America's new frontier. Explorers, including Daniel Boone, blazed paths across the Appalachian Mountains, establishing some of the first settlements outside the original 13 colonies.

Much of the area is heavily forested, with the extreme east and southeast parts quite mountainous. Davy Crockett was born here, and the state of Franklin, which never quite made it to statehood, was formed here several years before Tennessee became a state.

The Mountainous East. As the name implies, this area is probably the most rugged of all Tennessee terrain. The 500,000-acre Great Smoky Mountains National Park and its foothill communities provide beauty incomparable to what you'll find elsewhere in the southeast US.

Throughout the area, several museums have dedicated their collections and grounds to the preservation of mountain life, and many communities have preserved that lifestyle by their very existence.

Plateaus & Valleys. Forested and rugged, the Cumberland Plateau rises like a gigantic wall that spans the width of the state, forming the western boundary of the Tennessee Valley.

Although relatively flat, the area has many spectacular streams that have carved out deep gorges in the sandstone, making it one of the best areas in the state for whitewater enthusiasts. In fact, the 1996 Olympic Games whitewater events took place here.

The Heartland. Also known as Middle Tennessee, the area is a region of gently rolling hills, sloping green meadows, and miles of river and lake frontage.

At the heart of the area lies Nashville, "Music City," the home of the Grand Ole Opry. Musical attractions are popular in this area, as are Tennessee walking horse farms, sour mash whiskey distilleries, and the homes of two US presidents.

The Western Plains. An area of fertile bottomlands and dense hardwood forests, the Western Plains region is bordered on the east by the Tennessee River and on the west by the Mississippi.

A few of the state's most colorful folk heroes—frontiersman Davy Crockett, train engineer Casey Jones, and *Walking Tall* sheriff Buford Pusser—have strong roots here, as do *Roots* author Alex Haley and the King of Rock 'n' Roll, Elvis Presley.

The 520-mile-long state is divided into seven telephone area codes, 423, 731, 865, 901, 931, 629, and 615; about half of it lies in the Eastern Time zone and half in the Central zone.

Although care has been taken to ensure accuracy in all listings in this book, visitors are advised to call ahead before traveling any great distance. Life throughout Tennessee is slow-paced and mellow, so if a day appears to be going a bit slow, it isn't uncommon for a proprietor to close early and go fishing. Phone numbers, websites, and admission prices have been included in listings where appropriate.

Most of the attractions are open on a year-round basis, but some cut operations a bit during the winter months.

Before venturing forth, you may want to contact the state tourism bureau and load up on brochures and maps of the areas you plan on visiting. In the material you receive from the state, there will be a list of local tourism bureaus that will be able to provide even more specific information.

Contact the ***Tennessee Department of Tourist Development*** (Wm. Snodgrass/Tennessee Tower, 312 Rosa L. Parks Ave., Nashville, TN 37243; 615-741-2159; tnvacation.com).

Tennessee State Symbols

- **Bird:** Mockingbird
- **Insects, two of them:** Firefly and ladybug
- **Gem:** Tennessee river pearls
- **Tree:** Tulip poplar
- **Rock:** Limestone
- **Wildflower:** Passion flower
- **Flower:** Iris
- **Songs, five of them:** "My Homeland, Tennessee," "When It's Iris Time in Tennessee," "My Tennessee," "Tennessee Waltz," and "Rocky Top"
- **Animal:** Raccoon
- **Amphibian:** Tennessee cave salamander
- **Reptile:** Box turtle
- **Butterfly:** Zebra swallowtail

Bed-and-Breakfast Inns

Bed-and-breakfast inns can be found throughout the state. Many are listed in this book. Here are two contacts to call for information on more locations:

- **Natchez Trace Bed & Breakfast Reservation Service** (615-522-4865; natcheztracetravel.com) provides information on lodging along the Natchez Trace Parkway

- **Bed and Breakfast Association of Tennessee** (865-376-0113; tennessee-inns.com)

SELECTED TOURISM WEBSITES & TELEPHONE NUMBERS

Chattanooga
(800) 322-3344
chattanoogafun.com

Cherokee National Forest
(877) 692-6050
fs.usda.gov/cherokee

Gatlinburg
(800) 588-1817
gatlinburg.com

Historic Rugby
(423) 628-2441
historicrugby.org

Knoxville
(865) 523-7263
visitknoxville.com

Maury County Convention & Visitors Bureau
(888) 852-1860
visitmaury.com

Memphis
(901) 543-5300
memphistravel.com

Nashville
(800) 657-6910
visitmusiccity.com

Northeast Tennessee Tourism Association
(423) 262-0238
northeasttennessee.org

Pigeon Forge
(865) 453-8574
mypigeonforge.com

Smoky Mountains and Townsend Tourism
(800) 525-6834
smokymountains.org

Southwest Tennessee Tourism Association
(731) 616-7474
visitswtenn.com

State of Tennessee Tourism
(615) 741-2159
tnvacation.com

Tennessee Department of Environment and Conservation
(888) 891-8332
tn.gov/environment

Tennessee Farm Winegrowers Association
tennesseewines.com

Tennessee Overhill Heritage Association
(423) 263-7232
tennesseeoverhill.com

Tennessee State Parks
(615) 532-0001
tnstateparks.com

Upper Cumberland Tourism Association
(931) 537-6347
uppercumberland.org

The First Frontier

Corner of the Frontier

Bristol is about as far north as one can go in the state and stay in Tennessee. In fact, about half the city is in Virginia. The state line runs down the middle of State Street in the heart of the downtown shopping district. But other than the small state markers embedded in the street between the double yellow lines, there's little evidence that the city has two mayors, two city councils, and two telephone area codes.

A big, old-fashioned neon sign forms an archway across State Street, near Randall Street, and proclaims Bristol is a good place to live. It was erected in 1910 as a symbol of unity between the two Bristols. Arrows point to the Tennessee and Virginia sides.

Although Nashville, about 300 miles to the west, gets credit for being the center of country music, it was here in Bristol that the **Carter Family** and **Jimmie Rodgers** recorded the first country-and-western music that was distributed nationwide. That recording took place on August 2, 1927, and put the area on the musical map. A monument honoring those musical pioneers stands at Edgemont Avenue and State Street. Farther

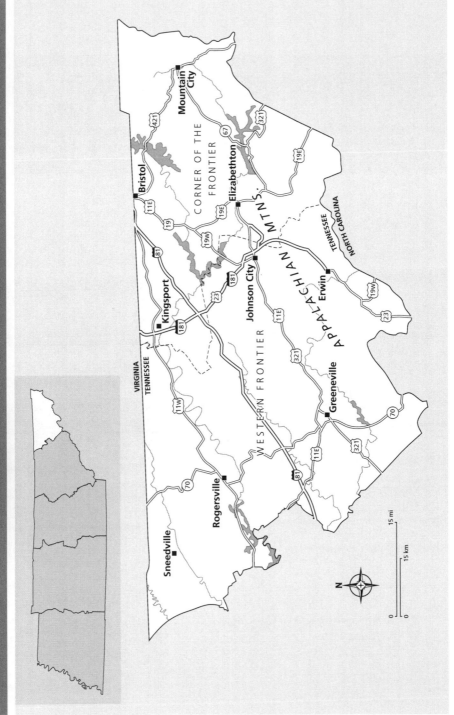

down State Street, a large mural on the side of a building presents a visual memorial to that event.

The performing arts are alive and well in Bristol at the historic **Paramount Center for the Arts** (518 State St.; 423-274-8920; paramountbristol.org). It's a circa 1931 theater restored to its original art deco style and is now listed on the National Register of Historic Places. Theatre Bristol calls the Paramount home for its own productions, and the venue is the site of other touring shows and concerts, as well as local meetings and seminars. It's a great place to watch a show.

Tennessee Ernie Ford was born Ernest Jennings Ford on February 13, 1919, in Bristol, and before he became the booming voice behind many hit country songs, including "Sixteen Tons," "The Shot Gun Boogie," and "Mule Train," he was a radio staff announcer and a bombardier during World War II. He earned the nickname "The Ol' Pea-Picker" due to his catchphrase, "Bless your pea-pickin' heart," which he began using during his disc jockey days on KXLA in Pasadena, California. He was elected to the Country Music Hall of Fame in 1990 and died in October 1991.

Today the house where Ernie Ford was born has opened as a lasting memorial to the city's favorite son. Located at 1223 Anderson Street, the home is garnished with memorabilia of his long musical and television career. The home isn't open on a regular basis; contact the **Bristol CVB** (423-989-4850; bristolchamber.com) for hours and more information.

If you feel like stepping over the state line, visit the **Birthplace of Country Music Museum** (101 Country Music Way; 423-573-1927; birthplaceofcountry music.org) in Bristol, Virginia. Opened on August 1, 2014, the museum is an affiliate of the Smithsonian Institution and houses interesting artifacts related to the famous 1927 Bristol Sessions. Just two months after Charles Lindbergh made the first flight across the Atlantic in his *Spirit of St. Louis*, record producer Ralph Peer was conducting important recording sessions that would preserve the precious music of Bristol—both Tennessee and Virginia—for posterity. During those sessions, Peer recorded 19 performers (or groups of performers) doing 76 songs. Considered the "Big Bang" of modern country music, the Bristol Sessions were once described by Johnny Cash as "The most important event in the history of country music."

The museum also features special exhibits and has a performance theater, radio station, learning center, and museum store. Since 2012, the museum has hosted the Bristol Rhythm & Roots Reunion during the third weekend in September. The festival usually hosts more than 130 bands on 20 stages in downtown Bristol.

AUTHOR'S TOP TEN PICKS

Appalachian Fair	Kissing Bridge
Archie Campbell Days	Tennessee Ernie Ford Home
Bays Mountain Park	Tennessee Wilderness Road
Cooper's Gem Mine	Trade Days
Heritage Days (Rogersville)	Unicoi County Heritage Museum

Race fans head to **Bristol Motor Speedway** (866-415-4158; bristolmotor speedway.com) to watch the cars go round and round. Constructed in 1960, the speedway held its first NASCAR race on July 30, 1961, and is one of the most popular NASCAR tracks because of its two-pit road, terrific steep banking, all-concrete surface, and stadium-like seating. If noise helps add to the thrill, Bristol Motor Speedway has been named one of the loudest NASCAR tracks.

Southwest of Bristol, Johnson County is surrounded by the hills of the Appalachian Mountains, and the businesses and attractions reflect that way of life quite nicely. Throughout the county you'll see small handwritten signs hanging from mailboxes advertising handmade quilts or birdhouses for sale.

In **Mountain City**, about the only thing you won't find are crowds. Within a few-block area of the downtown section, you'll come across numerous antiques and gift shops selling a variety of neat things.

A great place to start your East Tennessee mountain trek is at the **Johnson County Welcome Center & Museum**, located at 716 S. Shady St. on US 421 in Mountain City. In addition to maps, brochures, and great stories from the attendants, there's a historical museum with a large selection of Native American and pioneer artifacts. One of the coolest exhibits is Jessie Murphy's wedding gown. Jessie married Robert Ferdinand Wright on June 7, 1905, in Mountain City. Along with the dress are her shoes and pictures of the church and wedding party. The center is open 8:30 a.m. to 5 p.m. daily year-round, weather permitting. For information call (423) 727-5800, or log on to johnsoncountytn.gov.

South of Mountain City on US 421 is **Trade**, the oldest unincorporated community in the state. It's the spot where, in 1673, the first English-speaking white man set foot on Tennessee soil. Situated on an old buffalo trail, the community flourished as a resting place for those traveling the three major paths through the wilderness that crossed at this point.

By the 1790s the area had a country store, a post office, a blacksmith shop, and a handful of cabins, and today it's about as low-key as it was then—no big signs and no souvenir shops. ***Trade Days*** are held each June, when the entire county comes out to celebrate the heritage of the area.

Wilderness Road, one of the three major paths that converged at Trade, continues through East Tennessee to Cumberland Gap, where it heads northward into Kentucky and on to the "Great American West." Today the ***Tennessee Wilderness Road*** tour follows as closely as possible the original trail of the pioneers. The leisurely drive along the path takes you through a landscape of spectacular valleys dotted with church spires, old towns, and, if you take the time to explore on your own, plenty of unique experiences. Use the designated roads as your main route, but don't hesitate to follow a few side roads now and then to experience even more. There is also a full-color brochure and map, America's First Frontier tour, available for this part of the state. For more information contact the ***Northeast Tennessee Tourism Association*** (423-262-0238; northeasttennesse.org).

In ***Kingsport*** early travelers through the area exchanged their Virginia currency for Tennessee money at a stagecoach stop known as the ***Exchange Place*** (423-288-6071; exchangeplace.info). Today the small farm-like village and crafts center is open Sat and Sun May through mid-Oct. Admission is free during regular events. A small admission is charged for festivals and other special events. The ***Fall Folk Arts Festival*** and an open-house celebration take place during the last weekend of September. There are a lot of really neat traditional Christmas events here as well, including a Yule log burning. The village is located just off US 11W at 4812 Orebank Rd.

Unlikely as it may seem, a major US boatyard was in operation along the Holston River in Kingsport in 1802. William King's boatyard had a reputation for quality that stretched as far as New Orleans. On the hill across the stagecoach road from the yards was the always busy ***Netherland Inn*** (423-765-0937; thenetherlandinn.com), an inn and tavern where the likes of the state's three presidents, Andrew Jackson, Andrew Johnson, and James K. Polk, whiled away hours with their friends. The inn has been restored and is open to the public as a museum. Several other buildings on the property, including a shop and wagon shelter, have also been restored. A log cabin that was moved here from Virginia and served as Daniel Boone's home from 1773 to 1775 is now a children's museum; it is a must if there are any small travelers with you. Start your visit at the Log Cabin Visitors Center and Gift Shop, located behind the inn at 2144 Netherland Inn Rd. The former boatyards are now a city park that stretches for miles down the river. Open weekends only from 2 p.m. to 5 p.m. May through Oct. Admission is charged.

Within the city limits of Kingsport, tucked away between Holston River Mountain and Bays Ridge, is the secluded and tranquil ***Bays Mountain Park***

(423-229-9447; baysmountain.com). The 3,550-acre city-owned facility has a wildlife park, a planetarium, a wildlife tour on the 44-acre lake, a natural history museum, 38 miles of hiking trails, an Adventure Ropes Course complete with a 300-foot zip line, and the unique *Harry Steadman Mountain Heritage Farmstead Museum.*

The museum contains a collection of old tools and implements the founders of the area used in their daily lives. Donated by local families, the museum's collection gives a glimpse into the difficult challenges faced by the early pioneers. In the park, there's an unusual gray wolf habitat and a snake habitat.

yumyum

The first *Cracker Barrel Old Country Store and Restaurant* opened in Lebanon on September 19, 1969, and there are now 645 stores in 44 states, with 50 of those in our own state. That means you're never far from a great plate of country cookin'!

The park is a great way to spend a quiet, laid-back afternoon away from the crowds usually associated with natural parks of this size. The park is located 3 miles off I-181 at 853 Bays Mountain Road, and it is open daily year-round. Check the website for current hours. Their entrance fee is $5 per car.

The city fathers of *Blountville* say that there are more original log houses along their city's main street than in any other town in the state. Whether that's true or not, there are a great many vintage buildings to see here. One of those, *The Deery Inn*, played an important part in the frontier era of this part of the state. Built during the late 1700s, the building is actually three structures: a 2-story hewn-log house, a 3-story cut-stone house, and a 2-story frame structure, all built adjacent to one another and joined together. Now known as the *Deery Inn Museum*, it offers group tours. Contact the museum at (423) 323-4660, or visit historicsullivan.com/tourism_deeryinn/html.

Everyone gets a chance to relive the old panning days when they stop by *Cooper's Gem Mine* (1138 Big Hollow Rd.; 423-323-5680; coopersgemmine .com). Here you can buy a bucket of ore starting at $7 and take it out back to the stream, step up to the flume, wash away the sand and dirt, and what you find, you can keep! The shop is open year-round and sells specialty crafts and jewelry; the sluice is usually open Mar through Oct. Closed Sun.

A walking-tour map of Blountville is available, and most of the buildings are decorated and open to the public around Christmas.

Perhaps one of the most historically significant structures in the state is *Rocky Mount*, a 2-story log cabin in *Piney Flats* near Johnson City. Built in 1770, Rocky Mount is the oldest original territorial capitol in the US and one of the oldest buildings in the state.

It was the capitol of "The Territory of the United States south of the river Ohio" from 1790 until a new capitol was built in Knoxville. With 2 stories and 9 rooms, pine paneling, and real glass windows, the structure was a mansion by frontier standards, and it quickly became a gathering place for people across the entire frontier.

Today the house is open to the public, as is the adjoining ***Overmountain Museum*** (888-538-1791; rockymountmuseum.com), which shows the early life of the area. First-person interpretation provides visitors with a true sense of what was taking place in 1791. Guides talk with you as they would have in that year and stay in character for your entire visit. The museum is on US 11E and open Tues through Sat, Mar through mid-Dec. Admission is $10 for adults, $8 for senior citizens, and $5 for children.

Sycamore Shoals (1651 W. Elk Ave; 423-543-5808; sycamoreshoalstn.org) in ***Elizabethton*** was the first permanent settlement outside the 13 colonies and was a muster point for the Overmountain Men on their way to the battle of King's Mountain. Today it is a State Historic Area and offers a reconstructed Fort Watauga that interprets the role this area played in the early settlement of what is now Tennessee and in the expansion of America's western boundary. An outdoor drama, *Liberty! The Saga of Sycamore Shoals*, and is presented in July in the Fort Watauga Amphitheater. An interpretive museum tells the story of the area through three-dimensional interactive exhibits. Open year-round with free admission, the museum also has a theater with a film.

OTHER ATTRACTIONS WORTH SEEING

Bristol Caverns
Bristol
(423) 878-2011
bristolcaverns.com

Dickson-Williams Mansion
Greeneville
(423) 787-7746
Mainstreetgreeneville.org

Farmhouse Gallery & Gardens
Unicoi
(423) 743-5963

Hands-On! Discovery Center
Gray
(423) 434-4263
visithandson.org

Museum of Ancient Brick
Johnson City
(423) 282-4661
generalshale.com

Tipton-Haynes State Historic Site
Johnson City
(423) 926-3631
tipton-haynes.org

Wetlands Water Park
Jonesborough
(423) 753-1553
wetlandsjonesborough.com

There are three hiking trails ranging from easy to moderate in the park's 45 acres, and there are several boat launch ramps for the lake. Beautifully shaded and peaceful, this is truly an off-the-beaten-path mixture of history and recreation.

One of the state's remaining original covered bridges crosses the Doe River in downtown Elizabethton and is the focal point for the city's riverside park. Built in 1882, *The Elizabethton Covered Bridge* (423-547-3850; Elizabethton .org) is the oldest such structure in the state. The *Covered Bridge Celebration* takes place in June. Activities include concerts, crafts show, antique car show, and kids' games and contests.

For many years, a tall Fraser fir tree on Elk Street near downtown Elizabethton was considered the tallest such tree in the world. Then the gloomy day came when officials found it was only the second tallest. But since the tallest is never decorated at Christmas, they now decorate the fir in Elizabethton, making it the tallest decorated Fraser fir in the world. While you are in the area, pick up a free walking tour map of downtown Elizabethton; there are some great buildings here. Maps are available at the Elizabethton/Carter County Chamber of Commerce at 500 Veterans Memorial Parkway (423-547-3850; elizabethton chamber.com).

About 20 miles southeast of Elizabethton at 527 Route 143 is *Roan Mountain State Park* (423-547-3900; tnstateparks.com/parks/roan-mountain). The park itself lies at the foot of Roan Mountain, one of the highest peaks (6,285 feet) in the eastern US, but that's not what makes this park so special. On the side of that mountain is one of the largest rhododendron gardens in the country. More than 600 acres of color bloom each June, making the area a striking display of pinks and purples. The *Rhododendron Festival*, held in mid-June, features native arts and crafts, mountain music and dancing, local food festivals, and wildlife tours. The park is also the best place in the area to view fall foliage. A campground and cabins offer overnighters grand vistas of the mountains.

Walking and hiking trails line the mountain with numerous scenic overlooks. The *Dave Miller Homestead* (800-250-8620), a preserved farm, is tucked in a hollow atop Strawberry Mountain. The Miller family first settled in the area around 1870 and for generations lived in virtual seclusion. Today the farm is preserved intact and serves as a model of early Appalachian life. The park is open year-round; the homestead is open 9 a.m. to 5 p.m. Wed through Sun Memorial Day to Labor Day and weekends in Oct. Admission is free.

Farther down US 321 toward *Johnson City* at 2313 Elizabethton Hwy. is the *Sinking Creek Baptist Church* (423-928-3222; sinkingcreek.org), the oldest church congregation in the state, having been established in 1773. Next to its new church building, built in the 1960s, is the congregation's former place of worship, a log church built in 1783. It has been renovated, but many of the logs are from the original church. Occasionally the old log church is host to weddings and Sunday and Wednesday services. Reece Harris, pastor of the congregation for 51 years, once told me that the sight of the log church provokes "a sense of pride knowing that Christians have been on this creek bank for a long time."

Johnson City resident John Tipton was a participant at the 1776 Constitutional Convention, and today the home he built in 1784 is a significant piece of restored history. At the ***Tipton-Haynes State Historic Site*** (2620 S. Roan St; 423-926-3631; tipton-haynes.org), 10 original and restored buildings still stand on the property. A cave and a spring here were resting places for the early white explorers, and it is believed that Daniel Boone set up a hunting camp near the spring. The cave can be visited today. The site is open year-round.

> ## agreatname
>
> The name "Tennessee" originated from the old Yuchi Indian word *tana-see,* meaning "the meeting place." White men traveling the area in the 1700s associated the word with the name of a Cherokee village and as the name of a river in Cherokee Territory.

While walking through Johnson City, notice the great brick sculptures, created by Johnny Hagerman, a brick sculptor for General Shale Brick. The company, headquartered here, has plants throughout the South and Midwest and is the nation's leading brick maker.

South of I-81, on Highway 36 headed toward Johnson City, is the little community of ***Boone's Creek***. Daniel Boone loved this area, and he came back often to hunt. On one of his trips he brought along William Bean, who liked the area so much he decided to settle his family here in 1769, thus making them the first permanent white settlers in Tennessee. He built his first cabin on the site of Boone's hunting camp next to Boone's Creek. A monument now marks that spot.

Check the schedule to attend services at ***Boone's Creek Christian Church*** (305 Christian Church Rd.; 423-282-0248; boonescreekcc.org). ***The Sounds of Boone's Creek Museum and Opry*** (525 W. Oakland Ave., Ste. 1; 423-461-0151; boonescreekhistoricaltrust.org) shares local artifacts and sounds from Tennessee's oldest community. The museum is open 10 a.m. to 6 p.m. Tues through Sat. The museum is staffed by volunteers, so call ahead to make sure it is open. Saturday evening is Opry night with a local featured musician, followed by an open mic.

Out on Old Gray Station Road, off Highway 36, is a small waterfall that Boone once hid under to escape the Indians. The waterfall has eroded over time, but you can still see it right after you turn onto Old Gray Station Road. Approximately 2 miles farther down the road, you'll find a historic marker showing where Boone carved his own monument into a beech tree: D. BOON CILLED A BAR in 1760. The tree is now dead, but a short walk off the highway will take you to the spot, which is fenced in.

Western Frontier

The Unicoi County seat community of *Erwin* probably holds the distinction of being the only town ever to put an elephant on trial for murder, find it guilty, and carry out the death penalty.

"Murderous Mary," a circus elephant who trampled her owner to death, was hanged from a railroad derrick before 5,000 spectators in 1916. Newspaper clippings and photos of that event are but a few of the interesting items in the **Unicoi County Heritage Museum** (423-743-9449), housed in a century-old home on the grounds of the **National Fish Hatchery** (529 Federal Hatchery Rd.; 423-743-4712).

The hatchery was established in 1894, and the 10-room superintendent's residence was constructed in 1903. By the early 1980s the house wasn't being used by the superintendent, so the federal government signed an agreement allowing the county to use it as a museum. In addition to the story of Murderous Mary, various displays highlight local pottery production and the history of local railroading. On the second floor is a replica of the city's Main Street as it looked a century ago. "Grandmother's Attic" holds a collection of quilts, antique dolls, and children's toys, all displayed as they might be in your own grandma's attic.

Outside, the fish hatchery is still in operation and produces about 10 million rainbow trout eggs each year. Free tours are available at the hatchery as well as at the museum. Bring your lunch; the entire area is a beautiful parklike setting, complete with a picnic pavilion and restrooms.

A fun event to catch in Erwin each fall is the **Apple Festival** (423-743-3000), held the first full weekend in October. There is continuous music, dancing, handmade crafts, the famous **Blue Ridge Pottery Club Show and Sale**, and various local food vendors.

The 16 counties that now make up the eastern tip of Tennessee were at one time united in an effort to become a state by themselves. The framework for the would-be state of Franklin was set when about 30,000 white settlers

TOP ANNUAL EVENTS

JUNE

Covered Bridge Celebration
Elizabethton
(423) 547-3850
elizabethtonchamber.com

Rhododendron Festival
Roan Mountain State Park
(423) 547-3900

JULY

Liberty! The Saga of Sycamore Shoals Outdoor Drama
Elizabethton
(423) 543-5808

Uncle Dave Macon Days
Murfreesboro
(800) 716-7560
uncledavemacondays.com

SEPTEMBER

Fall Folk Arts Festival
Kingsport
(423) 288-6071
exchangeplace.info/

OCTOBER

Apple Festival
Erwin
(423) 743-3000
unicoicounty.org

Heritage Days
Rogersville
(423) 272-1961
rogersvilleheritage.org

National Storytelling Festival
Jonesborough
(800) 952-8392
storytellingcenter.net

crossed the Appalachian Mountains and founded several settlements in this area, which was a part of North Carolina at the time.

Leaders met in *Jonesborough* and created a bill of rights for their new state and requested that the lawmakers of North Carolina allow its creation. They refused, but Franklin, under the leadership of John Sevier, continued the battle for several years, until 1788. Several skirmishes between Franklin and North Carolina militia took place in the area.

Although never recognized as an official state, Franklin operated like a sovereign government with an assembly, administered justice, and negotiated treaties with Native Americans.

Eight years after the fight for the quasi state ended, Sevier became the first governor of the state of Tennessee, which incorporated the former boundaries of Franklin. Jonesborough, chartered in 1779, seventeen years before there was a Tennessee, holds the distinction of being the oldest incorporated area in the state. And thanks to an ambitious restoration effort, much of the city appears as it did more than a century ago. Jonesborough was the first Tennessee town placed on the National Register of Historic Places.

There are more than 27 points of interest on the walking tour map of the historic downtown area, including the historic **Chester Inn Museum** (116 W. Main St.; 423-753-4580; storytellingcenter.net), where a young Andrew Jackson stayed while working on his law degree in 1788. Now owned by the state of Tennessee, the inn is a museum and houses the **International Storytelling Foundation**. A gift shop on the first floor offers a wide variety of storytelling tools, including books and tapes.

Many of the old buildings along the main streets now house a wide array of specialty shops. One particular structure, the **Old Town Hall** (144 E. Main St.; 423-753-2095), was restored in 1982 and contains about 50 crafts-oriented shops.

The **Hawley House** (114 E. Woodrow Ave., Lot #1; 423-753-8869; hawleyhouse.com) is the oldest house in the state's oldest town. Built in 1793, the house now offers the **Hawley House Butterfly Cottage**, which was constructed from a Southern Living Cottage plan. The one-bedroom cottage offers a kitchenette with breakfast foods provided. Rocking chairs on the front porch overlook Hawley House grounds. Prices start at $135.

The **Jonesborough Washington County History Museum** (423-753-9580; jonesborough.com) is inside the visitor center at 117 Boone St. and a good place to begin your visit to this historic area. Brochures, maps, and a short film will get you started in the right direction. The museum is open Mon through Sat.

There are two great festivals in town you won't want to miss. An old-fashioned, family-oriented July 4 celebration known as **Historic Jonesborough Days** features arts and crafts, southern cooking, and clogging. In early October, the **National Storytelling Festival** is a celebration of the country's top storytellers. Call (423) 753-2171 or (800) 952-8392; their website is storytelling center.net. For information about Historic Jonesborough Days, contact the Jonesborough Visitors Center at jonesborough.com or (866) 401-4223.

If you're in this part of the state during late Aug, be sure to visit the **Appalachian Fair** (423-477-3211; appalachianfair.com), which is held at the fairgrounds in Gray. This 6-day event is the largest fair in East Tennessee. There are all kinds of live Appalachian crafts demonstrations, farm and home exhibits, and various agricultural exhibits and competitions. This is truly an old-time country fair, complete with demolition derbies, mud drag racing, baby shows, baking contests, and top-name country music entertainment.

Contrary to the myth promoted by Walt Disney, Davy Crockett was not born on a mountaintop in Tennessee; he was born along the banks of the Nolichucky River, near the mouth of Limestone Creek. Today that birth spot, just outside the small community of Limestone, is preserved as the **Davy**

The Bad-Shot President

Once, a long time ago, a small crowd of onlookers followed a fiery lawyer named Andrew Jackson from a courtroom in Jonesborough to a nearby meadow, where Jackson and his opponent, attorney Waightstill Avery, squared off, and a duel began.

Crack! A pistol shot rang out. Crack! Another shot.

Yet both men still stood, unharmed. Each dueler, it seems, had fired into the air, and a deadly conclusion was avoided. Moments later, the two adversaries shook hands.

Jackson went on to become the seventh president of the US.

Crockett Birthplace State Historic Park (423-257-2167; tnstateparks.com/parks/david-crockett-birthplace).

Born in 1786, David (he never signed his name Davy) went on to become the "King of the Wild Frontier." His name and legend can rightfully be claimed by many areas in the state. He was born here in the east, he ran a gristmill in middle Tennessee, and he was elected to Congress from western Tennessee.

But here is where it all began. A reproduction of his birthplace cabin has been constructed, with the cornerstone of his original cabin on display. Probably the most unusual aspect of this park is the monument erected in the late 1960s by a local civic organization. In honor of Crockett's stature as a national hero, each of the 50 states is represented in the wall of the monument. Stones native to each state are incorporated in the wall and engraved with the respective state's name.

The park, located off US 11E at 1245 Davy Crockett Park Rd., has a campground, swimming pool, picnic facilities, and a visitor center. Open year-round.

Fifteen minutes down US 321 is the county seat city of ***Greeneville***, which happens to be the only Greeneville in the US that uses that third "e" in its name.

It was to this city that an 18-year-old boy moved in 1826 to establish a tailor business for himself. Several years later that boy, Andrew Johnson, became the country's 17th president. Today Johnson's Greeneville years are highlighted at the ***Andrew Johnson National Historic Site*** (423-638-3551; nps.gov/anjo), in the downtown section. His small tailor shop has been preserved and is inside the site's visitor center. Across the street is the brick home in which Johnson lived from the early 1830s to 1851. On Main Street is the Homestead, his home from 1851 to 1875, during which time he was vice president and then president of the US. The cemetery where he and his family are buried is a few blocks away. All four attractions are open every day except Christmas, Thanksgiving, and New Year's Day. The visitor center is located at the corner of College and Depot Streets. The visitor center and Homestead are free.

A walking tour map of Greeneville is available that highlights 36 historic areas or structures of the community.

Greeneville's **Tusculum University** (423-636-7300; tusculum.edu), founded in 1794, is the oldest college south of the Ohio River and west of the Allegheny Mountains. It was the 28th college founded in America, is the oldest college in the state, and is the oldest coed college associated with the Presbyterian Church. Eight buildings on the campus were constructed between 1841 and 1928 and make up the college's historic district. A walking tour of the campus is included in the city's walking tour brochure.

The college's **Andrew Johnson Library and Museum** (423-636-7300) is the state's largest presidential library and houses a great many of the president's books, papers, and manuscripts, as well as those of his family. In addition, the library houses almost 200 original Civil War–era newspapers from throughout the country.

tennesseetrivia

The nation's 17th president was laid to rest on a high hill known as Monument Hill in Greeneville. President Andrew Johnson was buried with his beloved American flag and his personal copy of the US Constitution.

At 3265 E. Andrew Johnson Hwy., look for **Pal's Sudden Service** (pals web.com) drive-through restaurant. You can't miss any of the 21 Pal's drive-thrus, all of which are located in East Tennessee and southwestern Virginia. While the restaurants probably don't stand out if you see them every day, those of us from outside the area should surely appreciate the unique architecture.

In fact, each location is vernacular architecture at its finest. There is no doubt what the restaurant sells: Huge hot dogs, fries, hamburgers, and soft drink containers bedeck each of the little square buildings. Colorful and fun, the buildings stand out from the urban clutter. The food and service are pretty good, too.

Tennessee's first newspaper was printed in **Rogersville** in 1791, and to celebrate that fact, the **Tennessee Newspaper & Printing Museum** (401 S. Depot St.; 423-272-1961; rogersvilleheritage.org) has been established in the city's old railroad depot, just down the street from the **Hale Springs Inn** at 415 S. Depot St.

Most of the old structures in downtown **Rogersville** have been restored, and the entire district is listed on the National Register of Historic Places. A walking tour of the historic district includes the **Hawkins County Courthouse**. Erected in 1836, the building is the oldest original courthouse still in use in the state. You can view the entire walking tour, including information on each site, online at rogersvilleheritage.org.

Most of the Main Street retail businesses now sell antiques or crafts, but there are still a few old-time offices and clothing stores along the way.

There's a fascinating natural phenomenon a few miles outside Rogersville on Ebbing & Flowing Spring Road that you won't want to miss. The **Ebbing & Flowing Spring** is one of only two known springs in the world to flow and stop at regular intervals. The underground hollow is filled slowly with water. As it nears the surface of the ground, suction is created, and the water begins to be siphoned out of the ground into the spring basin. The siphon continues to drain the hollow until it dries up, breaking the siphon and stopping the flow. It then fills up and starts all over again. This has happened for at least the past 200 years at 2-hour-and-47-minute intervals. The water remains at a constant 34 degrees.

Legend claims that any couple drinking from the spring at the height of its flow will marry within the year. The flat rock nearby was a favorite courting spot and the site of many marriage proposals.

The **Ebbing & Flowing Spring School** (423-272-1961; rogersvilleheritage .org) was built in the early 1800s by families of its first students. Generations of the Amis family, the original land grant owners, were taught here until the dismissal bell rang for the last time in 1956.

The Ebbing & Flowing Spring United Methodist Church met in the school when it was organized in 1820 until a permanent church was built between the school and the cemetery in 1898. It still stands today with its original timbers and interior and is used regularly by the congregation.

From the center of Rogersville, head east on old US 11W (not the bypass) for about a mile to Burem Road. Bear right at the Amis House historical marker, and go a little more than 2 miles and turn left on Ebbing & Flowing Spring Road, a narrow country road. You'll go by ruins of a stone mill on your right. In less than a half mile, you'll come to a stream crossing the road. Immediately to your left is the spring. The road on your right leads to the church and school.

Plan your visit to Rogersville in mid-October. That's when the popular **Heritage Days** take place. All the activities are reminiscent of a harvest celebration at the turn of the 20th century.

Out on US 11E at Highway 66 is the little community of **Bulls Gap**. Named after local gun maker John Bull, who settled here in the mid-1790s, this natural gap in Bays Mountain later became a strategic location when the railroad through here was completed in 1858. During the Civil War, both the North and South wanted to control the railroad through the mountains; as a result, Bulls Gap was the site of several skirmishes.

taxmoney atwork

There are 56 Tennessee state parks, with more than 1,000 miles of hiking trails to walk, 394 species of birds to watch, 20 waterfalls, and about 3,500 campsites. For specifics, phone them at (615) 532-0001 or go to tnstateparks .com.

Even though the area has more than 200 years of history and architecture going for it, the event that put it on the map more than anything else was the birth of comedian Archie Campbell, who went on to become a member of the Grand Ole Opry in Nashville and to star on the long-running television show *Hee Haw*. He died in 1987.

Today a reconstruction of his birthplace is open in the town park alongside the ***Bulls Gap Railroad Museum*** (153 S. Main St.; 423-393-4429; bullsgap museum.com). A fun time to visit is during Labor Day weekend, when ***Archie Campbell Days*** take place. In addition to the Campbell complex, there's an Old Town historic district walking tour featuring nearly 30 structures. Campbell's birthplace is 2.5 miles off exit 23 of I-81, at 139 S. Main St. Call (423) 235-5216 for further information.

Off Highway 31, 7 miles south of Sneedville, is ***Elrod Falls*** (423-733-4341), one of the great hidden treasures of this sparsely populated county. Flat Gap Creek cascades more than 100 feet to the lower pool, where swimming is permitted in the cool, deep water. Take the unnamed gravel road off Highway 31 at the sign for the falls and follow it approximately 1 mile to a small picnic area. Park there; the walk is a very short, easy one to the lowest of the three falls.

Places to Stay in the First Frontier

BLOUNTVILLE

Rocky Top Campground
496 Pearl Ln.
(423) 323-2535
rockytopcampground.com

BRISTOL

Fairfield Inn & Suites by Marriott Bristol
3285 W. State St.
(423) 574-4500
marriott.com

ERWIN

Nolichucky Gorge Campground
101 Jones Branch Rd.
(423) 743-8876
nolichucky.com

GREENEVILLE

General Morgan Inn
111 N. Main St.
(423) 787-1000
generalmorganinn.com

JOHNSON CITY

Carnegie Hotel & Spa
1216 W. State of
Franklin Rd.
(423) 979-6400
carnegiehotel.com

Doubletree Hotel
211 Mockingbird Ln.
(423) 929-2000
doubletree3.hilton.com

JONESBOROUGH

**Hawley House Butterfly
Cottage**
114 E. Woodrow Ave.
(423) 753-8869
hawleyhouse.com

Historic Eureka Inn
127 W. Main St.
(423) 913-6100
eurekajonesborough.com

KINGSPORT

Hampton Inn Kingsport
2000 Enterprise Pl.
(423) 247-3888
Hilton.com

LIMESTONE

**Davy Crockett Birthplace
State Historic Park**
1245 Davy Crockett
Park Rd.
(423) 257-2167
Tnstateparks.com/parks/
david-crockett-birthplace

**Home Place Bed &
Breakfast**
132 Church Ln.
(423) 921-8424

MOUNTAIN CITY

Prospect Hill B&B
801 W. Main St.,
(423) 727-0139
prospect-hill.com

Places to Eat in the First Frontier

HAMPTON

Captain's Table
2340 Hwy. 321
(423) 725-2201
Lakeshore-resort.com

Laurel Fork Restaurant
201 Hwy. 321
(423) 725-2091

JOHNSON CITY

The Firehouse Restaurant
627 W. Walnut St.
(423) 929-7377
thefirehouse.com

Gourmet & Company
214 E. Mountcastle Dr.
(423) 929-9007
gourmetandcompany.com

Harbor House Seafood
2510 N. Roan St.
(423) 282-5122
harborhousejc.com

JONESBOROUGH

The Black Olive
125 E. Jackson Blvd.,
Ste. 8
(423) 788-3618
theblackolive123.com

The Mountainous East

Of Lincoln & Boone

The little village of **Cumberland Gap** rests just a few miles away from one of the most historic natural passageways of all time. Much of the westward movement of early America came through this V-shaped indentation in the Appalachian Mountains, a wall of rock that stretches from Maine to Georgia.

It was 1775 when Daniel Boone and his 30 axmen hacked out the Wilderness Road through the gap to open up the "western frontier" and the fertile farmlands on the other side. It was the first road platted by a white man in the state. That byway became a major thoroughfare and later was a 4-lane paved highway for decades.

Now the Cumberland Gap Tunnel, which opened October 18, 1996, takes US 25E through the mountain instead of up and over the top.

At the top of the gap, a marker in the **Cumberland Gap National Historical Park** (606-248-2817; nps.gov/cuga) shows where the states of Kentucky, Virginia, and Tennessee meet. It is said that from the top, those three states, plus Georgia and North Carolina, can be seen on a clear day. A visitor center and museum are part of the park.

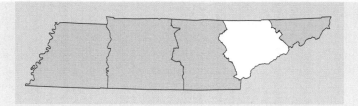

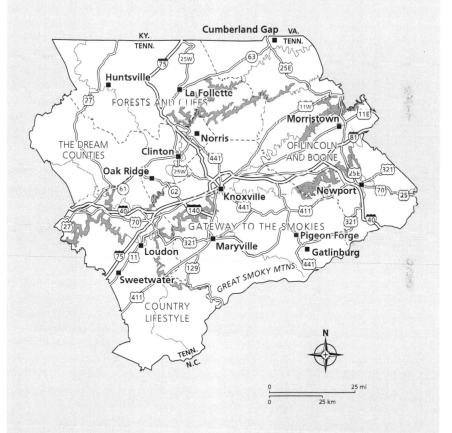

Cumberland Gap
KY.
TENN.
VA.
TENN.

Huntsville

La Follette

FORESTS AND CLIFFS

Morristown

Norris

THE DREAM
COUNTIES

Clinton

OF LINCOLN
AND BOONE

Oak Ridge

Knoxville

Newport

GATEWAY TO THE SMOKIES

Pigeon Forge

Loudon

Maryville

Gatlinburg

Sweetwater

GREAT SMOKY MTNS.

COUNTRY
LIFESTYLE

TENN.
N.C.

N

0   25 mi
0   25 km

To reach the park's visitor center, go through the tunnel to Middlesboro, Kentucky. Inside the center is an informative museum about the park, the gap, and early life in the area. A good way to see the terrain of the mountains is to drive 4 miles up to the Pinnacle, where you'll park in Kentucky, walk into Virginia, and overlook the village of Cumberland Gap in Tennessee. You can look down on the actual gap where Daniel Boone came through, and you'll see the old highway that follows the original Wilderness Road.

When old US 25E was built over the gap, much of it followed the Wilderness Road and was paved. Now that the tunnel takes all the traffic, that portion of 25E has been closed, all the paving removed, and the road restored to a primitive condition. The original dirt Wilderness Road, which can be seen from the Pinnacle, was reopened to foot traffic in mid-2002; we can all now walk exactly where those early settlers trekked in the late 1700s.

A fun, albeit somewhat tiring, side trip while you're in this area takes you to the mountaintop village where Sherman Hensley lived until 1951.

In 1904 he decided to get away from it all and moved, along with several relatives, to the mountaintop a few miles from Cumberland Gap. They all became self-sufficient when the rest of America was learning to rely more on one another for basic needs.

Since 1965 the National Park Service has restored parts of the **Hensley Settlement** (606-248-2817), including 12 homestead log cabins, several barns, many of the fences, the schoolhouse, and the cemetery. The public is invited to visit. It's not an easy place to get to, but what an adventure it is. The most popular way of coming in is on foot via a 3.5-mile path up the side of the mountain, or you can be shuttled there by park-operated vehicles, leaving from the visitor center daily from May through Oct. Tours are $10 adults, $5 senior citizens and children (ages 12 and under). Call for directions and a schedule of special events. Tours in 2019 were canceled due to unsafe road conditions, so be sure to call ahead to see if tours are offered.

AUTHOR'S TOP TEN PICKS

Davy Crockett's marriage license	Moonshine Capital of the World
Dollywood	Museum of Appalachia
Hensley Settlement	Ripley's Davy Crockett Mini-Golf
The Lost Sea	Rugby's Utopian Community
Mel's Diner	World's Largest Stalagmite

The village of Cumberland Gap was founded by English settlers and today shows a strong English influence in its architecture. The downtown section has been virtually untouched by modernization for more than 50 years. The opening scene of a movie was filmed here in 1988, and according to one of the downtown businessmen, only one sign had to be removed to make the village look like a small town of the 1930s.

On Wilderness Trail at the edge of town is the historic **Newlee Iron Works** iron furnace, built in the early 1820s. It was used to make iron that was shipped off to Chattanooga and to blacksmiths throughout the region. At its peak the furnace created more than 35 tons of pig iron a week. To the left of the furnace is a path that is part of the original Wilderness Road, which you can follow to get up to the historic gap itself.

There's a great website for Cumberland Gap and the surrounding Claiborne County area. Visit clairbornepartnership.com or call (423) 626-4149.

A few miles south on US 25E is **Harrogate**, the home of **Lincoln Memorial University** (423-869-3611; lmunet.edu). The school's mascot is the Railsplitters. Founded in 1896 as a living memorial to President Abraham Lincoln, the school's charter mandated the establishment of a museum to house memorabilia of the Lincoln era. Today the **Lincoln Library and Museum** (423-869-6235) on the campus houses the third-largest collection of Lincolniana and Civil War items in the world. At press time, the Lincoln Library and Museum was closed for a $3.6 million expansion project which is expected to be completed in late 2020. The project includes the addition of new galleries, an elevator, new restrooms, and a learning library to help visits experience the facility's extensive collection which covers the life of Abraham Lincoln, the Civil War, and the founding of the university. Call to be sure it has reopened.

One of the most significant historic items in the museum is the ebony cane the president was carrying on the night he was assassinated. A lock of Lincoln's hair is also on display. The **Lincoln General Store** is a fun stop where visitors can try out 19th-century games like pick-up sticks and checkers. Replica soldier items for sale include caps, haversacks, and canteens.

The school itself is beautiful and is a nice tribute to mountain life in East Tennessee. Take time to walk through the campus. Admission is charged for the museum.

High atop Clinch Mountain, about 5 miles out of Bean Station on US 25E, you'll find **Clinch Mountain Lookout Restaurant** (190 Look Mountain Rd.; 865-767-2511). It's not much to look at and the signs are falling down, but don't let any of that scare you away. The eatery is home to the famous vinegar pie. What a taste sensation. As the story goes, lemons were hard to get during the

OTHER ATTRACTIONS WORTH SEEING

Farragut Folklife Museum
Farragut
(865) 966-7057
townoffarragut.org

James White's Fort
Knoxville
(865) 525-6514
jameswhitesfort.org

Forbidden Caverns
Sevierville
(865) 453-5972
forbiddencavern.com

Museum of East Tennessee History
Knoxville
(865) 215-8830
easttnhistory.org

Great Smoky Mountains National Park
Gatlinburg
(865) 436-1200
nps.gov/grsm

Depression, so vinegar was substituted for lemons in pie making; some liked the taste so much, they never switched back.

Joining vinegar pie on the menu are ostrich burgers from a local farmer, hamburgers, and steaks. Breakfast is served all day. The outside tables have an astounding view of the valley and the Clinch River far below. It's open 7 days a week at from 8 a.m. to 6 p.m., and until 9 p.m. on Fri when live music is played. Karaoke is offered from 1 to 5 p.m. on Sun.

When Andrew Johnson came to Tennessee to establish a tailor shop, he spent a few months in Rutledge before relocating to nearby Greeneville.

A reproduction of Johnson's first shop has been built and is located in front of *Grainger County Courthouse*, on the original site.

A few blocks away is the circa 1848 *Grainger County Jail*, the oldest standing brick jailhouse in Tennessee. Restored by the county's historical society, the facility now houses the society and serves as a public meetinghouse for the area's clubs and organizations. Inside, the original metal stairs and wall partitions are intact.

In the 1790s Davy Crockett's dad opened a small 6-room tavern near present-day *Morristown*. That's where little Davy spent his early years. In the 1950s a reproduction of that tavern was built on the original site, and today the *Crockett Tavern Museum* (2002 Morningside Dr.; 423-587-9900; crockett tavernmuseum.org) serves as a frontier museum honoring the Crockett family and other early Tennessee pioneers. The tavern is full of period utensils and furnishings. It's open Tues through Sat, 11 a.m. to 5 p.m., Apr through Oct. Admission $5 adults, $1 students, and free for children under 5.

The first patented flying machine in America was developed by Melville Murrell, a Morristown preacher. Patented in 1877, a good while before the Wright brothers' flight, the ***Murrell Flyer*** flew several hundred yards under bicycle-type power. Parts of the original flyer, including its wings and some of the frame, are on display at the city's Rose Center. A video presentation features interviews with some of Murrell's descendants and several photos of the plane itself.

Built in 1892 and saved from destruction in 1975 by a community action group, the ***Rose Center*** (442 W. Second St. N; 423-581-4330; rosecenter.org) was the area's first school. It now serves as a community cultural center and includes a history museum, art gallery, exhibit space, and gift shop.

Each October, the ***Mountain Makins Festival*** is held on the grounds of the Rose Center and features one of East Tennessee's finest juried crafts shows. Two music stages spotlight various forms of local mountain music and other activities. Admission is $7 adults, $1 children (ages 6 to 12), and free for children under 6.

Downtown Morristown is a busy business center, and there are several antiques and collectibles shops along Main Street.

Cosby was settled in 1783 by a corn farmer searching for a quiet, peaceful life. Corn remained the main crop for many years, and it didn't take long before the discovery was made that it was easier to transport corn in the liquid form known as moonshine. For many years the area was known as the ***Moonshine Capital of the World***.

Apples are now considered one of the area's biggest cash crops, and there are five or six major orchards that sell directly from their farms. Also, many

TOP ANNUAL EVENTS

APRIL

Dogwood Arts Festival
Knoxville
(865) 637-4561
dogwoodarts.com

Townsend in the Smokies Spring Festival
Townsend
(865) 448-6134
Smokymountains.org

MAY

British Festival
Rugby
(888) 214-3400
historicrugby.org

NOVEMBER–FEBRUARY

Winterfest
Pigeon Forge, Gatlinburg & Sevierville
(800) 251-9100
mypigeonforge.com

smaller orchards have been planted and produce excellent crops. Look for APPLES FOR SALE signs along the roads.

One of the most popular year-round apple producers of the area is the **Carver's Orchard & Applehouse Restaurant** (423-487-2710), located on US 321 South at 3460 Cosby Hwy., about 5 miles from I-40. This is a family farm orchard; the Carvers have been growing apples in the area since the 1940s when Kyle Carver planted apple trees in his cornfield. The orchard now boasts more than 40,000 trees and 126 varieties of apples. The best time to visit is between mid-Aug and Dec—that's when most of the action takes place. They grow and sell many different varieties of apples on the farm and are known widely for their fresh fried apple pies. For a couple of bucks, you get a huge, tasty, magnificent, and hot fried treat. Forget your diet. You can't find pies of this quality just anywhere.

Along with their apples, the Carvers also sell grapes, peaches, fresh vegetables, honey, jellies, jams, apple butter, molasses, cider, and other seasonal items. Ice cream and several apple products, including both fried and baked apple pies, are available. Stacy's Candy Store features locally produced chocolate candies and other homemade delicacies.

Carver's Restaurant is located in the barn. According to Irene Carver, who runs the eatery for the family, the menu is "great country cooking," and "everything" is made from secret recipes and

doubleletterduo

Tennessee and Mississippi are the only two states having three sets of double letters in their names. And they border each other!

"that's why it's all so good." Well, secret or not, the chicken potpies are exceptional. Of course, there are a lot of apple products on the menu, including apple fritters, apple pie cake, fried apples, and baked apple pies. The restaurant is open daily 8 a.m. to 8 p.m.

Down the road from Carver's is a historical log cabin that houses **Foothills of the Smoky's Quilt Shop** (423-487-3866; foothillsofthesmokys.com). If you're a quilt maker, the shop carries a full line of fabrics, quilt kits, and supplies.

Next to the rustic log cabin store, owner Fredia Haley has created a quilters' getaway, a kind of bed-and-breakfast for quilters. "It's a retreat where people can come and concentrate on nothing but quilting," said Fredia. This refuge is located at 3892 US 321, just a few miles off I-40. Take exit 435 for Newport, and head toward Cosby. The shop is open Mon through Sat 9 a.m. to 5 p.m. Call first during winter, as they may close at times.

The ramp is an onion-like vegetable native to the foothills of the southern Appalachian Mountains. The odd-looking plant has been described as the "vilest-smelling, sweetest-tasting vegetable in the world." Early settlers attributed special medicinal qualities to the ramp.

Raw, parboiled, fried, or scrambled in eggs, it was regarded as a necessary spring tonic to ward off the sluggishness of winter. In the 1950s Cosby introduced the ramp to the rest of the world when it established its first annual spring festival in the plant's honor. Each May thousands come to the Cocke County Fairgrounds in Newport for the annual *Newport Kiwanis Ramp Festival* to enjoy activities and eat truckloads of ramps.

In the county seat of *Newport*, the *Cocke County Museum* (433B Prospect Ave.; 423-623-3382) is located upstairs in the Community Center building. Among items on display are many from Grace Moore, an internationally known opera singer and movie star who was born in the southern part of the county. The museum also houses a permanent collection of antiques and artifacts, many of which are displayed in three period rooms: Victorian Parlor, Early Bedroom, and Pioneer Kitchen. The museum is open only on Wed from 1 to 5 p.m. Downstairs are the chamber of commerce and tourist information offices. This is a good place to start a tour of the county and admission is free. Call the chamber at (423) 623-7201 or go to cocke-county-partnershipchamber-of -commerce.business.site.

One of the classiest bed-and-breakfast inns in this part of the state is just outside Newport off English Mountain Road at 1500 Pinnacles Way. *Christopher Place* (423-299-4062; christopherplace.com), which classifies itself as an "Intimate Resort," is a true Four Diamond Smoky Mountain resort. *Vacations* magazine named the inn "one of the Top 10 romantic inns in America." Great views of the mountains, big and hearty breakfasts, and a nightly five-course dinner by candlelight are only a few of the amenities. Others include a heated pool, tennis courts, billiard room, fitness room, and a library filled with books, music, and movies.

Ten different rooms, all with private baths and luxurious furnishings, range in price from $150 to $330 per night. If you're looking for the best mountain view the inn has to offer, ask for the Roman Holiday Room.

If you're looking for more of a rustic, off-the-beaten-path place to stay, you're only 15 miles away when you're in downtown Newport. To find *Meadow Creek Mountain Rustic Resort* (423-623-7543; meadowcreek mountain.com), head out on US 321 to Parrotsville, the state's third-oldest town. Then you'll turn left, then right, then left, and then at the fork, you'll . . . well, you get the picture. You're better off calling first. This place is way out there in the proverbial boonies. It's located deep in the beautiful Cherokee National Forest on 100 acres of pristine mountain property.

There are 4 individual cabins, sleeping anywhere from 2 to 10 per night, plus a 6-bedroom, 6-bath lodge with kitchen. These are full-size cabins, each with bedrooms and private baths, air-conditioning, fireplaces, a gas grill and a hot tub on a private deck, satellite TV, and a kitchen. You can bring your own horse, or you can rent one from Diane and Charlie Phillips, the proprietors of this fun, unique getaway and giddy-up resort. In-season prices per cabin start at $110.

You can grab some grub at the resort's *Crazy Horse Cafe* or create some fixin's in your own kitchen. The *General Store* sells basic merchandise, plus it has a lending DVD and book library and wireless Internet.

Located next to the popular Lake Douglas, *Dandridge* holds the distinction of being the only town in the US named for *Martha Dandridge Washington*, George's wife, and today has a well-preserved downtown historic district to be quite proud of. Self-guided tour maps are available throughout town and at the *Jefferson County Museum* (865-397-4904; jeffersoncountytn .gov), located on the first level of the circa 1845 county courthouse. One of the unique holdings of this regional history museum is Davy Crockett's marriage license. Admission is free, and the museum is open during courthouse hours.

This community was quite the crossroads through the years. It was a regular stop for boats carrying provisions up and down the French Broad River, it was a major stage stop, and it was a road traveled by the stock traders operating between Tennessee and the Carolinas. As we know, wherever travelers gather, there will always be an abundance of taverns. Today three are still standing in Dandridge.

Almost swallowed by the waters when the Tennessee Valley Authority (TVA) dammed the river to create Lake Douglas in the early 1940s, Dandridge was saved thanks to local protests and the intervention of President Franklin D. Roosevelt. The million-dollar dike of native stone that holds back the waters today serves as backdrop to many of the historic buildings along Main Street. The lake dominates the outdoor activities in Dandridge as well as the entire county. The yacht club holds a July 4 boat parade, various fishing tournaments run throughout the year, and the lake is always dotted by the colorful sails of pleasure boaters enjoying themselves.

As a result of the dam and the abundance of water, the TVA built a hydroelectric plant that is still in operation today.

If possible, plan your visit to the area for the first Saturday in October. That's when Jefferson City's *Old Time Saturday* festival takes place. This one-day event mixes entertainment and food with a festive open-air market featuring local arts and crafts.

The **Glenmore Mansion** (865-475-5014; glenmoremansion.com) is considered by many architects as an almost perfect example of Second Empire architecture. Built in 1869, the 27-room, 5-story mansion is fully furnished with antiques of the period. In eastern Tennessee, where most historical preservation efforts are saved for pre-1850 architecture, it's good to see something from the Victorian era. The mansion is located at 1280 N. Chucky Pike in Jefferson City. It's open Sat and Sun afternoons 1 to 5 p.m., May through Oct and for special events. Admission is $7 for adults and $5 for school-age children.

Great Smoky Mountains National Park

As the most visited national park in the country, with 10 million visitors a year, the **Great Smoky Mountains National Park** (865-436-1200; nps.gov/grsm) is hardly off the beaten path. But the 500,000-acre facility is so large and has so many nooks and crannies that it isn't difficult to get away from the madding crowds.

There are established camping areas throughout the park, but camping is also permitted in the undeveloped regions. Special backcountry permits are needed for that.

The **Sugarland Visitors Center**, located 2 miles inside the park from Gatlinburg, has maps and other information about the entire park, as well as exhibits on what one will most likely see during a visit.

Featuring more species of plants than any other area on our continent, this official **International Biosphere Reserve** is a true gem in Tennessee travel opportunities.

Within the boundaries there are 16 peaks towering above 6,000 feet, including **Clingmans Dome**, which, at 6,643 feet, is the highest point in Tennessee.

One of the park's most unusual attractions is **LeConte Lodge** (865-429-5704; lecontelodge.com), a great (but rugged and rustic) place to stay while in the mountains if you enjoy walking. In fact, that's the only way you can get there, and it's not the easiest walk you'll ever make. The lodge rests atop the third-highest peak in the park, making it the highest guest lodge in the eastern US. The shortest (and steepest) hike to the lodge is 5.5 miles long, which is about a 4-hour hike for a person in good condition. Once there you'll find no electricity, phones, or showers—just a great view and wonderful food. The lodge can host up to 60 guests per night housed in one of the seven rough-hewn cabins or the three multiroom lodges. All units are equipped with kerosene lanterns for light and propane heaters for warmth. It does get quite chilly in the mountains. Rates start at $154.50 per adult and $87.50 per child ages 4 to 12, per night, and include dinner and breakfast. Wine is available with dinner

Be(ar) Aware

The Great Smoky Mountains National Park is home to about 1,800 black bears. Here are a few bear facts: During the spring and summer, bears are most active in early morning and late evening. Momma bears and their newborn cubs leave their winter dens in late March or early April. Bears usually mate in July. Bears are good tree climbers and swimmers. They also can run about 30 miles per hour. Do not approach a bear if you see one. Black bear attacks are rare, but they have happened.

at $12 per person per night for those 21 and older. The lodge is open late Mar through late Nov.

The tourist destination city of *Gatlinburg* is near the main entrance to the park and considered its main gateway. Souvenir and craft shops and various attractions line the main streets, while honeymoon houses and motels line the backstreets.

Gatlinburg officials have put together one of the most helpful tourism websites in the state: gatlinburg.com. You can also call (800) 588-1817 for information. Among the attractions here you'll find something to please everyone. The parkway strip is lined with fun, colorful, and often macabre things to see and do. Don't miss *Ripley's Believe It or Not!*, up from the *Guinness World Records Museum*, across from the *Sky Lift*, and under the *Space Needle*.

High atop Mt. Harrison, overlooking Gatlinburg, is the *Ober Gatlinburg Amusement Park and Ski Resort* (800-251-9202; obergatlinburg.com). It's a fun, year-round facility that has a mountain resort feel to it even though it's just up the mountain from Gatlinburg's touristy downtown area.

In the summer there are amusement rides, an alpine slide, a water ride, miniature golf, go-karts, and other outdoor fun. In the winter there is skiing. Indoors, and open year-round, is a large ice-skating rink, shops, a lounge, restaurants, and a wonderful little fudge maker!

Gatlinburg's *Ober Gatlinburg's Wildlife Encounter* is located here and provides some great close-up views of the bears. The Wildlife Encounter is also home to river otters, bobcats, raccoons, skunks, flying squirrels, turtles, snakes, and birds of prey. Note that some animals hibernate in the winter and may not be available for viewing.

A quick but somewhat expensive way to get to the top is via the celebrated tramway. It's free if you have ski lift tickets, and it takes you directly to the top of the mountain. If you have a car full and want to save some money, you can drive to the top and park directly adjacent to all the activity.

The tram is at Traffic Light #9. If you want to drive, go to the end of the parkway; just before you enter the national park, turn right for Ski Mountain Road.

If you're looking for some of the best fine artwork and crafts the state has to offer, a drive through the **Great Smoky Arts & Crafts Community** (865-436-6921; gatlinburgcrafts.com) is a must. It's an 8-mile auto loop that features more than 100 independent artists and craftspeople with cafes, restaurants, and lodging sprinkled throughout. Many shops are grouped with others in large complexes, while some are set off by themselves.

Designated as a **Tennessee Heritage Arts & Crafts Trail**, the community was established in 1937. Along the route, artisans whittle, paint, sew, cast, weave, and carve to create original pieces of art, such as candles, baskets, quilts, brooms, pottery, jewelry, dolls, ceramics, scrimshaw, leather, stained glass, fine photography, and just about anything else you can think of. In all, there are 78 stops. Most of the shops are open daily during the summer usually from 10 a.m. to 5 p.m. They may close completely during the winter or at best have reduced hours of operation. Call first—individual shop numbers are available on the group's website. (Speaking of calling, you're in the mountains here and there's a very good chance your cell phone won't work, so plan accordingly.)

For a relaxing and environmentally friendly ride, park the car in town and go green. Take an old-fashioned trolley to the **Gatlinburg Arts & Crafts Loop** for only $1. The trolley can be boarded at the Gatlinburg Mass Transit Center at Traffic Light #5. The trolley runs daily Apr through Oct and Mon through Sat in Nov and Dec. Exact change is required for the trolley, and it takes about an hour for the trolley to run the entire loop. A good place to start (and finish) the loop is 3 miles out of Gatlinburg from Traffic Light #3, on US 321. You'll see a big green sign with GREAT SMOKY ARTS & CRAFTS COMMUNITY printed in white letters with arrows pointing the way. Turn left onto Glades Road near McDonald's, and the art-venture begins.

You'll definitely want to stop at the **Glades Arts & Crafts Center**, one of the first major complexes on the right, at King Road. There are nine shops here, and across the street in the Morning Mist Village, there are nearly 25 more arts and crafts shops.

What started as a co-op for female artists, the **Cliff Dwellers Gallery** (668 Glades Rd.; 865-436-6921; cliffdwellersgallery.com) is now owned by six local artists who represent approximately 60 other local artists, both male and female. Their building was originally built in downtown Gatlinburg in 1933 and moved to its current location in 1993. On special days you might find a craft demonstration by a participating artist in anything from glass working and painting to creating wooden bowls on a lathe. This is one of the most interesting stops along the trail.

At the end of Glades Road, just around the corner on Buckhorn Road, is Hemlock Village, with several different shops. The largest is **Highland Craft Gallery** (865-430-8951), which represents more than 70 different artists offering an eclectic selection of fine crafts. By the way, a photo of many of the represented artists hangs on the wall, so you can see whom you're buying from.

And if you're still hungry, check out the charming **Wild Plum Tea Room** (865-436-3808; wildplumtearoom.com) in a log cabin setting, just past Hemlock Village at 555 Buckhorn Rd. Open only for lunch, this popular eatery, known for its signature chicken salad and Wild Plum Tea, is a peaceful and relaxing stop along the way as you ponder what great art must find its way into your suitcase.

Since parking is at such a premium in Gatlinburg, perhaps the best deal in town is the 50-cent ride on its rapid transit system, **the trolley** (865-436-3897; gatlinburgtrolley.org). During peak season the entire city can become one large parking lot, so find a place to park on the edge of town or at your hotel and rely on the trolley. The trolley has more than 100 boarding stops.

The nation's earliest Fourth of July parade takes place on the streets of Gatlinburg each year at 12:01 a.m. July 4. Floats, bands, and huge helium balloons go by as more than 80,000 annually gather for the **"Midnight Parade."**

The **Hillbilly Golf Course** (865-436-7470) may well be one of the most unusual miniature golf courses in the world. To get to the first hole, you must ride an incline up to a point 300 feet above the city. Two 18-hole courses, with all sorts of mountaineer hazards, including a genuine outhouse and a moonshine still, are carved out of the mountainside. It's near Traffic Light #2 at 340 Parkway.

If you happen to be a Ripley's fan, Gatlinburg is heaven. Five of the company's top attractions are located in the city, including the high-tech and high-fun **Davy Crockett Mini-Golf** course (865-430-8851; ripleys.com/Gatlinburg/mini-golf), located at Traffic Light #1 at 188 Parkway. Here you'll find two 18-hole courses with animated figures and interactive holes. Where else can you be chided by a couple of old crows if you miss a putt? This neat place stands out from all the other miniature golf courses in the area! Open year-round, weather permitting.

Moving on down the parkway toward the Great Smoky Mountains National Park, on your right at Traffic Light #5 at 88 River Rd. you'll find the world-acclaimed **Ripley's Aquarium of the Smokies** (865-430-8808; ripleyaquariums.com/Gatlinburg). The fun starts here as you drive up. It's one of the most amazing structures in the state, and there's a real sense of arrival. Inside, there are many great exhibits, including a moving walkway under a large habitat that houses sharks (some up to 11 feet) and thousands of colorful tropical fish. Another fascinating exhibit contains jellyfish highlighted by special lighting and classical music. You'll rarely see anything more calming and surreal in your life. Open daily, year-round.

At Traffic Light #7 at 800 Parkway is **Ripley's Believe It or Not! Odditorium** (865-436-5096; ripleys.com/gatlinburg) of the weird and unusual. From shrunken heads and matchstick sculptures to vampire-killing kits and pieces of the Berlin Wall, the odditorium has one-of-a-kind items. The 16 themed galleries on three floors showcase such oddities as a car completely covered in crystals and the Last Supper artwork made out of lint. A fun place for everyone in the family! Open daily, year-round.

Ripley's Moving Theater (865-436-9763; ripleys.com/Gatlinburg/moving-theater) and **Ripley's Haunted Adventure** (865-430-9991; ripleys.com/Gatlinburg/haunted-adventure) are located next to each other at Traffic Light #8. Both are open daily, year-round. You'll ride along with the 5-D film at the Moving Theater, which is quite fun. Remember to hold on, and eat lunch afterward, not before! Get a chance to explore your nightmare at the Haunted Adventure. Created on the site of the old Grimsby & Streaper Casket Company, the haunted house has live actors and classy scare techniques and is quite a long walk through. They suggest you hold hands to keep from getting lost. Not a bad suggestion. Must be at least 6 years old to enter.

The **Peddler Steakhouse** (865-436-5794; peddlergatlinburg.com) has the best view, the best ambience, and the best salad bar of any restaurant in town. Located at 820 River Rd., the restaurant and bar are on the edge of the river, and even if you're not lucky enough to get a window table, you still have a lot to look at. The Peddler is actually constructed on history. The restaurant was built around the C. Earl Ogle cabin. Ogle was the descendant of one of the first pioneer families. Materials from four other original homesites were used to complete the structure. People come from all over for the steak, huge salad bar, and grilled fresh salmon. The place is always busy, and although they don't take reservations, you can call ahead and get your name placed on the waiting list. If you get there and there's a long list, go back to the lounge, which also offers great river views. If you find a table you like there, go ahead and order and enjoy your meal in the bar. It's the same menu as the dining room. The locals love this place, and it has been locally owned and operated since 1977.

Known for romantic wedding chapels, Gatlinburg and the Smoky Mountains offer plenty of opportunities for those looking for a memorable wedding. If you're on the market for something quite different and a bit funky and fun, call the Hillbilly Minister (865-436-3817) and he'll arrange a true **Hillbilly**

Wedding for you. The minister says he offers a "nontraditional and no-frills approach, yet with reverence and dignity." Wearing bib overalls, the minister will perform "a simple basic Christian ceremony" for $75. Marriage is at the Unique Chapel or Wedding Garden. The minister will give you the address.

And speaking of memorable, a great home base while you're enjoying the area is one of the nearly two dozen bed-and-breakfasts in the Smokies. They are all unique, with different amenities, and all offer spectacular breakfasts. Find a listing of the best at smokymountainbb.com.

With 200 booths of nationally known craftspeople living and working around the Smoky Mountains region, you can only imagine the scope of arts and crafts, paintings, furniture making, and wood carvings you'll find at the *Gatlinburg Craftsmen's Fair*, held twice a year at the Gatlinburg Convention Center (Traffic Light #8). There's a weeklong summer event in July and a 2-week fair in mid-October.

In addition to local and regional craftspeople, the best from around the country also take part in these events, and there is always live music, from bluegrass to mountain music, being performed on the trade show floor. Admission is $8 for adults, free for children 12 and under. Find out more at (865) 436-7479 or craftsmensfair.com.

Head north on US 441 out of Gatlinburg, go through a part of the national forest, and 5 miles later you'll be in *Pigeon Forge*, where a 50-cent trolley ride with 50 stops helps you avoid traffic congestion. Similar to Gatlinburg in its attractions, this city's main draw is country singer Dolly Parton's theme park, *Dollywood* (800-365-5996; dollywood.com). Country music prevails in the park, as do country crafts and good country cooking.

Even if you're one who doesn't like theme parks, chances are very good you'll love this place, which is more of a trip into mountain culture than it is an amusement ride park. Craftsmen's Valley offers a shady walk through a genuine holler past all sorts of working craftspeople, chefs cooking in huge cast-iron skillets over open fires, and a winding brook. The steam train takes you on a 5-mile journey to the top of the ridge and back and is one ride you definitely need to take. The Thunderhead wooden roller coaster offers a 100-foot drop at speeds of 55 mph. Whew!

The Barnstormer offers the thrills that daring stunt pilots of the 1920s might have felt as they zoomed over the fields of nearby farms. Located in the Owens Farm section of Dollywood, the Barnstormer has two pendulum arms with seating back-to-back for 32 riders. With a maximum speed of 45 mph, the Barnstormer reaches an exhilarating 81 feet in the air.

America's first wing coaster, the Wild Eagle soars 21 stories above Dollywood to give riders the sensation of flying. With nothing but air above and

Origins of a Legend

The fourth of 12 children of Robert Lee and Avie Lee (Owens) Parton, **Dolly Parton** was born and raised in a ramshackle cabin in Sevier County, TN. The local country doctor, Dr. Robert F. Thomas, who delivered Parton on January 19, 1946, was paid a sack of corn-meal for his work. The family struggled to make a living, but life was good, Parton said. "You know, we had it kind of hard, but not any more than most folks. I had an incredible family, and we had so much love, we didn't know we were poor."

Music was an important part of Parton family life. Before she learned to read or write, Dolly Parton was "making up" her own songs. When Parton was 7, her Uncle Bill Parton gave her a guitar. Three years later, she got a big radio job. "My first break came from a gentle-man named Cas Walker in Knoxville," Parton said. "He had a chain of grocery stores, but he also had a radio show on every day. He hired me."

Her career steadily climbed and in 1959, Parton made her debut at the Grand Ole Opry. The day after she graduated from high school in 1964, the 18-year-old packed her card-board suitcase and moved to Nashville to seek her fortune—and found her husband. "I met Carl my first day in Nashville at the Wishy Washy Laundromat," she said. Owner of an asphalt paving business in Nashville, Carl Dean has always shunned publicity.

Parton's initial success came as a songwriter, writing hit songs for Skeeter Davis and Hank Williams Jr. About this time, Porter Wagoner was looking for a new "girl singer" for his syndicated television show. Parton accepted the job in 1967, signed with RCA Records in 1968, and joined the Grand Ole Opry in 1969. Her career was in high gear.

After several hit duos with Wagoner, Parton left the show in 1974, writing the song "I Will Always Love You" for Wagoner. It reached No. 1 for the first time in 1974.

Despite all the awards and international acclaim, Parton has never forgotten her roots. In the early 1980s, she began musing about projects to help her Tennessee hometown. The result was Dollywood Family Amusement Park in 1986 in Pigeon Forge. The name had stuck in Parton's mind from her first visit to Los Angeles. She had looked up at the land-mark Hollywood sign and thought, "I would like to change that H into a D."

But she hastens to add that the theme park is "much more about the mountains and the people who live there than it is about me. I saw Dollywood as a chance to honor them. It brought a lot of jobs to the area for my kinfolk and others to work."

In 1987 came Dolly Parton's Stampede dinner theater with an emphasis on down-home cooking and a modern-day Wild West revue. The 299-room DreamMore Resort & Spa opened in 2015 next door to Dollywood and Dolly's Splash Country waterpark.

Parton herself has produced a children's picture book, *Coat of Many Colors*, based on her hit song of the same title. The story tells of a coat she owned as a child that her mother had stitched together out of many different pieces of cloth. Although the other children at school made fun of her, Parton took pride in her coat and the love that her mother had sewed into it. Her mother died in December 2003. Her father died in 2000.

Visitors to Chasing Rainbows, the Dollywood museum devoted to Parton's life, can see a replica of that childhood coat, as well as family photos and other memorabilia. As for any advice to others, Parton said, "I'd say trust in God and follow your dreams. One of my favorite quotes is 'To see a rainbow, you have to put up with a little rain.'"

below them, riders are seated on either side of the track rather than in a train directly on the rails. Definitely a "wind-beneath-your-wings" feeling.

There are plenty of other great rides, but most people don't come to Dollywood for the rides. The live shows, as you can imagine, are quite well done, with many of Dolly's relatives performing. Food? Did I mention that the food here is about the best you'll find at any theme park in the world? Great southern cooking at its finest! Throughout the year there are special festivals inside the park, including a traditional Smoky Mountain Christmas celebration and a fall Harvest Festival. A summer concert series features more than 40 top names in country music.

The 30,000-square-foot Eagle Mountain Sanctuary houses the country's largest presentation of non-releasable bald eagles. To inspire others to follow their dreams just as she did, Dolly Parton created the state-of-the-art Chasing Rainbows museum with Dolly's lavish gowns, awards, keepsakes, and personal mementos. Parked in front of the museum is Dolly's home on wheels, a 1994 Prevost bus. Dolly's bus bedroom features three clocks—one set on Dollywood time, one on Nashville time, and one on Los Angeles time.

In 2019, Dollywood opened the $37 million Wildwood Grove encompassing 6 acres. The signature piece is The Wildwood Tree, a sparkling butterfly tree that lights up at night with 650 multicolored butterflies and almost 9,000 leaves. Fun rides include the Dragonflier suspended roller coaster, Black Bear Trail ride, Treetop Tower ride, Great Tree Swing, and Frogs & Fireflies, where riders hop on the back of a frog ride for a fun chase around a lily pad. At the Wildwood Grove grand opening, Dolly said that the rides are based on the animals and things she grew up with in her mountain home. "Everything in the park has a little something to do with me," she said.

"After 3, next day free" is the policy here. Travel into the area, pay to get in after 3 p.m., and have a nice relaxing dinner at one of the park's restaurants. Leave, get a good night's rest, and come back the next day for free!

Next door is **Dolly's Splash Country** water park. You won't find a tropical theme here. No pastels or palm trees. Instead you'll find a re-created Smoky Mountains watering hole, complete with waterfalls, winding streams, and plenty of earth tones and rustic architecture. It's a fun and laid-back way to cool off. The RiverRush is Tennessee's first and only water coaster. An impressive 4 stories high with a 25-foot drop, the RiverRush "launches" 4-person rafts on a merry ride over 1,175 feet of hairpin curves, tunnels, and hills. RiverRush travels on a track that covers more than an acre in near the park's Big Bear Plunge.

In the Cascades, more than 25 interactive water elements are part of the fun. The 8,000-square-foot lagoon-style pool offers slides, waterfall, geysers, water jets, bubblers, and more. Live bands perform every Sat in July and Aug.

Dollywood is open from spring through the first week of Jan; the water park is open from May through Labor Day. A money-saving combo pass is available if you want to go to both parks.

If you haven't driven through Pigeon Forge lately, you're in for a surprise. Where the Music Mansion used to be at 100 Music Rd., there is now an upside-down building. That's right. **WonderWorks** (865-868-1800; wonderworksonline .com) looks as though it has been picked up and tossed upside down. Sure makes you wonder. And that's the whole point. Everything in WonderWorks is fun and has some sort of educational purpose.

WonderWorks mixes fantasy and reality. It's a place where the unexplainable comes to life and natural mysteries are explored. This is all done with sophisticated graphic and audio techniques. WonderWorks even has a tale to explain how it came to be. The story is pure fantasy, of course. Legend has it that an experiment on a remote island off the Atlantic coast went awry. During an attempt to harness the power of a man-made tornado, the giant swirling vortex spun out of control and took on a life of its own. The energy vortex was so powerful that it sent the entire structure skyward, hundreds of miles away, where it landed upside down in the heart of Pigeon Forge. The attraction has more than 100 interactive, hands-on exhibits.

It also offers a great magic show. Enjoy **The Wonders of Magic** as Terry Evanswood uses comedy, music, impersonations, sleight of hand, illusions, and Houdini-type escapes in a 75-minute magical variety show for all ages. He tops off his show with a message that proclaims hope and love to be the real magical wonders of the world. The show is $18.99 for all ages.

An iceberg in the heart of Pigeon Forge? And a huge cruise ship? Folks have been known to stop and stare. No wonder. The **Titanic Museum Attraction** (800-381-7670; titanicpigeonforge.com) towers 100 feet above the parkway and holds 400 priceless artifacts in 20 galleries. Built half scale to the original, the eye-catching building is a permanent 2-story museum shaped like *Titanic* herself. The structure is "anchored" in water to create the illusion of *Titanic* at sea. A 2-hour self-guided tour is designed to give guests the feeling of actually being a passenger on *Titanic*'s 1912 maiden voyage.

When they come aboard, visitors are given a boarding card with the name of an actual passenger. At the end of the tour, they discover whether their character survived or perished. The museum does an excellent job of helping visitors get to know real passengers through their stories, personal memorabilia, photos, cards, and letters. Everything on display once belonged to a *Titanic* passenger or crew member. The memorabilia was either taken off the ship at the time of the sinking or was found floating in the debris field. Save time for

Titanic Survivor's Story Told at Pigeon Forge Museum

The first time I met Marshall Drew, he pulled out a well-worn book. "This," he said with a chuckle, "is an announcement of my death."

Of course, the published account of his demise was wrong. In fact, Drew lived almost three quarters of a century longer. But many of the passengers he was traveling with on that long-ago trip were not so fortunate. Drew was one of the survivors of the sinking of the *Titanic*. I had interviewed him years ago in Massachusetts. Now I was seeing his name listed on the passenger memorial for the *Titanic* Museum in Pigeon Forge.

To travel on the mighty *Titanic* was a big adventure for an 8-year-old boy, Drew said when I interviewed him. Accompanied by his aunt and uncle, the child was on his way back home to America. He had lived with his aunt and uncle since the death of his mother when Drew was two weeks old. It was the *Titanic*'s maiden voyage, and the luxury ship had been widely billed as unsinkable. Capt. E. J. Smith and his White Star Line employers had been hoping to win the blue ribbon awarded to the fastest ship afloat. Therefore, as historians have since noted, some of the usual safety precautions were disregarded.

Drew remembered that the evening of the sinking a sumptuous dinner had been served and that he had sat in the foyer to watch some of the great people in all their finery. Some of the richest people in the world were aboard the *Titanic*, and some went down with her—Col. John Jacob Astor, Benjamin Guggenheim, Mr. and Mrs. Rothschild, Isadore Strauss and his wife, who refused to leave him for the safety of a boat.

At 11:40 p.m. on Sunday, April 14, 1912, Drew was in a bunk in the stateroom he shared with his aunt and uncle. "I remember a jar and the sensation of motion," Drew recalled. The jolt was caused when the *Titanic* hit an iceberg ripping a 300-foot hole in her hull below the waterline.

"A steward knocked on our door to tell us to get dressed and come up to the boat deck," he continued. As Drew walked topside with his aunt and uncle, he recalled that "it was very cold and the water was calm like a millpond. The sky was black and the water was black so that you couldn't see any difference between them—it was totally black."

To cries of "Women and children first," Drew and his aunt were put into Lifeboat 11, the only lifeboat out of all 16 that was filled. "My aunt said good-bye to my uncle. She never saw him again."

Although reports have varied, Drew said he "distinctly remembered" hearing the band playing as the lifeboats were rowed away. The band was all lost.

The only time he was scared, Drew said, was when the lifeboat was lowered down the side of the liner. "They were supposed to have a lifeboat drill that Sunday but didn't and the ropes on the davits didn't work," he said. "The lifeboat went down by a series of jerks. First the bow would be up in the air, then the stern would be. I was afraid we were going to be dumped into the sea."

Drew recalled hearing an explosion before the *Titanic* sank. "The engines broke loose and fell through the hull. The forward funnel fell, too, and shot sparks like fireworks into the black sky."

The great ship began the downward plunge that would take 1,516 souls to a watery grave. Drew fell asleep in a lifeboat of strangers and awoke to find daylight and towering icebergs all around him. "They looked more like ice islands."

Drew was one of the survivors who were picked up by the *Carpathia*, a Europe-bound liner with a capacity load of passengers. Arriving at the rescue ship, Drew recalled that children were hauled up in canvas bags. "The kids were all screaming, but I thought it was a pretty good ride until a sailor dumped me out on the deck."

In all the frenzy, no one asked the child his name. That is why Drew's name was not on the list of survivors and the first book published in 1912 on the *Titanic* disaster listed Marshall Drew as going down with the ship. It was impossible to get an accurate list of survivors. Drew remembered waiting with a group of people in New York. To amuse himself, the child was handed a paper and pencil. His drawing? A great ship steaming on a sea rough with high waves. "I remember a photographer took a picture of it so I ended up in the newspaper," Drew said.

He also was reunited with his tearful family who weren't sure what they were going to find. Drew grew up, settled down in Waverly, RI, and tried to put the past behind him. He became a teacher and a talented painter. He married and had one daughter. But he always felt an icy chill go down his spine whenever April came around, he said.

With the popularity of the *Titanic* attraction, I wondered what Drew would have thought about the continuing interest in the tragedy that happened more than a century ago. Probably, he would have responded the way he often did—with a shrug, a good-natured chuckle, and a reminder that life is too short no matter how long we live. Marshall Drew died of cardiac arrest on June 6, 1986, at age 82.

"I could easily have died before I really lived," he used to say. "Let that be a lesson to you—enjoy each day that you have."

the gift shop. One of my favorite items is the *Titanic* "survival kit"—a box of chocolates that are quite good.

Located at 2134 Parkway, the Titanic Museum Attraction is open daily 9 a.m. to 9 p.m. Advance purchase is suggested as tickets sell out quickly. Tickets are $27 plus tax for adults; $14 for children (ages 5 to 12); free for ages 4 and under.

Sounds of "Silent Night" fill the air. Santa Claus greets children of all ages. Stockings are hung by the chimney with care. And glittering Christmas trees brighten the winter night. Scenes like this are familiar during the holiday season. But at **The Inn at Christmas Place** (888-465-9644; innatchristmasplace .com), it is Christmas every day. Opened June 15, 2007, the Smoky Mountains destination at Traffic Light #2A at 119 Christmas Tree Lane on the Parkway has been drawing visitors no matter the season. The Inn at Christmas Place is open year-round and filled with all the joys of the holiday season—no matter what the weather may be outside. Featuring the mountain village architecture of the European Alps, the inn offers luxurious old-world charm including copper-crowned turrets, a stone-terraced courtyard, two large ponds with natural stone waterfalls, and landscaped gardens.

Uniformed bellmen and caroling figurines welcome guests through custom-etched glass doors into a holiday wonderland. Guest rooms are also clad in holiday finery, including 2- and 3-room suites with full-size decorated trees, fireplaces, 2-person whirlpools, and private balconies overlooking the courtyard. A stay at the inn includes a complimentary breakfast with country-style buffet items and an omelet bar. Santa shares his cookies with guests nightly from 8:30 to 10:30 p.m. at the front desk.

Santa is at the Inn every morning except Wed and Sun. He has Story Time in the lower lobby on Sat, as well as concerts in the evening on Tues, Thurs, and Sat. Call the hotel to verify Santa's schedule since St. Nick sometimes has to fly back to the North Pole.

Across the parkway from **The Incredible Christmas Place and Village** shops (800-445-3396; christmasplace.com), the inn is within easy walking distance of many Pigeon Forge attractions. For guests who appreciate the inn's decor so much that they would like to add it to their own homes, most of the items on view are sold at The Incredible Christmas Place and Village shops at 2470 Parkway. Not surprising, since the Biggs family who started The Incredible Christmas Place more than 2 decades ago are also owners of The Inn at Christmas Place.

Dolly Parton's Stampede (865-453-4400 or 800-356-1676; dixiestampede .com) has an interesting concept for a dinner theater at 3849 Parkway. While eating a southern feast, patrons watch a live show in the central dirt-covered arena. The Western Show features 32 horses, Conestoga wagons, pig racing, bull riding, steer wrestling, and a bunch more good-old-boy activities. For added flavor, a friendly competition divides the audience into two sides. Reservations are sometimes necessary. The Dixie Belle Saloon opening act begins 50 minutes prior to Dolly Parton's Stampede and is well worth arriving early to see.

During the Christmas holidays, the Stampede is magically transformed into a fairyland complete with evergreens, twinkling lights, and holiday music.

Santa's Elves from the North Pole and the South Pole get into a friendly rivalry while serving a four-course holiday feast. Before the show, guests are invited to stroll down Horse Walk to get an up-close view of the stars of the show.

Another feature of the Dolly Parton's Stampede is the ***world's largest stick-horse collection***, which is displayed throughout the venue. An offhand comment is what started it all. Dan Cavanah had a friend in Seattle with many fine horses. When he retired, Cavanah told his buddy that he would gather an even larger herd, the biggest in all of Florida. When he got home from visiting Seattle, Cavanah received a gag gift from his pal—a stick horse to get him started on his herd. That was in 1990. Since then, Cavanah has collected more than 500 stick-horse pieces. In November 2002 he was honored by the *Guinness Book of World Records* for having the world-record stick-horse collection.

As his collection increased, Cavanah decided he wanted to display his stick horses where others could enjoy them. After checking out various places, Cavanah settled on the Dolly Parton's Stampede in Pigeon Forge. With its horse-related show, Cavanah figured his make-believe mounts would fit right in. The stick horses were delivered to the Stampede in April 2004. The amazing collection is displayed everywhere inside the Stampede, from the theater to the entrance hall to the carriage room and from the lobby to the gift shop. There's a Davy Crockett stick horse, an orange one autographed by country singer Tammy Wynette, a Lone Ranger stick horse, Gumby's horse Pokey, Roy Rogers's Trigger, and many more. Some have wheels that make a galloping noise, while others have reins with bells, yarn manes, and moving mouths. A 1950s model is battery operated to make a whinnying sound.

Another unique dining opportunity in Pigeon Forge is ***Mel's Diner*** (119 Wears Valley Rd.; 865-429-2184; melsdinerpf.com), where the good ole days of rock 'n' roll are featured on the menu, on the walls, and on the jukebox. Located one road west of the parkway, in an authentic stainless-steel diner,

A Veterans' Thank-You

Pigeon Forge throws a big party each August to say "thank you" to our country's military veterans. The city is loaded with activities, including a land and air parade, lectures, educational forums, keynote speeches by well-known American veterans, a military history book fair, static aircraft displays, canteen dances, war story storytelling, and a huge picnic. The 2-week ***Celebrate Freedom*** event is sponsored by the city of Pigeon Forge, with help from the University of Tennessee and the Center for the Study of War and Society. Contact them at (865) 453-8574 or mypigeonforge .com.

Mel's features a fun, tasty menu. The half-pound burgers are called Jukebox Heroes, and among the offerings are the Beach Boy Basic Burger, the Chubby Checker Cheeseburger, Marilyn's Mushroom Burger, and the Little Deuce Coupe Cajun Burger. The Sandwich Favorites include the Hot Diggity Dog, the Bette Davis B.L.T., James Dean Grilled Chicken, the Elvis Country Club, and the Doo Wah Diddy Philly Chicken Cheese. Starters include Fonzarelli Cheese Sticks, Potsy's Potato Salad, Ralph Malph Nachos, and Chachi's Cheese Nachos. The kid's menu is called Little Anthony's, and the wonderful thick and creamy milkshakes can be found under the Shake, Rattle & Roll heading.

Next to the vintage jukebox is a sign that reads IF MUSIC IS TOO LOUD, YOU'RE TOO OLD, and near the cash register a sign proclaims IF YOU THINK YOU HAVE A RESERVATION, YOU'RE IN THE WRONG PLACE. This is a fun, quality eatery. Open daily.

The country's first indoor vertical wind tunnel, **Flyaway Indoor Skydiving** (Traffic Light #5, 3106 Pkwy; 865-453-7777 or 877-293-0639; flyawayindoor skydiving.com), bills itself as America's "most unique" sports attraction. You suit up and ride in a vertical wind tunnel with wind speeds up to 115 mph, and as you float and fly in the air current, you're never more than 5 or 6 feet from a padded landing spot or from the arms of your personal flight attendant. Each flyer receives training, and the entire experience will last about an hour and 15 minutes with about 3 minutes of airtime. A video machine is running so that you can take your experience home with you and impress your friends. The flight costs $34, plus tax, and anyone under 18 must be accompanied by a parent.

Imagine climbing into a huge balloon and bouncing down a hill. That's the basic idea behind an attraction known as Zorb at the **Outdoor Gravity Park** (203 Sugar Hollow Rd.; 865-366-2687; outdoorgravitypark.com). These heavy-duty balloons, however, are 11 feet high and 11 feet round. Known as an OGO, the transparent sphere is constructed of more than 300 square feet of plastic. Riders roll down a 700-foot-long hill just along the Smoky Mountains. Choose the adrenaline rush that suits you: one of four track options and eight ride variations. Adding even more excitement, some of the orbs can take up to 3 riders. The result is a lot of slipping, sliding, spinning, and hilarious laughs as the action-filled ride careens down the slope. Wet zorbing is available year-round. Dry zorbing is only available in the fall, winter, and early spring. The dry option rolls only on the fast straight tracks. Zorb is open year-round, and rides start at $17.

Applewood Farms is located just off US 441 at 240 Apple Valley Rd., right where Pigeon Forge and Sevierville meet. Part of a working apple orchard, the barn was converted into a cider mill in 1981, just in time to attract people from 45 different states and 10 foreign countries who were in the area visiting the

Childhood Literacy One of Dolly Parton's Loving Legacies

Growing up in the Great Smoky Mountains, Dolly Parton read a book that helped change her life. Although her father couldn't read or write, he encouraged his children to embrace education and was proud to see his daughter enjoy "book learning."

"I am '*The Little Engine That Could*,'" Parton said. "That is my favorite book, next to the Bible."

The classic story tells the tale of a determined little engine that, despite its size, triumphantly pulls a train full of toys to the waiting children on the other side of the mountain. "It was always my dream to be a star, to travel around the world," Parton said. Although the odds may have been against her, Parton succeeded in her dreams to become one of the world's best-known and most-beloved entertainers. She also created a program, Dolly Parton's Imagination Library in 1996, to help other children dream and succeed.

"I never in a million years thought we would help give away more than 120 million books," Parton said. Currently 1.4 million children receive a book each month. Through the program, children from one month old to five years old receive a free, brand-new, age-appropriate book once a month in the mail. The first book is *The Little Engine That Could*. The last book when a child turns 5 is *Look Out Kindergarten Here I Come*.

"At the end of the program, each child has a 60-volume library," says David Dotson, CEO of the not-for-profit Dollywood Foundation. "There are currently 1,700 communities in five countries participating in the program. There is at least one participating community in all 50 states."

Parton says it is important to help children develop a love for reading while they are young. "That's when they are most impressionable," she says. "I know how, if you can read, you can self-educate yourself."

1982 World's Fair in nearby Knoxville. Today, in addition to the cider mill, they have a bakery, a winery featuring apple and other fruit wines, an apple butter kitchen, a fudge kitchen, a candy factory, an ice-cream factory specializing in apple-flavored ice cream, a smokehouse, a Christmas and candle shop, and a gift shop featuring crafts, gifts, and souvenir items. In 1987 their old farmhouse home was turned into the *Applewood Farmhouse Restaurant* (865-428-1222; applewoodfarmhouserestaurant.com). On the menu you'll find traditional items such as prime rib and steaks, plus downhome favorites like beef liver and onions, country-fried catfish, meatloaf, and chicken and dumplings. But save room for some wonderful apple dessert. The homemade apple pies are always a favorite, but the apple fritters, accompanied by homemade

Hike with a Personal Guide

If you've thought about hiking in the Smokies but felt you didn't know enough about the mountains or about hiking, here's a unique opportunity to enjoy the area on foot. Liz Domingue, owner of **Just Get Outdoors**, located in Townsend, is a noted naturalist and wildlife biologist whose interest in and study of the natural world has been a lifelong pursuit and joy. She is tuned in to nature and to the personal needs and aspirations of her customers. Give her a call and she'll custom-fit a hike to your interests and skill level. She is an expert on birds, wildflowers, and salamanders of the Great Smoky Mountains and can talk with you about the natural as well as the cultural history of the mountains as she points out all the various flora and fauna. She also knows where all the neatest views and waterfalls are located. Prices start at $85 per person for half-day hikes for groups of two to four and $40 each for children ages 4 to 15. Full-day prices start at $100 each for two to four hikers and $45 for children ages 4 to 15. Liz also offers family and group discounts. Reach Liz at (865) 977-4453, or visit justgetoutdoors.com.

apple butter, are also high on the list for apple lovers. Located across the road from the Little Pigeon River, there are plenty of huge shade trees to sit under while you wait your turn. There was such a demand for their food that the owners decided to build a second eatery on the property in 1995 so that they wouldn't have to turn away so many hungry friends. Now the **Applewood Farmhouse Grill** (865-429-8644) offers the same menu, plus some lighter options for those who want to sample the different foods without digging into a full meal. Open daily for breakfast, lunch, and dinner. There are special meals and hours for Thanksgiving and Christmas.

About 4 miles north on US 441, or the **Dolly Parton Parkway**, as they call it around here, is the downtown section of Dolly's hometown, **Sevierville**. Stop and ask about her and you'll be amazed at how many "good friends" this lady has. Less commercial than the other communities along US 441, the downtown section has retained most of its small, mountain atmosphere. On a walking tour of 26 historic landmarks, you'll get to see a life-size bronze statue of Dolly.

Home to more than 600 animals representing over 130 species, **RainForest Adventures Discovery Zoo** (109 Nascar Dr.; 865-428-4091; rfadventures.com) takes you on a fun journey into the mysteries of the world's rain forests. In here you'll find hundreds of cool-looking species in natural habitats. Look close, because they'll be looking back at you. There are birds, bugs, snakes, amphibians, and mammals with fascinating critters galore. Open daily year-round, 9 a.m. to 5 p.m. Located at stoplight 13.4, adjacent to Tanger Outlet Mall.

Heading to **Knoxville** from Sevierville on US 441/411, you'll pass an abundance of antiques and craft shops, potteries, and souvenir and gift shops. When the highways split, continue on US 441 into Knoxville until you cross the Tennessee River. That big golden ball you see high in the air to your left as you cross the river is the **Sunsphere** (810 Clinch Ave.; worldsfairpark.org), the 266-foot-high hexagonal streel structure is topped with a 75-foot gold-colored glass sphere. The Sunsphere was the centerpiece of the **1982 World's Fair**.

The Sunsphere offers a marvelous view of Knoxville from a 4th-level Observation Deck, which features 360-degree views of the original 1982 World's Fair site, downtown Knoxville, the Tennessee River, the University of Tennessee, and the great Smoky Mountains. There is no admission charge to visit the Observation Deck which is usually open from 9 a.m. to 10 p.m. Access is from double elevators facing the lake at the base of the Sunsphere.

Adjacent to the fair site is the **Knoxville Museum of Art** (1050 Worlds Fair Park Dr.; 865-525-6101; knoxart.org), with a fine permanent collection as well as 12 exhibitions a year to choose from. On most Friday nights during the year, a special Alive After Five program features jazz and blues music from 6 to

Bush's Beans Museum

Strange as it may sound, **Bush's Beans Company** didn't start with beans. The family business began as a tomato cannery in 1897. As Americans clamored for the convenience of canned fruit and vegetables, Bush Brothers & Company added peaches, blackberries, hominy, and green beans to its canning line.

During the Great Depression, inexpensive food like the development of Pork & Beans in 1934 became a popular addition to family dining tables. When World War II ramped up, the Bush Brothers canned and shipped cans of tasty Pork & Beans to American troops overseas.

Before long, families were putting canned Bush's beans into baked beans. That gave Condon Bush the idea that his company should make its own canned baked beans. In 1969, the facility's Bush's Baked Beans was developed based on a secret family recipe. The result proved to be the biggest success in company history.

Today, visitors can tour the free **Bush's Beans Visitor Center & Museum** (865-509-3077; bushbeans.com) at 3901 US 411 in Chestnut Hill, browse in the gift shop and visitor center, learn the history of family dog Duke, and dine in Bush's Best Family Café where diners love the baked beans and the special pinto bean pie for dessert. Bush will proudly share the recipe for the pinto bean pie.

"But don't ask for the secret family recipe for our baked beans," said manager Scott Schroeder. "The secret recipe is protected by lasers in the museum. That's a recipe the family won't share."

8:30 p.m. The $8–10 admission gets you the music and access to the exhibits. A cash bar and light appetizers are available. The museum is open Tues through Sun with free admission.

A great way to start a visit in Knoxville is at the ***Knoxville Visitor Center*** (800-727-8045; visitknoxville.com), located downtown at 301 S. Gay St. The Knoxville Visitor Center has four different areas in one location. It's the place to pick up printed information or get questions answered at the visitors' desk. Then there's the gift shop, which carries locally made products such as candles, pottery, and paintings. The Parlor offers snacks and drinks, and a stage inside the visitor center is the site of live music at noon every day, except Sun. The music is broadcast live on the WDVX radio station as the Blue Plate Special. Open daily.

The ***Women's Basketball Hall of Fame*** (700 Hall of Fame Dr.; 865-633-9000; wbhof.com) is easy to find. Just look for the big basketball. The facility sits under a huge 30-foot-wide, 20,000-pound orange basketball. Although I have never counted them, officials say there are 96,000 pebbles on that ball.

See the Warbirds

The ***Tennessee Museum of Aviation*** is home to resident warbirds and is intended to be patriotic, educational, and entertaining. It certainly achieves all three! Even if you're not particularly interested in aviation or war history, this is a compelling, emotional stop. We guarantee you'll end up with a couple of lumps in your throat.

Located in a 50,000-square-foot hangar next to the Gatlinburg Pigeon Forge Airport, along Dolly Parton Parkway at 135 Air Museum Way in Sevierville, the museum has a collection of functional warbirds, including two rare P-47D aircraft, a P-47 Thunderbolt, a Mig-17, and a T-6 trainer. Planes will be flown in, flown out, and rotated in the exhibit lineup.

Exhibits include a comprehensive historical timeline, uniforms, memorabilia, plane engines, and jeeps. Among the prized possessions is the Congressional Medal of Honor presented to aviator general Jimmy Doolittle in 1942. Also on display is an in-depth look at the roots of flight through the eyes of the Wright Brothers; it showcases their first 10 years of flying experimentation, complete with models of nine of the planes they built during that time.

The mission of the privately owned museum is to preserve an understanding and appreciation for the aircraft and those who flew them to change the course of American history. There is a gift shop, and the museum is also home to Tennessee's Official Aviation Hall of Fame. Open year-round, Tues through Sat 10 a.m. to 6 p.m. from Mar 1 through Nov 30, from 10 a.m. to 5 p.m. from Dec through Feb. Closed Thanksgiving and Christmas Day. Closes at 3 p.m. on Christmas Eve. Just call (866) 286-8738, or visit tnairmuseum.com.

I'll take their word for it. Inside the entranceway is a spectacular 17-foot-tall, 3-player bronze sculpture. There are exhibits, videos, and memorabilia from all facets of women's basketball—from collegiate to professional. The Hall of Fame is open Tues through Sat Labor Day through Apr. 1 and Mon through Sat May 1 to Labor Day. Closed major holidays. Admission is $7.95 for adults, $5.95 for seniors and children ages 6 to 15.

Knoxville is the site of the main campus of the ***University of Tennessee***, where the Volunteers play their football games in the 95,000-plus-seat ***Neyland Stadium***. It's only natural that tailgate partiers would adapt to the unique position of the stadium next to the Tennessee River. The Volunteer Navy, as it is called here, starts gathering as early as the Thurs before a Sat game, and by game time as many as 300 boats have tied up. The only traffic these folks have to contend with is walking across the street to the stadium. Washington State has the only other major college stadium in the nation accessible by water.

Colorful "Big Orange" football is king in the fall, but the pinks and whites of flowering dogwood dominate the city's attention each spring. City officials estimate that about a million such trees bloom in their city each year. Why is Knoxville so decked out in beautiful trees? The story goes that it is all the result of a perceived insult. Seems that in 1947, New York newspaper reporter John Gunther came to town and looked around. Then he returned to his New York home and wrote a scathing article.

"Knoxville is the ugliest city I ever saw in America, with the possible exception of some mill towns in New England. Its main street is called Gay Street; this seemed to me to be a misnomer." Understandably, those words riled some Knoxville folks tremendously. They not only got riled, they decided to do something about living in "the ugliest city." Members of the Knoxville Garden Club, led by Betsey Creekmore, Martha Ashe, and Betsy Goodson, joined with other concerned citizens to begin a civic beautification project—the Dogwood Trails. Today, the city has more than 85 miles of dogwood trails in 12 neighborhoods throughout the city. A ***Dogwood Arts Festival*** (865-637-4561; dogwoodarts.com) is held annually during late April, with arts, crafts, and other activities. Bus tours for $5 a seat leave from the festival grounds at Market Square Mall.

You won't find any chain stores or nationally known restaurants in the ***Old City area*** (800-727-8045; knoxville.org) of Knoxville. What you'll find instead is a several-block area of one-of-a-kind shops, restaurants, bars, and music clubs that feature everything from jazz to reggae.

The hub of the Old City is at the junction of Jackson Avenue and Central Street in the northeastern section of downtown Knoxville. The area is a product of the period when the railroad made the city a center for commerce by delivering merchandise to the many huge 19th-century brick warehouses in the neighborhood.

The Old City's charm adds a perfect backdrop to various festivals and events during the year. Don't miss the fun.

In Morningside Park, near downtown, is the largest statue of an African American in the US. The 13-foot-tall bronze statue honors Tennessee's own **Alex Haley**, author of numerous books, including the novel **Roots**. Designed for interaction, the statue depicts Haley with an open book as if he's reading to children; it's a popular setting for photos.

Dedicated in 1998, the **War Dog Memorial** commemorates all the dogs that served during World War II. It's located in front of the University of Tennessee's Veterinary Hospital at 2407 River Dr. A touching memorial, the sculpture features a Doberman pinscher to represent the hundreds of dogs that served.

The **Bijou Theatre** (803 S. Gay St.; 865-522-0832; knoxbijou.com), Knox-ville's third-oldest building, is on the National Register of Historic Places and is a fun place to attend a concert or a live stage production. The restored relic houses all sorts of events, plays, and concerts throughout the year.

The **Three Rivers Rambler** train excursion (865-524-9411; threerivers rambler.com) is one of the best in the South. The 90-minute trip aboard a coal-fired steam engine runs parallel to the Tennessee River, providing some great views. It passes through the historical areas of the city, past industrial plants, and through farmland.

Where the Holston and French Broad Rivers converge to form the head of the Tennessee River, the train crosses the Holston River on the historic Three Rivers Trestle. On the way back, the engineer will usually slow way down or stop on the trestle, allowing passengers to take in a fabulous view.

There is food and drink in the club car, and passengers are permitted to bring a picnic lunch if they desire.

You can choose to ride in a plush circa 1925 Pullman car, a circa 1932 enclosed passenger car, or an open-air gondola car. Adult rates are $28.50, senior citizens $27.50, and children (ages 3 to 12) are $16 with $7.50 for tod-dlers ages 1 and 2; infants free. The train loads at Volunteer Landing, down-town on the Tennessee River, and runs Sat and Sun from late Mar through Dec, except for Sat home football games.

East Tennessee's preeminent fair, the **Tennessee Valley Fair** (865-215-1471; tnvalleyfair.org), takes place in early September each year in Chilhowee Park, 4 miles east of downtown. There's top-name entertainment, livestock and agriculture shows, carnival rides, and plenty of great old-time fair flavor. Admission is charged.

Another example of the old-time company town is found along US 129 south of Knoxville. Incorporated in 1919, the city of **Alcoa** was created by the Aluminum Company of America (ALCOA). Corporate offices are in Pittsburgh, but the southern plant opened in 1913 in a town called North Maryville. Six years later, with the financial help of the corporation, the city was created and its name changed.

birthplaceofa phrasemaker

"Damn the torpedoes! Full speed ahead." That well-known command was given by David Farragut, a Civil War admiral of the Union navy during the battle of Mobile Bay. He was born in Knoxville, and today the community where he grew up is named for him.

Sam Houston, Davy Crockett's good friend, came to Blount County with his family when he was 14 years of age and in due time developed a fascination with the lifestyle of the neighboring Cherokee Indians. Soon he was adopted by the Cherokees, who called him The Raven.

He left the Indians to take a teaching position in a one-room schoolhouse near Maryville. He had little formal education but had read every book he could get his hands on, had won every spelling contest he entered, and could recite large portions of Homer's *Iliad* from memory. His teaching career lasted one term. In March 1813, he gave up teaching to enlist in General Andrew Jackson's army to fight the Creek Indian War.

The schoolhouse where he taught still stands and is considered the oldest original schoolhouse in the state and the only building left having a close association with this famous soldier and statesman. Built in 1794, the school now houses many Houston artifacts, including a pair of lead knuckles with his name carved in the soft metal. The guide at the **Sam Houston Schoolhouse** (865-983-1550; samhoustonhistoricschoolhouse.org) speculates whether he used them to keep order in the classroom.

The site also includes a visitor center and museum exhibits. It's located 6 miles north of Maryville at 3650 Sam Houston Lane, off Highway 33. Open 10 a.m. to 5 p.m. Tues through Sat. The Schoolhouse closes the last Sat before Christmas and reopens the first Tues in Feb. Admission for adults, $3; children under 10 free.

Before the Smoky Mountains became a national park in 1935, the little community of **Townsend** was a major lumbering center. The **Townsend Visitors Center** (800-525-6834; smokymountains.org) at 7906 E. Lamar Alexander Pkwy is the place to start your visit to this part of the state.

The Little River Railroad and Lumber Company, headed by Colonel W. B. Townsend, set up mills and harvested logs from the rich, fertile forests that are now federal lands. Today, very little of that heritage exists except in memory and old photos. In the center of town you'll find the **Little River Railroad and Lumber Company Museum** (7747 E. Lamar Alexander Pkwy.; 865-661-0170; littleriverrailroad.org). Among its memorabilia are a restored Shay Engine No. 2147 that was used locally during the early 1900s and an L&N Class NE Little Woody vintage caboose.

A restored train depot serves as a museum that's filled with memorabilia and photos of the early railroad and lumbering industries. It's open daily during the summer; weekends Apr, May, Sept, and Nov. Grounds and outdoor exhibits are always available during the off-season. Admission is free.

Sandy Headrick is one of the dedicated group members that run the museum, and she can be found across the street at the resort facility she owns and operates with her husband, Don. The Tudor-style **Highland Manor Inn** (865-448-2211 or 800-213-9462; highlandmanor.com) has a classy country inn atmosphere. The views from the balconies offer a spectacular vista of the Smokies, and several rooms have private whirlpool baths. It's located up on a hill, off US 321, near the center of town at 7766 E. Lamar Alexander Pkwy. In-season room rates start at $80.

Townsend calls itself "The Peaceful Side of the Smokies," referring to the fact that it is still quite laid-back and low-key, while the cities on the other side of the mountain, Pigeon Forge and Gatlinburg, are bustling tourist magnets. However, there is still a great deal to do here, especially if you love the outdoors.

You're only 8 miles from one of the national park's premier attractions when you're in Townsend. **Cades Cove** was a thriving mountain community in the 1850s with about 685 residents and 15,000 acres of usable farmland under cultivation. Today, the area remains as it was then, with original buildings in original locations, so visitors can get a true sense of the spaciousness of early mountain life. An 11-mile self-guided auto loop tour gives the best idea of the culture of the region. Most homes, churches, and stores are open to the public.

The **Foothills Parkway**, which runs from US 321 near Walland for 17 miles, is a magnificent stretch of road that provides some great scenic pull-off opportunities that give you superb panoramic views of the mountains.

While it's always beautiful around here, our favorite time to visit is in the spring. Wildflowers seem to be growing everywhere you look. The mountains and valleys are carpeted with mountain phlox, dwarf irises, trilliums, and pink lady's slippers. Dogwoods, redbuds, and azaleas also add their color. The temperatures are usually comfortable, and the hiking and biking are superb. If you're interested in hopping on a horse and doing some trail riding in the mountains, contact the expert horsemen at the **Davy Crockett Riding Stables** (505 Old Cades Cove Rd.; 865-448-6411; davycrockettridingstables.com).

Billing itself as the "greatest sight under the Smokies," the **Tuckaleechee Caverns** (865-448-2274; tuckaleecheecaverns.com) is a fun diversion if you get tired of always going up into the mountains. Here's your chance to go under things. It's always 58 degrees, and some of the formations and cave rooms are quite spectacular. These lovely caverns are open Mar 15 to Mar 31 from 10 a.m. to 5 p.m.; Apr 1 to Oct 31 from 10 a.m. to 6 p.m.; and Nov 1 to Nov 30 from 10 a.m. to 5 p.m. The Caverns is located off US 321. Admission is $18 adults, $8 children (ages 5 to 11), and free for children under 5.

Country Lifestyle

Sequoyah was an uneducated, crippled Cherokee half-breed who was shunned by his peers for much of his life until, in 1821, he introduced an alphabet to his people. It was so easy to learn that soon thousands were using it. Before long, the Cherokees were more literate than most of the white men living in the area.

Sequoyah is the only man to single-handedly develop and perfect an alphabet. In doing so he endowed an entire nation with learning. The story of Sequoyah is told in the **Sequoyah Birthplace Museum** (423-884-6246; sequoyahmuseum.org), which is located south of Vonore at 576 Highway 360 and is owned and operated by the Eastern Band of Cherokee Indians. The only Indian-operated historical attraction in Tennessee, it's found on the shores of Tellico Lake, 37 miles south of downtown Knoxville.

The museum is dedicated to this brilliant Native American, but it also tells a great deal about the Cherokee as a nation. Displays range from Native American artifacts to a *Blondie* comic book written in the Cherokee alphabet. An adjacent gift shop offers a wide variety of Cherokee crafts, works of art, and related books. Open daily, year-round except Thanksgiving, Christmas, and New Year's Day; admission for adults, $5, children under 12, free.

Along US 11 a few miles from Sweetwater lies the little town of **Niota**, which you may remember from national news reports a few years back. It was put on the map when the town was run by an all-female government. Coincidentally, this was the home of Harry Burn, the Tennessee legislator who cast the deciding vote to ratify the amendment to the US Constitution that gave women the right to vote.

The main attraction here is the **Niota Depot** (423-568-2584; niotatn.org), the oldest standing railroad depot in the state. Built in 1853 from handmade baked bricks, the building now houses the town offices. If you'd like a tour, stop by and someone will take you on a guided walk through the historic building, or contact them in advance for more tour information.

Along Highway 68, just outside Sweetwater, you'll find something quite amazing "under the beaten path." It's the ***Lost Sea Adventure*** (423-337-6616; thelostsea.com), an attraction that the *Guinness Book of World Records* calls America's largest underground lake. It's a 4.5-acre "bottomless" lake 300 feet underground.

The 55-minute tour is an easy walk down to the lake. There's not a single step to concern yourself with, since all paths are sloping and include handrails. Glass-bottomed boats take you out onto the water, and white trout will gather around the boat as you approach their end of the lake. The tour guides are local and have quite a few interesting stories to tell. They might even try to scare you a few times as you walk along.

Trade Faire Follies

Trade fairs were the commercial centers of an English community during the 18th century. Streets were filled with vendors and craftspeople selling all sorts of essentials. Puppet shows were presented for the kids and theatrical plays for the adults. Farmers would bring their oxen to trade and their handiwork to sell.

In America trade fairs were abundant throughout most of the colonies and were originally set up to resemble those in Britain. However, it wasn't long until Americans came up with their own version of this annual social event. Sporting challenges, including fistfights and running races, were held; fortune-tellers foretold ladies' dreams for the coming year; and circus performers and gypsies would appear for both fun and profit.

It's not often in today's society that one gets the opportunity to walk among the sights, sounds, and smells of those early social gatherings. However, early each fall, more than 100 reenactors regularly gather at Fort Loudoun State Historic Area to put on an early trade fair, both for their own fun and for the public's education.

At the *18th Century Trade Faire*, you can sample the foods and the crafts of the 1700s, enjoy period musical entertainment, and see how good we really have it today! You'll have the opportunity to interact with costumed reenactors—from British and French soldiers to ladies with small children—all of whom will be more than happy to talk with you and explain the way of life they are re-creating.

It all takes place at the 1,200-acre *Fort Loudoun State Historic Area*, one of the earliest British fortifications on the Western Frontier, built in 1756. Today the area houses an interpretive center offering information and artifacts excavated from the ruins prior to the fort's reconstruction. Numerous other unique events take place on the grounds during the year, including a warm and wonderful Christmas celebration. Located 30 miles south of Knoxville, off US 441 in the town of Vonore. Call (423) 420-2331, or go to fortloudoun.com for more information.

The Lost Sea has been designated as a Registered Natural Landmark by the US Department of the Interior because of the lake phenomenon and the abundance of rare crystalline formations throughout the cavern system. Open year-round except for Thanksgiving and Christmas; admission for adults $21.95; children (ages 4 to 12) $12.95.

Back in 1958, members of the Tellico Plains Kiwanis Club started talking about the lack of roads from Monroe County across the mountains into North Carolina. That put plans in motion, and in 1996 The *Cherohala Skyway*, also known as the Ribbon in the Sky, opened as a $100 million, 43-mile scenic stretch of pure, uninterrupted mountain beauty. It runs along the ridge for a portion, down into the valleys for a while, and provides amazingly colorful vistas from 5,000 feet up, from the dogwoods and redbuds in the spring to the oranges, reds, and browns of the fall.

The road gets its unusual name from a combination of the two national forests where it begins and ends: the Cherokee in Tennessee and the Nantahala in North Carolina.

In *Tellico Plains*, enter the Skyway via Highway 165. There are plenty of brochures out about the road, and you can see some stunning photographs of the highway at cherohala.com, or call (800) 768-7129.

The *Tellico Ranger Station* of the Cherokee National Forest (250 Ranger Station Rd.; 423-253-8400; tellico-plains.com), just off the Skyway. Sited at an old Civilian Conservation Corps camp, the visitor center is located in a building built by the CCC in the 1930s. An exhibit area has a display of CCC items, including photos, caps, coats, and equipment. The folk here know the area quite well and can help you custom-build a day in the forest. There are plenty of maps and brochures, as well as a gift shop. Open Mon through Fri 8 a.m. to 4:30 p.m.

To reach the ranger station, take the Skyway out of town; the river will be on your right. Approximately 5 miles out of town, you'll see Forest Service Road 210 forking off to the right and continuing along the river. Take it; the station is less than half a mile down the road on your left. The river will still be on your right.

As a little boy, Charles Hall used to love to listen to tales told by local men around the old potbellied stove at his father's country store. Hall became fascinated with area history. Even as a child, he began collecting memorabilia that might have been lost over the years. Today, we are all the richer for this man's vision.

The *Charles Hall Museum* (229 Cherohala Pkwy.; 423-253-8000; charleshallmuseum.com) in Tellico Plains has grown to more than 6,000 artifacts and thousands of historical pictures and documents. The huge collection contains coins and currency, guns, historic equipment, telephones, and much more. It is now showcased in two museum buildings. Among the first white settlers in the area, Charles's mother's family settled in Tellico Plains in 1830. His father's family settled in the area in 1908. Hall has spent his life serving the community he loves. His list of offices held is quite impressive—mayor for 31 years, alderman-recorder for 2 years, justice of the peace for 6 years, and county commissioner for 6 years. Hall and his wife Billie Nell were also former owners of the Tellico Telephone Company.

Open daily 10 a.m. to 5 p.m. from Mar through Dec, open 10 a.m. to 5 p.m. Fri through Sun in Jan and Feb. Free admission.

It may be wise to fill up your tummy before heading to the mountains, and in Tellico Plains, the popular ***Tellihala Cafe*** (128 Bank St.; 423-253-2880; tellicafe.com) is the place to do it. There's an enormous selection, but if you're stopping for lunch, try the fried or broiled Tellico trout or the country-fried steak. You'll also find tantalizing choices on a special Barbecue Menu. It's open daily for lunch and dinner.

The people of the Coker Creek area are still shouting, "There's gold in them thar hills!" The community has been celebrating the ***Autumn Gold Festival*** (423-261-2242; tennesseerivervalleygeotourism.org) each October since 1968 to highlight the area's two forms of gold: the golden color of the leaves as they turn each fall and the gold that can still be found in the creeks of the area. The festival salutes the gold-mining heritage of the region, which goes back to the late 1820s.

Organizers bring down a few truckloads of dirt from the mountain gold mines so that festivalgoers have a better chance of finding some real gold when they participate in one of the major events, panning for gold. There are also board splitting, syrup making, gospel and country music, and arts and crafts. The festival is held at Coker Creek Village at 12528 Highway 68 in Coker Creek.

herewecome

Tennessee earned its nickname, the Volunteer State, from its remarkable record of furnishing volunteers in the War of 1812 and the Mexican War.

Coker Creek Crafts Gallery (423-261-2157; cokercreekgallery.com) is 1 block off Highway 68 on Hot Water Road. Turn onto Hot Water across from the fire station in town. Owned by Ken and Kathleen Dalton, the business specializes in high-quality crafts and visual arts. The Daltons' baskets are widely known and are in craft collections and museums all over the country. Closed Jan through Mar, it's open the rest of the year Tues through Sat.

The ***Crosseyed Cricket*** (865-986-5435; crosseyedcricket.com) advertises that it's more than "just a place to stay." Located at 751 Country Lane a few miles from exit 364 on I-40, about 20 miles southwest of Knoxville in Lenoir City, the Cricket is a campground in a beautiful rural setting and open year-round.

Roane County is dominated by the Tennessee Valley Authority's (TVA) ***Watts Bar Lake***. With 783 miles of lakefront, water-oriented activities are quite popular. Numerous marinas with boat rentals are scattered throughout the county. Once on the lake, island hopping is a popular activity. Hundreds of small islands make perfect secluded areas for picnicking and swimming.

Watts Bar Lake is one of several TVA lakes throughout the state that make up the chain called the ***Great Lakes of the South***. Many families live on the lake in houseboats. One colony is located just west of Kingston off US 70.

A driving tour of the county has been developed, as has a backcountry trail driving tour. Brochures and maps for both are available from the ***Roane County Visitors Bureau*** (1209 N. Kentucky St.; 865-376-4201; roanetourism .com), one block north of I-40.

The ***Roane County Museum of History & Archives*** (865-376-9211), located in the old county courthouse, features local and state history from prehistoric time to World War II. The building, with tall white columns, is only one of the seven remaining antebellum courthouses in the state. The museum explains how Kingston was the "Capital for a Day," and how a young Sam Houston clerked at a local hardware story. Located at the corner of Kentucky and Cumberland Streets at 119 Court St. in Kingston, it is open Mon through Fri 8:30 a.m. to 4:30 p.m. for free.

Fort Southwest Point (865-376-3641; roanetourism.com) in Kingston is the only fort in the state that has been reconstructed on its original foundation. The completed sections of the fort so far include the barracks, blockhouse, and more than 250 feet of palisade walls. A separate building houses the welcome center and the ***Fort Southwest Point Museum***. Work began on the site in the early 1970s, with a lot of construction still to do, according to officials.

The fort is located on a 30-acre hill overlooking Watts Bar Lake. Take Highway 58 south out of town; go 1 mile and the fort is on your right at 1225 S. Kentucky St. Fort Southwest Point is open Tues through Sat from 10 a.m. to 4 p.m. Staff members dress in period costumes and re-create activities from the fort's past during Living History Days each summer and Colonial Christmas Candlelight Tour in December.

West of Rockwood off US 70, high atop "the mountain" (as locals call it), is a Forest Service–run fire tower. Although visitors are not supposed to climb to the top of the tower, the picnic area around the bottom offers a magnificent bird's-eye vista of Rockwood and Watts Bar Lake. There are several shaded picnic tables and barbecue grills for the public to use. Open daily during daylight hours only. If you're driving through Rockwood during the Christmas season and see a huge star shining brightly to the west, this is where it's plugged in.

The Dream Counties

During the 1880s and 1890s, *Oliver Springs* was a central railroad town for the local coal miners. The area was booming by 1895 when the Oliver Springs Hotel opened and created a strong demand for passenger rail service to the area. As a result, the town built a new rail depot in 1896 to serve the increased needs.

That depot still stands today and is the home of a museum that highlights the area's growth to fame and fortune, although the hotel burned in 1905 and was never replaced, and the town hasn't had passenger service for decades. The town's library and museum are located in the restored depot. A reconditioned caboose sits out back, as do several other large pieces of local memorabilia. Located on the corner of Winter's Gap Road and Walker Avenue at 301 Kingston Ave., admission is free. You can reach the depot at (865) 403-5959 or oshistorical.com.

shhh!don'ttell anyone

The *World War II Secret City Festival* takes place in June each year and features tours, diverse entertainment by national acts, a WWII reenactment, arts and crafts, and children's activities. Festival is held at A.K. Bissell Park at 969 Oak Ridge Turnpike. Call (865) 425-3610, or visit their website at secretcityfestival.com.

In 1942, as World War II was raging, President Franklin D. Roosevelt approved the proposal by Albert Einstein to proceed in making a secret weapon. The Army Corps of Engineers chose an isolated 60,000-acre site here in Anderson County. Within one year, three defense plants were built and a *Secret City* for 75,000 people was cut out of the wilderness.

Throughout the war years *Oak Ridge*, the name given the community, remained under direct supervision of the government and was surrounded by a tall barbed-wire fence. Only a handful of the workers knew the true nature of the project, and all were sworn to secrecy. It was not until the dropping of the first atomic bombs in 1945 that the inhabitants behind the fence learned that they had been members of an important team of the famed *Manhattan Project*. *Oak Ridge National Laboratory* produced the uranium 235 and plutonium 239, the fuel necessary for the atomic bomb.

The fences came down in 1949, and the city was incorporated. Today, more than 4,000 buildings exist as a link to this era of secrecy. All three plants are still there, but the main emphasis in Oak Ridge now is energy research.

The original graphite reactor, the oldest continuously operated nuclear reactor in the world, is located in the Oak Ridge National Laboratory and open to the public. A map of the 38-mile self-guided motor tour of the entire area and other information on the area are available at the **Convention and Visitors Bureau** (1400 Oak Ridge Turnpike; 865-483-1321; exploreoakridge.com). Since September 11, 2001, some areas have been closed to the public.

bringhome dinner

The Clinch River has the highest trout catch rate of any stream in the eastern US.

The US Department of Energy has developed one of the world's largest energy exhibitions. The **American Museum of Science and Energy** (115 E. Main St.; 865-294-4531; amse.org) includes interactive exhibits, live demonstrations, computer displays, and filmed interpretations. All forms of energy and their relationship to humanity are explained. One favorite demonstration, especially of the young, makes a person's hair stand straight up on end. Open year round Tues through Sat 9 a.m. to 5 p.m.; Sun and Mon 1 p.m. to 5 p.m. Closed Thanksgiving Day, Christmas Day, and New Year's Day. Closing time is extended by one hour in June, July, and Aug. The admission fee is $8 for those 18 years of age and over, $5 for those 6–17, $5 for senior citizens and active military personnel, and free for kids under 6.

The story behind the creation of the living areas of Oak Ridge is an amazing one. Five home designs were created and assigned to workers according to family size and job importance. Neighborhoods centered on the town site, which was designed to offer shopping and recreation. The high school, multifamily housing, and the hospital were also built near the town site. Now known as **Jackson Square**, a walking tour of that original town site is available. You can get information on the tour at the visitor center.

The **Appalachian Arts Craft Shop** (2716 Andersonville Hwy.; 865-494-9854; appalachianarts.net) is on Highway 61 about a mile after it crosses I-75 in Clinton. The center was started in 1970 to "enrich the souls and pocketbooks of low-income people." Today the nonprofit organization that runs the center works with local people to preserve traditional Appalachian crafts and techniques. All types of crafts are available. The center is open 10 a.m. to 6 p.m. Mon through Sat and 1 to 5 p.m. Sun. In Jan and Feb, the gallery is closed on Sun and Mon.

Museum of Appalachia

"We simply cannot appreciate where we are today, or understand where we are going tomorrow, unless we understand where, as a culture, we've been in the past."

—John Rice Irwin

John Rice Irwin can pinpoint when his passion began. Back in 1962, he was attending an estate auction near his home when he saw a family's treasures being sold. An old cedar churn, one buyer said, would make a fine lamp, once she was done with it. A wagon seat would be turned into a coffee table, another buyer vowed.

Rice was horrified. He knew the stories behind some of these artifacts. He also knew that history was quickly being lost. "Things mean little when they are separated from their history," he said.

So Rice began trekking over hills and hollows buying and preserving relics and the tales behind them. Before long, folks began stopping by his home to see the interesting items that Rice had and to hear him talk about them. What happened next was only natural. Irwin and his wife Elizabeth decided to open a museum. In the late 1960s, the **Museum of Appalachia** (865-494-7680; museumofappalachia.org) was opened at 2819 Andersonville Hwy in Clinton with one log building on a 2-acre plot. Now, it has grown to 65 acres with dozens of authentic log structures and over 250,000 items—most of them with their stories, of course.

Most of the buildings were saved and moved from within a 200-mile radius of the museum. "It was not my intention to develop a cold, formal, lifeless museum," Irwin said. "Rather, I aimed for the 'lived-in' look, striving for, above all else, authenticity."

That is why, Irwin says, dwellings "appear as though the family had just strolled down to the spring to fetch the daily supply of water."

Some of the most joyous memories of his childhood, Irwin said, were listening to the stories told by old folks. "I was very lucky to know all four of my grandparents," he said. "They taught me a great deal and had a great influence on me."

Those ancestors often didn't have photographs or recordings but they would pass down their stories and their relics from one generation to another. Even back then, Irwin worried that so much was being lost. Sharing a quote from his friend Alex Haley, Irwin explains that "When an old person dies, it's like a small library burning."

The author of *Roots*, Haley visited the Museum of Appalachia in 1982 and became fast friends with Irwin. So impressed was the famous author with what he saw that he built a home across the road from the museum. "The day Alex Haley came to my house, we had soup beans and cornbread," Irwin recalled. "Then he used my phone to call his secretary and said, 'I'm moving to Tennessee.'"

Buildings include the Appalachian Hall of Fame with artifacts and stories about notable, colorful and unusual folks from the surrounding area "It's important to preserve these things that almost certainly would have been lost and their history lost with them," he said. "It's a shame that so many fascinating and meaningful stories are already gone."

Take for example, Gol Cooper's glass eye and a penknife on display. Cooper lived between Clarksville and Pris, Tennessee, in a place his grandfather had named Needmore because he said everybody there "needed more" than they had. In 1910, young Cooper was tying his shoe and had an opened penknife in his hand. He was stooped over, pulling tight the string when it broke, thrusting the knife blade through his eye.

"Gol's father had an eye made for him and he wore one until he died in 1979 in Norris where he had been employed by the Bureau of Mines for many years," Irwin said. The eye and the knife were presented to the museum by Cooper's daughter.

One of the most unusual stories must be the one about Charlie Fields. Fields never learned to read or write. After his father died, Fields stayed on to care for his mother. When she died, he started his now famous hobby of painting everything in sight in red, white and blue, most often with stripes and especially polka dots.

The museum display on Fields can create sensory overload. A replica of his bedroom with all the things he painted in his unique fashion could make your eyes swim. Born in 1894, Fields was a retired farmer who never married. The walkway leading to his house had concrete painted with red and white polka dots everywhere. Polka-dotted car tires also lined each side of the walk.

"You hear a lot of people say that they don't like history," Irwin summed up. "But they do like people and they do like stories. Well, that is history."

Less than a mile down the road from the crafts center is the **Museum of Appalachia** (2819 Andersonville Hwy.; 865-494-7680; museumofappalachia .org) in Clinton. Founded by John Rice Irwin in 1960, the museum is considered one of the most authentic representations of early Appalachian mountain life. Dozens of cabins and buildings have been moved here and preserved in the spaciousness of their original locations. More than 250,000 items are on display. Live music and demonstrations abound as employees go about living and working in a mountain village. *Roots* author Alex Haley said he loved the museum so much that he "built a home in sight of it." He lived across the street until his death in February 1992. Open daily, year-round from 9 a.m. to 5 p.m.; admission is $18 for adults, $15 for senior citizens, $10 children ages 13 to 18, and $6 for children ages 5 to 12.

If you can, plan your visit during one of the three "authentic" annual events: *July 4th Celebration, Tennessee Fall Homecoming* in October, or Candlelight Christmas.

The nearby city of **Norris** (800-524-3602; yallcome.org) is a great little community. Planned and built by the Tennessee Valley Authority (TVA) in 1934 as a demonstration of sound community development, the town features a greenbelt, a town forest that protects the city's water supply, and houses placed in a parklike atmosphere. Now an independent municipality, Norris has preserved its original look. Brochures and information are available at the police and fire departments.

The Tennessee Valley Authority Act was signed into law by President Franklin D. Roosevelt on May 18, 1933, and within a few weeks the TVA's first flood-control project, the Norris Dam, was started. As the oldest TVA facility, the dam is open to visitors on occasion, although the entire operation is now run by remote control. No tours are given, but you can drive across and get some great photos.

The dam and the lake are part of the **Norris Dam State Park**, as is the **Lenoir Family Museum** (865-494-7645; cityofnorris.com). Made up primarily of Helen and Will G. Lenoir's "junk" collection, items in the state-run facility date from prehistoric times to the present. The place is filled with artifacts that visitors are encouraged to pick up and touch. As the guides walk visitors through, they tell stories that bring the items to life. Many of the stories are more fun than the items themselves. To get the full benefit here, take the tour first and listen to the stories, then go back through and look at the displays at your own pace.

The museum's most treasured artifact is a European barrel organ with tiers of hand-carved wooden figures. Research shows it was made in Germany in 1826 and probably brought to America by a traveling showman. Admission is free. Open daily during summer; Wed through Sun only for the rest of the year.

Outside, the TVA has gathered two additional buildings. The **Caleb Crosby Threshing Barn**, built in the early 1800s, was one of the first threshing barns to be built in the US. It's full of pioneer machinery, including a wooden treadmill made in 1855. Across the field from the barn is a 1798 gristmill where corn is ground during the summer months. A gift shop is on the upper level. The entire setting is very rustic and just a short distance from the dam and a picnic area.

If it's rugged wilderness and wild whitewater you're looking for, follow US 27 north to **Wartburg** and the **Obed Wild and Scenic River** (423-346-6294; nps.gov/obed). The area is managed by the National Park Service and the Tennessee Wildlife Resources Agency and consists of four streams within the same watershed. Over the years, they have carved their way through the landscape and have created beautiful gorges, some as deep as 500 feet.

During the rainy season, December through April, the streams provide some of the finest, most technical whitewater in the nation. Some primitive camping is allowed. The visitor center for the area is located at 208 N. Maiden St., next to the Federal Building in Wartburg.

Frozen Head State Natural Area (423-346-3318; tnstateparks.com/parks/frozen-head) was named for a 3,324-foot peak in the Cumberland Mountains, the top of which is often shrouded in ice or snow. You enter this peaceful area through a vestige of densely forested, unspoiled mountain terrain. A vintage fire tower, which is accessible only by a walking trail, offers a spectacular panorama of this majestic part of the state. The park is located off Highway 62, east of Wartburg at 964 Flat Fork Rd.

Of the three utopian experiments in Tennessee during the late 1800s, **Rugby**'s was the largest and has left us with the most evidence of the dream ers' struggles.

Today 20 of the 70 original buildings of **Rugby's Utopian Community** (423-628-2441; historicrugby.org) still stand and have been preserved or restored. A few are still inhabited by descendants of the original settlers.

In 1880, English author-reformer Thomas Hughes launched this colony with the dream that it would be "a centre in which a healthy, reverent life shall grow." At its peak in 1884, the population was about 450. Today, Rugby has about 85 residents.

Hughes's vision of a utopian existence in the wilderness of Tennessee brought a taste of British culture along with it. Most of the settlers were young British of good family, and today their colorful Victorian legacies line the streets, making Rugby one of the most unusual communities in the state.

A journey through town should begin at the old **Rugby Schoolhouse**, which now serves as a museum and visitor center. In addition to the school, historic buildings open to visitors include the **Christ Church, Episcopal**, with its original hanging lamps and 1849 rosewood reed organ, and the **Thomas Hughes Free Public Library** (423-628-2441), which still contains what is regarded as the best representative collection (7,000 volumes) of Victorian literature in America.

Two historic structures have been restored and now offer overnight accommodations with historical accuracy. The **Pioneer Cottage**, **Percy Cottage**, and the **Newbury House Inn** are available with prior reservations. For dining,

capitaldujour

Four cities have served as Tennessee's state capital:

Knoxville, 1796–1817

Kingston, 1807, for one day only

Murfreesboro, 1817–1826

Nashville, 1826–present

the *Harrow Road Café* (423-628-2350) offers such taste pleasers as Welsh Rarebit, bangers and mash, and fish and chips. The cafe also offers ales, wines, and cocktails.

If you're into ghosts and stories of haunting, you'll get your fill during your tour of Rugby's historic district. If your guide doesn't talk about the various sightings through the years, make sure you ask. Rugby is located on Highway 52 a few miles west of US 27. Structures are open year-round except for Thanksgiving Day, Christmas Eve, Christmas Day, and New Year's Day; during Jan, tours are by appointment. Housing, shops, and a restaurant are open year-round.

Approximately 1 mile west of Rugby is the *Grey Gables Bed and Breakfast Inn* (2487 Rugby Pkwy.; 423-628-5252; greygablesbedandbreakfasttn.com). The magnificent home was built in 1990 for the purpose of setting up a classy inn that would combine the best of Victorian English and Tennessee country heritage. Decorated with country and Victorian antiques, the inn reflects the grace of the English and the cordiality of this area.

Innkeeper Linda Brooks Jones not only has a great 10-bedroom inn, but you'll have to loosen your belt a few notches after you've eaten a couple of meals here. In fact, Jones's cooking has gone over so well, and so many people were asking for her recipes, that she has written her own cookbooks, called *The Table at Grey Gables* and *A Full Table at Grey Gables*. She was born and raised in the area, and the cookbook has not only recipes but also historical narrative about Rugby and her relationship with the locals through the years.

If you look around, you'll see a few photos of former president Jimmy Carter and his wife, the inn's most famous boarders to date. They stayed here on June 17, 1997, and Jones has some great, fun stories about the visit. If it's available, she may let you have the bed the famous couple slept in.

officially speaking

The Square Dance is the official folk dance of Tennessee, and there are ample opportunities to join in the fun throughout the state. A good place to find information is through the **Tennessee State Association of Square & Round Dance Clubs Inc.** at tnsquare dance.org.

In addition to the great hospitality and the yummy cooking, the hostess offers a full array of activities and themed events. Rates include an elegant evening meal and a hearty country breakfast. Reservations are required; rates are $145 double occupancy, $95 single occupancy, plus a 5 percent lodging tax. Call Jones, and she'll send you a calendar that highlights special themed weekends. Wheelchair accessible. The

Inn also offers Level 2 Nissan Electric car charges, the only Nissan electric car charges within 50 miles of Rugby.

In addition to the bed-and-breakfast duties, Jones's daughter Tiffany and husband Gary run the *R. M. Brooks General Store* (2830 Rugby Pkwy.; 423-628-2533; rmbrooksstore.com), just west of Grey Gables. Linda's grandparents started the store in 1930, and it has remained in the family since. The village post office was tucked away in a corner of the store for years, and when it moved, the family made sure that the old-time postal feel of the mailboxes remained. The family wants to keep it a "typical, working country general store" where you can buy sandwiches, hoop cheddar cheese, mousetraps, soup, and just about anything else. Plus they have a selection of antiques and local crafts on sale. As in most establishments of this type, you'll find a good supply of local characters sitting around the potbellied stove just about any time you drop in. The general store is open Mon through Fri 10 a.m. to 5 p.m., Sat 8 a.m. to 5 p.m.

Next to R.M. Brooks Store is the *Brooks Corner Campground & RV Park* (2830 Rugby Pkwy.; 423-628-2533). The campground has 7 sites with 30-amp and 3 with 50-amp service. A bathhouse and restrooms are provided. The campground is open all winter but the bathhouse is winterized. Rates are $10 for tent camping, $20 for a 30-amp site, and $30 for a 50-amp site.

Forests & Cliffs

The 673-acre *Cove Lake State Park* (110 Cove Lake Ln.; 423-566-9701; tnstate parks.com/parks/cove-lake) is on the banks of Cove Lake, near *Caryville*. Established in the 1930s as a recreation demonstration area by the TVA, the National Park Service, and the Civilian Conservation Corps, the lake is home to more than 400 Canada geese each winter. Open daily year-round, the park is visited by nearly one million people each year. Located in Cove Lake State Park, *Rickard Ridge BBQ* (131 Goose Ln.; 423-907-8202; rickardridgebbq .com) features, just as it says, barbecue chicken, pork, beef, ribs, and catfish. The restaurant is open year-round, too, and features live bluegrass music on Mon and Thurs starting at 6 p.m. The park's schedule changes seasonally, so give them a call to find out more. The ranger's station and the masonry fences around it were built by the Civilian Conservation Corps.

In the summer the park offers an Olympic-size swimming pool and a wading pool for children, tennis courts, and more than 7 miles of trails of which more than 3 miles are paved for multiple uses, including jogging and biking.

This entire county has been described by many as one big natural museum. Ruggedness is the key word here, and one access to that ruggedness is through the **Big South Fork National River and Recreation Area** (423-569-9778; bigsouthforkpark.com). Authorized by Congress in 1974, the park has been frequented mainly by those who have been willing to explore the wilderness on its own terms. During the last few years, more roads, overlooks, and river access sites have been built, opening up the 100,000-acre park to less adventurous visitors.

The Big South Fork River cuts a course through one of the most spectacular chasms east of the Mississippi. The gorge is rimmed by towering bluffs of weathered sandstone rising as high as 500 feet. It's considered to be one of the best whitewater rivers in the East. In all, there are more than 80 miles of prime canoeing waters within the park.

Camping is permitted just about anywhere in the park, and mountain bikes and four-wheeled off-road vehicles are permitted on designated trails and roads. There are three developed campgrounds and the **Charit Creek Lodge** (865-696-5611; ccl-bsf.com), which offers 5 private cabins that accommodate up to 12 guests each, 2 cabins that can house up to 6 guest each, and 1 cabin (corncrib) for up to 3 guests. There is no electricity here, and no vehicular traffic is allowed. The lodge has clean restroom facilities with showers available seasonally and serves a hearty breakfast at 8 a.m. and dinner at 6 p.m. Sack lunches are available for day hikers/riders by reservation 3 days in advance.

The most comfortable way to see the rugged terrain and the river is aboard the **Big South Fork Scenic Railway** (66 Henderson St.; 800-462-5664; bsfsry .com). The 3-hour narrated trip leaves from the historic coal-mining town of Sterns, Kentucky. The 7-mile trip takes you down gently to the bottom of the gorge, through a massive tunnel, and along high rock ledges. It then hugs the banks of the river, where you might catch a glimpse of whitewater aficionados.

One of the most scenic highways in this part of the state connects Jellico with La Follette. Although it seems much longer, US 25W curves and twists for 29 very interesting miles. The road offers some spectacular views as it follows the canyons through the mountains. This route is a great alternative to interstate driving, but you'll need to adjust your speed to the road conditions, and you'll probably want to pull off a couple of times to enjoy the scenery. Several bitter skirmishes were fought around here during the Civil War.

Since 1760, treasure hunters have searched this area for the legendary **Swift's Silver Mines**, where John Swift and his crew mined silver, minted coins, and took it all back to the colonies. The operation ended during the Indian Wars. Several years later, Swift came back but due to his failing eyesight was unable to locate his mines, which he insisted were still full of silver. Nobody has found those mines yet.

Places to Stay in the Mountainous East

CARYVILLE

Cove Lake State Park
110 Cove Lake Ln
(423) 566-9701
Tnstateparks.com/parks/
cove-lake

CUMBERLAND GAP

The Olde Mill Bed & Breakfast
603 Pennlyn Ave.
(423) 869-0868
oldemillinnbnb.com

GATLINBURG

Bearskin Lodge on the River
840 River Rd.
(865) 430-4330
thebearskinlodge.com

Buckhorn Inn
2140 Tudor Mountain Rd.
(865) 436-4668
buckhorninn.com

Elk Springs Resort
123 Silverbell Ln.
(865) 233-2390
elkspringsresort.com

Foxtrot Bed and Breakfast
1520 Garrett Ln.
(865) 436-3033
thefoxtrot.com

Gatlinburg Town Square
414 Historic Nature Trl.
(865) 436-2039
exploriaresorts.com

Great Smoky Mountains National Park
(865) 436-1200
nps.gov/grsm

Greystone Lodge on the River
559 Parkway
(800) 451-9202
greystonelodgetn.com

Laurel Springs Lodge Bed and Breakfast
204 Hill St.
(865) 430-9211
laurelspringslodge.com

LeConte View Motor Lodge
929 Parkway
(865) 436-5032
leconteview.com

Lodge at Buckberry Creek
961 Campbell Lead Rd.
(865) 430-8030
buckberrylodge.com

Margaritaville Resort Gatlinburg
539 Pkwy.
(865) 430-4200
margaritavilleresort
gatlinburg.com

Zoder's Inn & Suites
402 Pkwy.
(865) 436-5681
Zoders.com

JEFFERSON CITY

EconoLodge
531 Patriot Dr.
(865) 397-9437

KNOXVILLE

Cook Loft
722 S. Gay St.
(865) 310-2216
cookloft.com

Glenwood Inn Bed & Breakfast
214 E. Glenwood Ave.
(865) 368-9398
theglenwoodinn.com

Hotel Knoxville
501 E. Hill Ave.
(865) 637-1234
Marriott.com

Marble Hill Inn Bed and Breakfast
125 E. Glenwood Ave.
(865) 851-1966

Oliver Hotel
407 Union Ave.
(865) 521-0050
theoliverhotel.com

Tennessean Hotel
531 Henley St.
(865) 232-1800
thetennesseanhotel.com

Volunteer Hotel
1706 Cumberland Ave.
(865) 437-5500
thevolunteerhotel.com

Volunteer Park
9514 Diggs Gap Rd.
(865) 938-6600
volparktn.com

LENOIR CITY

Crosseyed Cricket
Paw Paw Rd.
(865) 986-5435
crosseyedcricket.com

PIGEON FORGE

Black Fox Lodge
3171 Pkwy.
(865) 774-4000
tapestrycollection3.hilton
.com

Dollywood's DreamMore Resort
2525 DreamMore Way
(800) 365-5996
Dollywood.com

Hearthside Cabin Rentals
702 Wears Valley Rd.
(877) 411-5855
hearthsidecabinrentals.com

Inn at Christmas Place
119 Christmas Tree Ln.
(865) 868-0525
innatchristmasplace.com

Inn on the River
2492 Pkwy.
(800) 388-1727
myinnontheriver.com

Margarita Island Hotel
131 The Island Dr.
(865) 774-2300
margaritaislandhotel.com

Music Road Resort Hotel
303 Henderson Chapel Rd.
(844) 993-9644
musicroadresort.com

Park Grove Inn
149 Community Center Dr.
(865) 429-2333
parkgroveinn.com

Ramsey Hotel and Convention Center
3230 Pkwy.
(865) 428-2700
myramseyhotel.com

Riverstone Resort & Spa
212 Dollywood Ln.
(866) 908-0990
riverstoneresort.com

Sunrise Ridge Resort
2301 Ridge Rd.
(865) 908-6040
diamondresortsandhotels
.com

Valley Forge Inn
32142795 Pkwy.
(865) 453-7770
valleyforgeinn.net

RUGBY

1880 Newbury House at Historic Rugby
1331 Rugby Pkwy.
(423) 628-2441
historicrugby.org

Grey Gables Bed and Breakfast Inn
5809 Rugby Hwy.
(423) 628-5252
rugbytn.com

SEVIERVILLE

Berry Springs Lodge
2149 Seaton Springs Rd.
(865) 908-7935
berrysprings.com

Blue Mountain Mist Country Inn and Cottages
1811 Pullen Rd.
(865) 428-2335
bluemountainmist.com

Clarion Inn Willow River
1990 Gov. Winfield Dunn Pkwy.
(865) 429-7600
choicehotels.com

Comfort Inn Apple Valley
1850 Pkwy.
(865) 428-1069
choicehotels.com

Hidden Mountain Resort
475 Apple Valley Rd.
(865) 453-9850
hiddenmountain.com

Lodge at Five Oaks
1650 Pkwy.
(865) 429-8300
thelodgeatfiveoaks.com

Oak Haven Resort & Spa
1947 Old Knoxville Hwy.
(800) 652-2611
oakhavenresort.com

Oak Tree Lodge
1620 Pkwy.
(865) 428-7500
theoaktreelodge.com

Wilderness at the Smokies River Lodge
1424 Old Knoxville Hwy.
(877) 325-9453
wildernessatthesmokies
.com

TOWNSEND

Dancing Bear Lodge Townsend
7140 E. Lamar Alexander Pkwy.
(865) 448-6000
dancingbearlodge.com

Gracehill Bed and Breakfast
1169 Little Round Top Way
(865) 448-3070
gracehillbandb.com

Highland Manor Inn
7766 E. Lamar Alexander Pkwy.
(865) 448-2211
highlandmanor.com

Richmont Inn
220 Winterberry Ln.
(865) 448-6751
richmontinn.com

Townsend Gateway Inn
8270 Hwy. 73
(865) 238-0123
townsendgatewayinn.com

Townsend River Breeze Inn
8242 Hwy. 73
(865) 448-2389
riverbreezeinn.com

Tremont Lodge & Resort
7726 E. Lamar Alexander Pkwy.
(865) 448-3200
tremontlodge.com

Places to Eat in the Mountainous East

BEAN STATION

Clinch Mountain Lookout Restaurant
17 Old Mountain Rd.
(865) 767-2511

COSBY

Carver's Orchard & Applehouse Restaurant
3462 Cosby Hwy.
(423) 487-2710
carversappleorchard.com

GATLINBURG

Buckhorn Inn Restaurant
2140 Tudor Mountain Rd.
(866) 941-0460
buckhorninn.com

Calhoun's
1004 Pkwy. #101
(865) 436-4100
calhouns.com

Crockett's Breakfast Camp
1103 Pkwy.
(865) 325-1403
crockettsbreakfastcamp.com

Greenbriar Restaurant
370 Newman Rd.
(865) 412-1576
greenbriarrestaurant.com

Ole Red Gatlinburg
511 Pkwy.
(865) 325-3101
olered.com

Pancake Pantry
628 Pkwy.
(865) 436-4724
pancakepantry.com

Park Grill
1110 Pkwy.
(865) 436-2300
parkgrillgatlinburg.com

Peddler Steakhouse
1110 Pkwy.
(865) 436-5794
peddlergatlinburg.com

Timbers Log Cabin Restaurant
600 Glades Rd.
(865) 412-1303
timberslogcabinrestaurant.com

Wild Plum Tea Room
555 Buckhorn Rd.
(865) 436-3808
wildplumtearoom.com

KNOXVILLE

Chesapeake's
600 Union Ave.
(865) 673-3433
chesapeakes.com

Copper Cellar
1807 Cumberland
(865) 673-3411
coppercellar.com

Lakeside Tavern
10911 Concord Park Dr.
(865) 671-2980
lakeside-tavern.com

Lonesome Dove Knoxville
100 N. Central Ave.
(865) 999-5251
lonesomedoveknoxville.com

Stock & Barrel
35 Market Sq.
(865) 766-2075
Thestockandbarrel.com

Tupelo Honey
1 Market Sq.
(865) 522-0004
tupelohoneycafe.com

PIGEON FORGE

Alamo Steakhouse
3050 Pkwy.
(865) 908-9998
alamosteakhouse.com

Bullfish Grill
2441 Pkwy.
(865) 868-1000
bullfishgrill.com

Dolly Parton's Stampede
3849 Pkwy.
(865) 453-4400
dpstampede.com

Huck Finn's Catfish
3330 Pkwy.
(865) 429-3353
huckfinnsrestaurant.com

Local Goat
2167 Pkwy.
(865) 366-3035
localgoatpf.com

Mama's Farmhouse
208 Pickel St.
(865) 908-4646
mamasfarmhouse.com

Mel's Diner
119 Wears Valley Rd.
(865) 429-2184
meldinerspf.com

Old Mill Restaurant
164 Old Mill Ave.
(865) 429-3463
old-mill.com/
the-old-mill-restaurant

SEVIERVILLE

Applewood Farmhouse Grill
220 Apple Valley Rd.
(865) 429-8644
applefarmhouserestaurant.com

Applewood Farmhouse Restaurant
240 Apple Valley Rd.
(865) 428-1222
applewoodfarmhouserestaurant.com

The Diner
550 Winfield Dunn Pkwy.
(865) 908-1904
thediner.biz

Five Oaks Farm Kitchen
1638 Pkwy.
(865) 365-1008
fiveoaksfarmkitchen.com

Holston's Kitchen
639 Dolly Parton Pkwy.
(865) 365-4205
holstonskitchen.com

SWEETWATER

Bradley's Pit Barbecue & Grill
517 New Hwy. 68
(423) 351-7190
bradleypitbbq.com

Dinner Bell
576 Oakland Rd.
(423) 337-5825

Plateaus & Valleys

Upper Cumberland

In a valley surrounded by the Cumberland Mountains a few miles from the Kentucky border, **Sergeant Alvin York**, one of America's most celebrated military heroes, was born and reared. Except for the 2 years he fought in World War I, Sergeant York spent his entire life in these mountains. But those 2 years put York in the history books and this part of the state on the map. Today the ***Sgt. Alvin C. York State Historic Park*** (931-879-6456) commemorates his life and career. The area is about 9 miles north of Jamestown on US 127 and is open daily.

York's one-man firefight with the German army in France's Argonne Forest on October 8, 1918, is now legendary. As a patrol leader, he killed 25 German soldiers and almost single-handedly captured another 132. As a result, he received more than 40 Allied decorations and worldwide publicity.

His modest upbringing here in the Tennessee mountains and his refusal to cash in on his popularity by selling out to the media won the hearts of millions, and he returned to the valley as a bona fide hero.

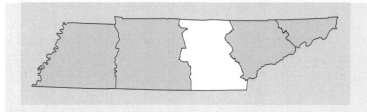

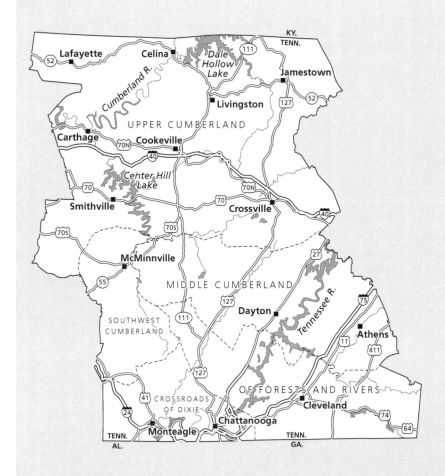

Lafayette

52

Celina

Dale Hollow Lake

111

KY.
TENN.

Jamestown

Cumberland R.

Livingston

127

52

UPPER CUMBERLAND

Carthage

70N

Cookeville

40

Center Hill Lake

70

70N

Smithville

70

70S

Crossville

40

70S

McMinnville

55

MIDDLE CUMBERLAND

27

127

Dayton

75

Tennessee R.

111

SOUTHWEST
CUMBERLAND

11

Athens

411

127

OF FORESTS AND RIVERS

41

CROSSROADS
OF DIXIE

Cleveland

74

24

Chattanooga

64

TENN.
AL.

Monteagle

TENN.
GA.

All along US 127, you'll find rural front yards loaded with items; in the cities you'll find sidewalks filled with merchandise. It's an almost endless supply of trash and treasures, and you'll find just about anything you'd ever want. Please be careful: US 127 is quite busy during the sale. Watch out for traffic and always use your turn signals if you are going to pull over. Held one weekend in Aug, Thurs through Sun. Call (800) 327-3945, or go online at 127sale.com to find out more.

Jamestown was popular with Native Americans and early travelers because of the many freshwater springs that came up through the sandy soil. In fact, the original name of the community was Sand Spring. One of the early settlers here was John M. Clemens, the father of Samuel Clemens, better known as Mark Twain. On Main Street, just off the courthouse square, **Mark Twain Spring Park** is on land adjacent to the Clemens homestead and still has a small spring that was once the source of water for the early residents. Although there is no evidence that Samuel Clemens ever visited here, he was conceived here. He was born 5 months after his parents moved to Missouri.

Three miles south of Jamestown on US 127 is the **Highland Manor Winery** (2965 S. York Hwy.; 931-879-9519; highlandmanorwinery.com), which has the distinction of being the oldest licensed winery in the state and the first American winery to be awarded the International Gold Medal for Quality in Madrid, Spain. This is one of more than 70 commercial wineries in the state, including 6 wine trails. (See Montgomery County in the Heartlands chapter for additional fruit-of-the-vine experiences.) The winery is open daily for tours and tastings.

Some huge pumpkins are grown each year in the area around Jamestown, and the pumpkin is king for a weekend early each October when the **Great Pumpkin Festival and Weigh-Off** (allardtfestival.blogspot.com) is held in nearby Allardt, southeast of Jamestown on Highway 52. The folks here have turned pumpkin and gourd competition into a reason to play. On Saturday morning, the weigh-offs begin to find the year's champion. Pumpkins from all over show up on the back of pickup trucks. We were amazed at our first sight of an 800-pounder.

World's Longest Yard Sale

The 690-mile US 127 Corridor Sale now runs from 5 miles north of Addison, Michigan, to Gadsden, Alabama. It travels through 6 states—Michigan, Ohio, Kentucky, Tennessee, Georgia, and Alabama.

From Hell-Raiser to Hero

Born December 13, 1887, in a two-room log cabin in Pall Mall, **Alvin York** was the third-oldest of 11 children. The York family barely eked out a living through farming and hunting. York had the equivalent of a third-grade education and earned a reputation as a hell-raiser. But that reputation changed in 1914 when York experienced a religious conversion.

After his best friend was killed in a bar fight, York attended a revival at the Church of Christ in Christian Union and was converted. Blessed with a good singing voice, York quickly became the song leader and Sunday-school teacher at the church.

Then came World War I. On April 6, 1917, the United States declared war on Germany. Less than two months later and just six months before his 30th birthday, York received his draft notice. Because of his church's stand against violence and war, York wrote at the bottom of his draft card: "Don't want to fight."

It made no difference. The excellent marksman who had no stomach for war was ordered to report to Camp Gordon, Georgia, for basic training. Then he would be shipped to France to fight. York's rise to fame resulted from his seemingly impossible firefight against the German Army in the Argonne Forest of France. York's platoon set out to capture a railroad defended by German machine gunners. Most of the squad was killed or wounded in a torrent of bullets.

Armed with a rifle and a .45 Colt pistol, York returned fire. With the uncanny marksmanship he developed while hunting in the Tennessee backwoods, York picked off soldier after soldier. Twenty-five Germans had fallen when the demoralized enemy troops threw down their weapons and surrendered. York and 7 of his men marched their captives back to the American lines, taking more prisoners along the way. They returned with 132 prisoners in tow.

But his family would not have known of his heroism were it not for a flood of newspaper and magazine articles. When he returned from France in May 1919, York was shocked to find that he was a bona fide American hero. Shortly after his return home, York married his longtime sweetheart, Gracie Williams. The couple moved into a new farmhouse on a 385-acre farm which grateful Tennesseans had contributed money to purchase. The Yorks had 10 children, with such famous American names as Betsy Ross, Woodrow Wilson, Thomas Jefferson, Andrew Jackson, and Sam Houston.

In 1954, York had a stroke and spent the last 10 years of his life bedridden. He died in 1964. Today, visitors can see the York home almost exactly as it was when the family lived there. The special bed where the old soldier spent his last years is still set up in the couple's bedroom. The historic area also contains a gristmill that Alvin York operated in the 1940s, a grocery store/post office he built and ran, and a re-created World War I trench.

In addition to all the noteworthy gourds, pumpkins, watermelons, and squash, dozens of local craftspeople set up in Bruno Gernt Park to sell their unique products. There's also music, an antique tractor show, a quilt show, a street dance, beauty pageant, auto show, a bake sale and auction, a parade, and of course plenty of pumpkin-flavored goodies. Admission to this great rural slice of life is free.

In the heart of the Upper Cumberland region, *Livingston*, the county seat, is rapidly becoming known for its quality crafts outlets. The downtown area around the historic courthouse is known as Court Square and is home to many retail shops, antiques stores, and crafts stores.

Counted among the antiques stores in downtown is the *Antique Market* (116 N. Court Sq.; 931-823-4943). Inside, you'll find more than 40 booths and two large rooms full of everything from fabulous antique jewelry to postcards to oak furniture. It's open Mon through Sat.

At 1825 Burkhart Rd., the *Livingston Antique Outlet* (517-548-5399; livingstonantiqueoutlet.com) features more than 200 dealers in a 33,000-square-foot red barn. Open daily.

Livingston throws some great parties, and it is Hometown USA at its finest. Call the Chamber of Commerce at (931) 823-6421 for a full listing, but two to keep in mind are Fall-O-Ween the Sat before Halloween, when more than 150 vendors and live music fill the Livingston Historic Downtown Square while children parade in trick-or-treat finery. Christmas in the County is always the day after Thanksgiving and the following two Fridays from 5 p.m. to 8 p.m. with carriage rides, late-night shopping, a tree-lighting ceremony, Santa visits, food, arts and crafts, and a lot of good-neighbor howdies.

Down in the southeast corner of Overton County is *Muddy Pond*, a small Mennonite community that happens to be way off the beaten path. Entrance

AUTHOR'S TOP TEN PICKS

Great Pumpkin Festival and WeighOff	Muddy Pond
Highland Manor Winery	Ocoee Whitewater Center
Homesteads	Rhea County Museum
Horsin' Around Carving School	Russell Stover Candies Factory and Outlet Store
International Towing & Recovery Hall of Fame and Museum	
	Tennessee's Badlands

to the community is off Highway 164, about halfway between Crawford and Monterey, or off Highway 62, 1 mile west of Clarkrange. In either direction you'll have a nice paved road for several miles before the gravel road begins.

There are several retail shops located back here, and many of the farmers sell fresh eggs and bread out of their homes. A horse-powered mill, the **Muddy Pond Sorghum Mill** (931-445-3509; muddypondsorghum.com), creates the product and is where the owners also sell homemade bread and fried pies. The mill is open Tues, Thurs, and Sat 7 a.m. to 4 p.m. in Sept and Oct. The **Muddy Pond Variety Store** (4066 Muddy Pond Rd.; 931-445-3357) makes its own sorghum and carries produce and vegetables as well. The **Muddy Pond General Store** at 3608 Muddy Pond Rd. has sorghum, cheeses, meats, quilts, pottery, outdoor furniture, and a large variety of gift and household items. The **Leather Shop** is a favorite with horse lovers. You can buy a saddle or a dog collar or a fancy belt with your name on it, custom crafted by Irvin Bauman. The **Country Porch** offers gifts and homemade ice cream. Most of the businesses are open Mon through Sat. Phone the Muddy Pond General Store at (931) 445-7829 for more information.

If you'd like to stay a while in Muddy Pond, the Horst family is happy to welcome guests at **Cabin in the Pond** (3100 Muddy Pond Rd.; 931-445-3743; mysite.twlakes.net). Several cabins and accommodations are available with lovely names like Whipoorwill Hideaway, Two's Company, and Lazy Days. Rates start at $99 per night.

There are a great many houses, fences, walls, and buildings around Crossville made of the famous Crab Orchard stone—a brownish-beige stone that is quarried along US 70 in the small community of Crab Orchard. The quarries are located along the north side of the highway and show years and years of mining operations.

Crab Orchard was a pioneer outpost in the 1700s, and those on a westward trek would stop here for a rest after going through the mountains and climbing onto the plateau. The crab apple trees were numerous, and the Indians caused no problems. It was a comfortable respite. In his 1985 novel, *Jubal Sackett*, Louis L'Amour wrote fondly of the area.

A few miles east on US 70 is the **Ozone Falls Natural Area**, where old-growth forests dominate. The highlight here is the magnificent 110-foot-high waterfall where Fall Creek cascades into the deep gorges below. How did it get its name? Local lore says that the area was named "Ozone" because of the "stimulating quality of the air" created by the mist that is generated when the water takes its long plunge. Park in the pull-out area along the highway, and you'll only have about a fifth-of-a-mile walk to the top of the falls. Be very careful. There are no guardrails or railings. If you follow the path, you'll walk right over the edge! Also be wary of slippery stones that you might step on as you lean over to take a look. Nearby **Cumberland Mountain State Park** (931-484-6138, tnstateparks.com/parks/Cumberland-mountain) is in charge of the area.

Looking for some great cheddar cheese? **Simonton's Cheese & Gourmet House** (2278 Hwy. 127 South; 931-484-5193; simontonscheese.com) in Crossville, is known throughout this part of the country for its 3-pound hoop of cheddar, made from grade A milk. It's sold here along with other specialty cheeses, jams, jellies, teas, candies, and hams. They carry more than 60 domestic and imported cheeses in all. Simonton's Cheddar even has a cheer: "Red as an Apple, Yellow as Gold, I am Delicious, I am Told ... TRY ME!" Simonton's is open Mon through Sat 9 a.m. to 5 p.m. and during the Christmas holiday season on Sun noon to 5 p.m.

Considered one of the South's top professional theater groups, the **Cumberland County Playhouse** (221 Tennessee Ave.; 931-484-5000; ccplayhouse .com) is located here in Crossville. With two indoor stages and an outdoor amphitheater, the playhouse features professional theater in an unlikely rural setting and draws audiences from a great distance. Ticket prices range from $20 to $30 for adults for most shows.

The **Stonehaus Winery** (2444 Genesis Rd.; 931-484-9463; stonehauswinery .com) offers free nitty-gritty tours daily with all aspects of the winemaking process shown. Unlike a lot of wineries, which give superficial tours, these guys take you from A to Z, from crushing to bottling—and of course they have a

OTHER ATTRACTIONS WORTH SEEING

Creative Discovery Museum
321 Chestnut St.
Chattanooga
(423) 756-2738
cdmfun.org

Cumberland County Playhouse
221 Tennessee Ave.
Crossville
(931) 484-5000
ccplayhouse.com

Key Park Log House
Lafayette
(615) 666-5885
maconcountytn.gov

Tennessee Aquarium IMAX 3-D Theater
201 Chestnut St.
Chattanooga
(423) 266-4629
tnaqua.org

Virgin Falls
Sparta
(931) 836-3552
spartatnchamber.com

tasting counter. However, if you want to buy a glass of wine, you'll have to buy a bottle. They'll open it for you and give you a glass, but Tennessee law forbids them from serving it to you. Open Mon through Sat 9 a.m. to 7 p.m. and Sun noon to 5 p.m. Located at exit 320 off I-40.

The *Vanity Fair Outlet Mall* (228 Interstate Dr.; 931-484-7165; vfoutlet .com), located across I-40 from the Stonehaus Winery, has enough shopping opportunities to keep you busy for hours.

South of Crossville, where Highways 127 and 68 split, is the planned community of *Homesteads*. The area, with its quaint little stone houses lining both highways, is often referred to as the "showplace of the New Deal."

In January 1934, following several years of hard times in the area, the local farm agent submitted an application to the government for one of the subsistence projects formulated by the Roosevelt administration. The application was accepted, and work began on the 10,000-acre project.

The plan was to build 250-plus homesteads, each of about 20 acres. The homesteaders were selected following a series of intense background checks and interviews of about 4,000 applicants. Cooperatives were established for the community, and family members went to these to make their families' mattresses, can their families' food, or weave at a loom house.

Today 218 of the 252 houses built are still standing. At the base of the 85-foot-tall octagonal tower that originally served as a water tower is a sandstone building that housed the administrative offices of the project. Today those offices serve as a museum depicting Roosevelt's homesteading project. If you want, you can climb the 97 steps to the top of the tower.

Of the 102 New Deal projects nationwide, the *Cumberland Homesteads* (931-456-9663; cumberlandhomesteads.org) was considered one of the most successful of all. Open Mon through Sat 1 p.m. to 5 p.m. from Apr through Oct. A small admission is charged. Each Dec, a lovely Christmas Tour of Historic Homestead Homes features the museum decked for the holidays in vintage decorations from the 1930s and 1940s.

More information on Crossville, Crab Orchard, and the rest of Cumberland County can be found on the chamber of commerce's website, crossville-chamber.com, or call (877) 465-3861.

Cannon County is known throughout the state for the number of fine craftspeople it has within its borders. Just about every craft you can think of is created here by superb artists. From potters to folk artists to basket weavers to chair makers, a great many craftspeople call Cannon County home.

Unfortunately, many of the gifted craftspeople don't like you to visit their home workshops unless they know you, preferring instead to sell their crafts through various shops and at craft shows throughout the Southeast. A directory

TOP ANNUAL EVENTS

JUNE

Defeated Creek Bluegrass Fest
Carthage
164 Marina Ln.
(615) 774-3230

Riverbend Festival
Chattanooga
180 Hamm Rd.
(423) 756-2211
riverbendfestival.com

JULY

Fiddler's Jamboree
Smithville
100-198 S. 1st St.
(615) 597-8500
smithvillejamboree.com

AUGUST

Red Apple Days
Auburntown
(615) 598 5578

Red Clay Cherokee Heritage Festival
Cleveland
1140 Red Clay Park Rd.
(423) 478-0339

SEPTEMBER

White Oak Craft Fair
Woodbury
1424 John Bragg Hwy.
(615) 563-2787
artscenterofcc.com

DECEMBER

**Christmas Tour of Historic
Homesteads Homes**
Crossville
2611 Pigeon Ridge Rd.
(931) 484 8520
cumberlandhomesteads.org

Monterey Christmas Parade
Monterey
(800) 264-5541
visitcookevilletn.com

listing more than 100 local craftspeople is available from the ***Arts Center of Cannon County*** (615-563-2787; artscenterofcc.com) in Woodbury. The Arts Center consists of a playhouse, art gallery, and concert venue in a single facility. The Arts Center is open Tues through Sat 10 a.m. to 4 p.m.

The county's craftspeople come out in force for the local ***White Oak Craft Fair***, held in September. Artists from other counties are invited to participate as well, making this a wonderful place to buy items you won't find in too many other locales. The fair is held at the Arts Center of Cannon County on John Bragg Highway (US 70-S), 1 mile west of town.

Check statewide crafts show calendars, or write the Arts Center of Cannon County, 1424 John Bragg Hwy., Woodbury 37190.

Up off Highway 96 at the very top of the county is the little community of ***Auburntown***, which holds Red Apple Days the first full weekend in August. A fundraiser for the Auburntown Volunteer Fire Department, the festival features music, games, craft and food vendors, fireworks, cornhole tournament, dog show, baking contest, bobbing for apples, and more. It is the social highlight of the area and a great place to catch up on all the gossip and to meet some great icons of rural America. Call (615) 598-5578 for more information.

Several bed-and-breakfast facilities in the state are also bona fide tourist attractions, and *Evins Mill* (615-269-3740; evinsmill.com) in *Smithville* is one of them. James Lockhart built his mill on this spot in 1824 and had a burgeoning business through the late 19th century. Tennessee state senator Edgar Evins purchased the property in 1937, renamed it, and had a 4,600-square-foot lodge built on the bluff overlooking Fall Creek and the mill.

Today, the lodge and the rustic cabins built along the bluff serve as a bed-and-breakfast. The restored mill, still with all its workings in place, is a full-service state-of-the-art conference center. The kitchen of the lodge has been turned into a modern operation with a full-time chef who provides lodging guests as well as conferencing business folks with gourmet meals. The huge stone fireplace and the original wood flooring add a neat, homey feeling to the environment. If you want someone else to do the cooking, this is a charming place to spend Thanksgiving Day. Roaring fire in the fireplace, good eating, and some great walking trails will help make the day a fun one for everyone! It's off US 70, 1.5 miles east of the junction of US 70 and Highway 56 at 1535 Evins Mill Rd.

The internationally famous *Old-Time Fiddler's Jamboree and Crafts Festival* (615-597-8500; smithvillejamboree.com) is held on the Smithville Square early each July, and for a country and Appalachian music fan, it's truly a piece of heaven. There are 28 categories of traditional music and dancing, including old-time bluegrass, clogging, buck dancing, old-time fiddle bands, five-string banjo, dulcimer, dobro, fiddling, and flat-top guitar, all for top prizes. The fiddle players have a fiddle-off to determine the grand champion fiddler. There are also seven categories for musicians under the age of 12. In addition, there are more than 300 traditional crafts booths, food stands, and other great things to do and see.

soconfusing

Short Mountain in Cannon County is actually the highest point between the Ozarks and the Appalachian Mountains.

In selecting the Grand Champion Fiddler from winners of the Junior and Senior Fiddle competition, each contestant plays three tunes: one hoedown or fast one, one waltz, and one tune of the fiddler's choice. The two finalists draw for position. The winner is asked to play a crowd-pleasing victory song after the award ceremony. This is a great educational experience as well as a fun, unique event to visit. The festival is free.

Back when this part of the state was known as the New Frontier, the **Wilderness Road** (US 70) was the main route through the state, connecting the frontier settlements to the west and the more civilized areas to the east. The Rock House stagecoach inn and tollhouse were strategically built at the point where an early railroad connection crossed the trail. Built between 1835 and 1839 of Tennessee limestone, the inn soon became a gathering place for the who's who of the American frontier.

Preserved through the years by caring friends, this piece of Americana is now open to the public on a limited basis. The Rock House chapter of the Daughters of the American Revolution is the caretaker of the property, now known as the **Rock House Shrine** (931-836-3552; tndar.org) state historic area, located on US 70, 4 miles west of Sparta.

While you're here, check out the great southern-fried catfish at the **Galley** (931-858-5695; edgarevinsmarina.com) restaurant down at the **Edgar Evins State Park** (931-858-2446; tnstateparks.com) marina. Located on Center Hill Reservoir, the restaurant is open daily Apr through Oct.

Cookeville, Putnam County's seat of government, had two early surges of commerce that resulted in two distinct downtown sections. The town had already established its square and business hub long before the railroads came through. When the rails came to town in 1890, they came through a residential area on the west side. That area soon became less residential and more commercial as business shifted from the established area around the courthouse to the new, prospering area around the depot. A large hotel was built, and warehouses and stores soon followed.

By 1910 a new passenger depot had been built, and the area was considered the Hub of the Upper Cumberland. Passenger service was terminated in 1955, but the locals were able to save the depot, which is now on the National Register of Historic Places and the site of the **Cookeville Depot Museum** (931-528-8570; cookevilledepot.com).

Inside is one of the best re-creations of an early depot in the state. Original fixtures, desks, time schedules, and the like have been preserved through the years. There are four rooms of exhibits, plus a caboose out back with more displays. Open Tues through Sat 10 a.m. to 4 p.m. Admission is free; its location is Broad and Cedar Streets at 116 W. Broad St.

Across the street from the museum, high atop an old dairy, you'll see a big, old-fashioned neon sign advertising Cream City Ice Cream. Atop the 1950s sign is a giant ice-cream sundae whose cherry bounces up and down (in neon) when the sign is turned on. Below the sign at 119 W. Broad St., stop in **Cream City Ice Cream & Coffee** (931-528-2732) for a sweet treat.

Fun-Filled Region

The region formed by the northern 14 counties in this area of the state is called the Upper Cumberland and is one of the most beautiful areas in the state for rolling hills, waterfalls, and foliage. A listing of sites, heritage trails, waterfalls, lakes, rivers, festivals, and accommodations can be found at uppercumberland.org. You can call the Tourism Association at (931) 537-6347.

The streets are rolled back in Cookeville the first weekend after Labor Day each year. That's when the ***Downtown Fall Fun Fest*** (931-528-4612; fallfunfest .com) is held around the courthouse.

The Fall Fun Fest runs both days and features live entertainment on two stages with a big headline act on Saturday night. One stage is reserved for the local acts that specialize in blues, jazz, and the Latin beat. Along the streets are food vendors and a top-notch crafts fair sponsored by the Tennessee Association of Craft Artists, which holds its big festival in Nashville about two weeks later. A couple dozen activity booths are set up for the kids. Considering everything there is to offer, this is one of the most fun-filled weekend events in the state.

Attention, all candy lovers: The ***Russell Stover Candies Factory and Outlet Store*** (931-526-8424; russellstover.com) is open Mon through Sat 10 a.m. to 6 p.m.; Sun noon to 5 p.m. Take the Cookeville/Algood exit off Highway 111, 3 miles north of I-40, and turn toward Cookeville. Almost immediately take a right onto 1976 Chocolate Drive. The store is on your left about 0.5 mile down the road.

Looking for some truly off-the-beaten-path, funky, laid-back outdoor fun? Cookeville's ***Hidden Hollow*** (931-526-4038; hiddenhollowpark.com) fills that bill. The place is hard to explain and is certainly something you don't see every day. Back in 1972, Arda Lee retired in order to live out his childhood dream and transformed an old, 86-acre discarded farm into a fun place to picnic. Among its offerings now are a small petting zoo with rabbits, goats, chickens, ducks, and other birds; a dandy beach complete with kiddie swimming pool; and cane-pole fishing in the pond.

Lee died in 2004 at the age of 88. With his death, the future of the park was in question, and the property went up for auction a few years later. Vince and Amanda Taylor stopped by the auction, although they had no intention of buying anything. However, when the bidding started, something got into the couple. Some say it was fate. For whatever reason, the Taylors raised their bid paddle and suddenly the property was theirs.

The couple, along with their two sons, Skylar and Dalton, works hard to maintain Lee's tradition and vision. When October rolls around, Vince begins the tedious task of stringing lights around the property for the holidays. The Taylors are at the park every night from Thanksgiving through New Year's Day, replacing bulbs and making sure all is bright.

Hidden Hollow also has a gingerbread house for the kids to play in, a covered bridge, a waterwheel, a wedding chapel, rock gardens, and fountains. Located at 1901 Mount Pleasant Rd., Hidden Hollow is open daily year-round. Admission is $4 per person, free for children 3 and under.

Gainesboro is the seat of Jackson County and has several antiques stores on the main square in the downtown area. It also has two drugstores, **Anderson & Haile Drugs** (101 E. Gore Ave.; 931-268-0233) and **Gainesboro Drugs** (100 E. Hull Ave.; 931-268-9919), which still have the old-fashioned soda fountains in operation.

If you think marbles are just for kids, then you haven't met the gang of marble players in *Celina*. For the group of dedicated players around here, the simple ring marble game is unheard of. What they play in "these here" parts is called Rolley Hole.

The game is a team sport, played on a 40-by-20-foot field called a marble yard. There are three holes evenly spaced down the middle. The object of the game is for each team of two to get their marbles into each hole in succession, down the court, back and down again, three times.

The top players make their own marbles or buy them from other local players. The best of the best was Dumas Walker, who died in 1991. He was the world champion Rolley Hole player, and people would come from miles to watch him play. If that name sounds familiar, the old marble player was saluted in a popular 1990 song by The Kentucky Headhunters.

In his memory the **National Rolley Hole Marble Tournament** (931-823-6347) is held each September at Standing Stone State Park in conjunction with the county's Homecoming Day celebration. Players from other Rolley Hole hotbeds, namely, Kansas City and parts of New Jersey and Kentucky, come to Celina to compete in that tourney. Several English players usually show up for that one as well.

The **Dale Hollow National Fish Hatchery** (931-243-2443; fws.gov/dale hollow), just north of Celina on Highway 53, produces yearly about 300,000 pounds of 9-inch rainbow trout, which are used to restock public waterways. They also hatch and ship about 500,000 fingerlings each year.

Most of the public waterways in the Southeast are too warm for trout to breed, hence the need for this facility. Trout fishing is allowed and encouraged on most dam and river sites owned by the government, so periodic restocking is necessary.

The hatchery offers self-guided tours, but there are plenty of workers around to answer any questions. The long greenhouse-type building is where the eggs are hatched, and then the small trout are taken outside to spend the rest of their time here in one of the more than 100, 8-by-100-foot concrete raceways.

Feeding times, early morning and late afternoon, are probably the best times to visit. The larger fish are fed food pellets from a truck. A certain amount of food drops down onto a base and then is blown across the water by a current of air. The smaller fish are fed by hand. Open every day year-round from 7:30 a.m. to 3:30 p.m.; admission is free.

During the first half of the 20th century, **Red Boiling Springs** was a bustling health and vacation resort known for its medicinal waters. The resort enjoyed its heyday in the years between the world wars, when as many as six large hotels and 10 boardinghouses were in business. Today the spa resort feeling hasn't totally vanished. The springs are still here, as are three of the hotels, and you can still get a mineral-water bath. A major flood in the 1960s wiped out much of the old-time charm, but the community has rebuilt and has restored much of that ambience.

Brenda Thomas realized back in the early 1990s that Red Boiling Springs still had a life to it and that some of the charm and history of the area could be brought back. She and her husband, Bobby, both born and raised in the area, bought and renovated **Armour's Red Boiling Springs Hotel** (321 E. Main St.; 615-699-2180; armourshotel.com), built in 1924. In fall 1999, Reba

What the Heck Is Poke Sallet?

There are only three **poke sallet** festivals in the US, and downtown Gainesboro is home to one of them. That distinction is something to be proud of, even though this is basically a festival to celebrate a weed. Poke sallet grows wild in the South and is cooked the same as (and tastes something like) turnip and mustard greens. Events that you won't want to miss include the poke sallet–eating contest, continuous country music, and the outhouse races. (No, not a race to the outhouse, but rather a race of outhouses.) The terrapin (turtle) races are also a highlight. Found locally in the countryside, the terrapins are placed in a circle by up to 60 contestants, and the first turtle to cross the outer line of the circle wins. There are also crosscut-saw contests, a hay bale roll, and the Miss Poke Sallet Festival contest. It has been held during early May each year for about 40 years; proceeds from the festival fund the Rescue Squad. Their number is (931) 268-0971, or you can visit gainesborochamber.com.

and Laban Hilton visited the inn and decided they wanted to own it. Then in 2008, Dennis and Debra Emery became the owners of this charming piece of Americana. They were quick to assure us that nothing has changed and the entire atmosphere that Brenda Thomas created is still there—along with a total renovation to make the hotel even lovelier. There are 15 rooms, including 3 suites, all with private baths. Rates are $57 single, $85 double, and $129 for suites (2 persons). Rates also are available for a full country breakfast; dinner is available for an additional $14 per person, plus tax. A treatment consisting of a one-hour massage and steam bath is $89, $79 for only a 60-minute massage, and $35 for only a mineral bath.

Just down the street is a 2-story brick hotel, the ***Thomas House*** (520 E. Main St.; 615-699-3006; thomashousehotel.com). Owned by Evelyn Thomas Cole, who was born and raised in the area, the hotel differs in style from the others in that it has a courtyard and a European feel to it.

This historic hotel was ravaged by fire in 2001 and was closed during much of the renovation. Now there are 15 guest rooms back in operation, as are the kitchen and dining room. Lunch and dinner are served family style, Mon through Sat, reservations required.

This town was famous for four types of water: black, red, double and twist, and free stone. Each is quite different in its mineral analysis, and each was considered a "cure" for different ailments. A self-guided tour brochure of the area is available at the small log cabin visitor center on E. Main Street.

Over in ***Lafayette***, the county seat, you don't have to have a map to find the biggest loafers in the county. On any fair-weather day, be it in January or June, you'll find a group of men of indeterminate age sitting under an old oak tree on the southeast side of the Macon County Public Square. With knives in hand, these whittlers have become part of small-town life around here. The chamber of commerce likes them because of their almost unlimited knowledge of the area. But you don't have to have kin in the area to ask after; just walk right up and start talking with them. Of course, you'll always walk away wondering whether the directions they gave you will really take you where you want to go or whether these good ole boys have played another trick on a city slicker.

Al Gore is from the small town of ***Carthage***, the county seat of historic Smith County. A good way to start your visit in this area is to stop by the ***Smith County Welcome Center*** (615-683-6410), located in a log cabin at mile marker 267 on I-40, in a rest area just east of the Carthage exit. It's 60 miles east of Nashville and is accessible from both east- and westbound traffic. Inside, you'll find plenty of printed information, plus people who not only know the area but knew Al Gore as a young boy who loved showing his cattle at the county fair. If the weather's cold, sit a spell in the rocking chairs in front of the fire-place; if the weather's nice, take a short walk down to Caney Fork River. It's a pleasant setting.

In downtown Carthage, the circa 1879 courthouse is a must-see. Built in the Second Empire architectural style, the building has undergone extensive renovation and is now listed on the National Register of Historic Places. A lot more history is alive and well in Carthage, including the old city cemetery and the circa-1889 Carthage United Methodist Church. The church has amazing stained-glass windows, with several dating back to when the church was built.

In 1936 the *Cordell Hull Bridge* replaced an old toll bridge. Named for the former secretary of state of the US, who served under President Franklin D. Roosevelt, the bridge's unique steel grid work makes it not only an interesting sight but also a great place from which to view the river valley.

Upriver about 5 miles from Carthage, the 12,000-acre *Cordell Hull Lake* (615-735-1023) was built by the US Army Corps of Engineers primarily for navigation, hydropower generation, and recreation. Construction began in 1963, and the lake was fully functional in 1973. The power plant visitor center is open every day Memorial Day through Labor Day. It's located on Highway 263 north of Carthage. There are 11 access areas to the lake with boat ramps, and there are eight different recreation areas, some with camping.

On Highway 25, about halfway to Hartsville, is *Dixon Springs*. It was founded by Revolutionary War major Tilman Dixon on a military land grant. There are many of the area's original homes still standing, including Dixonia, the home of Major Dixon, now a private residence. The *Smith County Chamber of Commerce* (615-735-2093) can provide more information on the area.

If Civil War history fascinates you, here's an unusual chance to find out quite a bit about General John Hunt Morgan and the Battle of Hartsville. A 17-stop self-guided tour of Hartsville starts at the site where General Morgan, known as the *Thunderbolt of the Confederacy*, crossed the Cumberland River with his troops the night of December 6, 1862, and ends at the Hartsville Cemetery, where more than 50 Confederate soldiers are buried.

The general and his men seized the *Hartsville Vidette* newspaper while raiding the town, and they ended up publishing it themselves when they could find the opportunity and paper. The newspaper still publishes and still bears that historic name. The tour brochure is available from the *Hartsville-Trousdale County Chamber of Commerce* (615-374-9243; hartsvilletrousdale .com), 328 Broadway Rm. 7.

Middle Cumberland

It's hard to believe that **Dayton**, a small city 40 miles north of Chattanooga, was probably a household word from coast to coast during the long, hot summer of 1925. That's when the silver-tongued orators William Jennings Bryan and Clarence Darrow engaged in a legal battle in the Rhea County Courthouse. The Scopes "Monkey Trial" let the world know that a Dayton outside of Ohio actually did exist. Although John Scopes, a schoolteacher, didn't reach the heights that the Wright brothers of the other Dayton did, he earned himself a place in history.

The Romanesque Revival, Italian Villa-style courthouse was built in 1891 and has been restored to its 1925 vintage. The Scopes trial courtroom is on the second floor and contains the original judge's bench, four tables, railing, jury chairs, and spectator seats.

The **Rhea County Heritage and Scopes Trial Museum** (423-775-7801; rheacountyheritage.com) is housed in the courthouse and contains exhibits, photos, and actual newsreel footage of what many still call the first major trial treated as a media event.

Scopes was accused of teaching the Darwinian theory of evolution to a high school biology class in violation of a recently passed Tennessee statute making it unlawful "to teach any theory that denies the story of the divine creation of man as taught in the Bible."

Scopes wasn't even the school's regular biology teacher, but a math teacher filling in. He was fined $100, a fee he never paid. In 2018, the museum underwent a major renovation project to add new floors, new exhibits, storyboards, and an interactive touch screen. The museum is open Mon through Fri 9 a.m. to 5 p.m. admission is free.

The **Scopes Trial Play and Festival** (scopesfestival.com) take place each summer in mid-July when a special drama is acted out in the courtroom where the trial took place. A crafts fair, an antique car show, and traditional music are all a part of the festival. Of course, there's plenty of great southern cooking available as well.

Like strawberries? If so, plan your visit to the Dayton area during the first or second week of May. That's when the annual **Strawberry Festival** (423-775-0361; tnstrawberryfestival.com) takes place, featuring the "World's Longest (line of people eating) Strawberry Shortcake" and 3 days of eclectic fun.

Other events include a carnival midway full of rides, various sports tournaments, an arts and crafts show, and a music festival.

An unlikely resident of the wonderfully named Soddy Daisy, Tennessee, is the **Horsin' Around Carving School** (8361A Dayton Pike; 423-280-4688).

Owner and chief carver Bud Ellis teaches classes, does historic carousel restoration, and enjoys talking about his art. He'll give you a free tour of the place—and for only $1,300 to $1,800, you can sign up, take a course in carving, and bring home your own carousel horse. The brass ring is extra.

Ellis is responsible for the restoration and the horse carving on the Coolidge Park Carousel, next to the Walnut Street Bridge in Chattanooga. The carving school is located behind the Walmart at the Soddy Daisy exit off US 27 North, 14 miles north of the Tennessee River.

Out on Highway 30 is the small community of **Meigs,** the county seat of Decatur, where a historic town square will attract your attention. Unlike many of the older courthouse squares, this one is a bit barren and free of large trees.

But in the shadow of the courthouse, you'll find the area's version of the **Spit and Whittle Gang**, a bunch of old-timers who gather each day to—well, you guessed it.

When you've worked up an appetite, stop at **Uncle Gus's Mountain Pit Bar B Que** (810 Peakland Rd.; 423-334-2487; unclegusbarbque.com), open Tues through Sat. Uncle Gus's features pulled pork, brisket, fried pickles, homemade potato salad, and peach cobbler. Breakfast also is served on Sat from 7:30 a.m. to 10:30 a.m.

In **Athens**, just off Highway 30, rests **Tennessee Wesleyan College** (423-745-7504; twcnet.edu), a liberal arts school established in 1857. The first building on campus, appropriately called the "Old College" building, is still standing and up until 1989 housed the county's heritage museum.

The structure, built in 1854 and also used as a hospital during the Civil War, faces the quad grounds of the school. Behind Old College on Dwain Farmer Drive, you'll find a marker explaining one of the most poignant legends in Tennessee history.

A wounded English officer from nearby Fort Loudoun was befriended by an Indian chief and nursed back to health by Nocatula, daughter of the chief. The soldier, given the name of Connestoga (the oak), was accepted into the tribe and married Nocatula. A jealous suitor attacked Connestoga with a knife. As he lay dying, Nocatula confessed her eternal love for him and plunged a knife into her breast.

The pair were buried together, and the chief placed an acorn in Connestoga's hand and a hackberry in Nocatula's hand, symbolizing undying love. From these there developed two trees that grew intertwined on this spot for more than 150 years.

After these two original trees died in 1957, two others were planted. Those have since died, and today the stumps are all that remain.

The *McMinn County Living Heritage Museum* (522 W. Madison Ave; 423-745-0329; livingheritagemuseum.com) is located in Athens's old high school building, about a half mile from downtown. The museum's collection of 19th- and 20th-century quilts is one of the finest in the state. In addition to the permanent display of quilts, a nationally known quilt show is hosted by the museum each year. Check to see when it will be held, as it varies from year to year.

There is also a great children's collection that includes china and bisque-head dolls, toys, and clothing, along with school desks, books, and maps dating from 1850. Admission is charged; open daily except Sun and Mon.

The *Mayfield Dairy* (806 E. Madison Ave.; 423-745-2151; mayfielddairy .com) has been serving the folks in this part of the state for more than a century with fresh milk products and some of the best ice cream you've ever wrapped your tongue around. The dairy now offers fun tours, which conclude at a gift shop and dairy bar where you can sample (for a price) some of the products you saw being made.

The *Swift Museum Foundation* (423-745-9547; swiftmuseumfoundation .org) at 223 CR 552 is housed here at the McMinn County Airport, which is also the Swift Aircraft international headquarters. The small planes with the homebuilt feel to them were first built in Texas in the mid-1940s and today have quite a fanatic following. You can learn the history and see a few of the planes at the airport, but if you really want to get a big dose of them, drop by in September each year. That's when the annual *Swift Fly-In* takes place, usually attracting more than 100 aircraft.

Out on CR 52, 8 miles west of I-75 at 198 CR 52, Dave and Vicki Rhyne make "fruitcakes for people who don't like fruitcakes." Really, that's their slogan. Dave told me his pecan fruitcakes don't have the raisins or citrus peel that the others do and that his contain 25 percent pecans by weight. Their *Sunshine Hollow Bakery and Exhibition Gardens* (423-745-4289 or 800-669-2005; sunshinehollow.com) pumps out about 10,000 pounds of the holiday treat each year.

When they aren't making fruitcakes, they are out in their greenhouse hybridizing daylilies and hostas. The farm is also home to National Daylily and Hosta exhibition gardens. Right now they grow and sell about 800 varieties of daylilies and 200 varieties of hostas. They sell them at the farm as well as by mail order. They have a 2.5-acre shade garden and a 7-acre daylily garden, displaying many of their varieties. For 5 weekends in June and July, visitors can enjoy the *Daylily Bloom Festival* and receive a free daylily. The store sells other items as well, including pecan pralines, chocolate-covered pecans, jams, and jellies. Lunch is served in June for individuals. For groups of 20 or more, lunch is available by reservation Mar through Oct. Admission is free.

At the turn of the 20th century, the site of present-day Etowah on US 411 was muddy farmland. Then news came that the Louisville and Nashville Railroad (known as the L&N) was to build a new line between Cincinnati and Atlanta. The land was purchased to build a rail center. A boomtown named Etowah soon sprang up, and the **L&N Depot** was built in 1906. It became the community's central point, from which social, economic, and cultural activities evolved for many years.

By 1974, passenger travel had declined to the point that the depot was abandoned and sat empty until the town purchased it in 1978. It was restored and placed on the National Register of Historic Places. It now houses a railroad museum that examines what it meant to be a railroad town in the "New South."

You've never seen a railroad depot like this one. As you drive up, the elegant Victorian structure looks more like a hotel or a beautiful private home than a railroad depot. It's made of yellow pine and has 15 rooms. The depot is also home to the Depot Gift Shop, but the building itself is the star here.

The grounds around the depot remain a community gathering spot and are the site of several fairs, festivals, and weddings during the year, including a popular old-time July Fourth celebration. The trainyard is still active and can provide rail buffs a fun time watching all the switching and maneuvering. You'll find it on US 411 in downtown **Etowah** (423-263-7840; tennesseeoverhill.com).

The city fathers of Etowah have also purchased the circa 1918 **Gem Theater** (423-263-3270; gemplayers.com) and have nearly finished restoring it to its cultural splendor. At one time the Gem was considered the largest privately owned theater in East Tennessee. Today it has a full schedule of live stage presentations at its 700 Tennessee Ave. location.

There aren't too many museums around that spotlight women in industry, but in the little village of Englewood you'll find such a place. This area of the state is unusual in that it was built on textile manufacturing, the one Appalachian industry that employed large numbers of women. The **Englewood Textile Museum** (109 N. Niota Rd.; 423-887-5455; tennesseeoverhill.com) traces the area's textile industry from 1850. Exhibits present examples of different textiles and machinery from 1890 and emphasize the role of working-class women in the mills, their home life, and their role in the development of the community. See Miss Ella's handmade trousseau and learn why she never wore it. Tour the restored "Little White House" birthplace of an early mill owner. The museum is open Mon through Sat 10 a.m. to 5 p.m. There is free admission, but help them out by placing a couple bucks in their donation bucket.

Adjacent to the Textile Museum is *The Company Store*, an antiques and "attic treasures" store. Local crafts and gift items are also available. To turn back the clock of this historic southern town, visit during "Englewood Celebrates" each year in June.

Southwest Cumberland

In *Tracy City* US 41, you'll find *Henry Flury and Sons* (223 Main St.; 931-592-5661) general store, which has had "staple and fancy groceries" for sale since 1905. The proprietors like to call their little establishment the "living museum of mountain life and the gathering place for friends."

Henry Flury and his three sons are all gone now, but Paul Flury, Henry's grandson, runs the store. "I guess you could say I'm the last of the Mohicans," he laughs.

Along with the groceries the store offers fresh meats, hoop cheese, produce, deli sandwiches, deli trays, and hand-dipped ice cream. Call ahead and they'll pack a picnic for you. The old wooden floors and the high ceilings are just what you would think you'd find in a store like this. Feed bags hang from the ceiling, baskets line the top shelves, and old time items are sitting around the shop. The local folk use the store as a handicraft outlet for their homemade products.

Stay on US 41 and head to *Monteagle*, where, just across I-24 on US 64/41A at 850 W. Main St. you'll find one of the best places for pit barbecue and hickory-smoked meats in the state. *Jim Oliver's Smokehouse* (800-489-2091; thesmokehouse.com) complex offers a great country store, meeting rooms, a lodge, a motel, cabins, a wedding chapel, and his famous restaurant. In all, he has 20 acres full of all sorts of things to do. The motel's swimming pool is a sight in itself; it's in the shape of a ham.

If you're heading toward Monteagle, make plans to stay at the *Edgeworth Inn* (931-924-4000; edgeworthinn.com), located on the grounds of the historic Monteagle Assembly at 19 Wilkins Ave. The inn, owned and operated by Jeanine Clements, is a first-class, 8-bedroom bed-and-breakfast. Built as a boardinghouse in 1896, the structure has been completely renovated to its Victorian splendor and offers guests a respite from the real world. The owner accepts pets and children. Rooms start at $160.

letmomvote

Women today can thank the state of Tennessee for helping them get their right to vote. It was the state's ratification in 1920 that added the 19th Amendment to the Constitution, giving women the right to vote.

Grundy County is gaining a national reputation as a mountain crafts center thanks to several artisans whose works are known and in demand from coast to coast. Many of these craftspeople have settled in the center of the county and have established homes and local ties.

On the other side of Beersheba Springs, Phil and Terri Mayhew live and work in an 1850s log cabin. Phil's work with high-fired, functional porcelain pottery is represented by 10 galleries in 12 states. Terri creates porcelain and hand-wrought silver jewelry. Phil, a former arts professor, has developed a porcelain that will fuse at a higher temperature, thus making it more durable and giving it a unique color range.

Although they do some shows and are still represented by some of the country's finest galleries, Phil and Terri do about half of their business out of their home. *Beersheba Porcelain* (931-692-2280; beershebaporcelain.com) has no showroom, no fancy gallery, just a lot of great art. In the warmer months they'll have stuff on the front porch; the rest of the year, "we kinda sleep and eat around our business" in the house, Phil said.

The Mayhew cabin is in the historic district, just off Highway 56. They have a small sign out front, so you'll have to look hard or you might miss it. If you do, drop by the *Beersheba Springs Market* at 19564 TN 56 (931-692-3314), the only store in town, and the friendly folk there will direct you to the Mayhews.

Beersheba Springs was a bustling resort area during the last half of the 1800s, and its grand hotel, which was built in 1850, is still standing. Down the road a couple of blocks from the Mayhews, the building is now owned by the United Methodist Church and used as a summer meeting facility. The view from the front of the hotel is nothing less than breathtaking.

When the hotel was active, stagecoaches would stop at the foot of the mountain and sound a horn once for each guest they had aboard for the hotel. By the time they reached the top, the hotel's band was ready to greet them. Dinner and a clean room had also been prepared.

The *Beersheba Springs Arts & Crafts Fair* (931-692-3691) takes place on the hotel grounds each August and is considered one of the best shows in this part of the state. The setting alone sets this show apart from most of the rest.

Cumberland Caverns (931-668-4396; cumberlandcaverns.com), located about 7 miles southeast of McMinnville just off Highway 8 at 1437 Cumberland Caverns Rd., is the second-largest cavern system in the US, after Kentucky's Mammoth Cave, and is a US National Landmark. Unless you happen to be an expert in this sort of thing, most of the tour through the cave reminds you of just about any other cave journey.

Howdy, Y'all Welcome

There's plenty of mountain hospitality at the annual *Mountaineer Folk Festival* at Fall Creek Falls State Park. Handmade mountain crafts, traditional mountain music, country cooking, bluegrass music, and pioneer skills demonstrations are plentiful. The festival is held in early September, so it's a great time to stock up on genuine Tennessee mountain-made Christmas gifts. At Highways 111 and 30, west of Pikeville. Call (877) 716-4493 or visit mountainglenonline.com.

One room here, however, is impressive no matter what your interests are. The **Underground Ballroom** is 600 feet long, 150 feet wide, and 140 feet high. It is the largest cave room east of the Mississippi River. The room's man-made amenities are built alongside the natural formations. Of these constructed features, the most amazing is the dining room, which will seat 500 for a banquet. High above the tables is a 15-foot, 1,500-pound chandelier from a theater in Brooklyn, New York. And all this is more than 300 feet below the hustle and bustle of the real world.

Falcon Rest (931-668-4444; falconrest.travel.com), in McMinnville, is both an elegant bed-and-breakfast and a tourist attraction. In fact, owners Charlien and George McGlothin had so many requests for tours of the house that they now offer daily ones from 9 a.m. to 5 p.m. for $13 for adults and teens and $7 for children ages 4 to 12. The hour-long tour, peppered with local color and anecdotes, is a great way to learn the history of this magnificent Queen Anne Victorian mansion, built in 1897 by entrepreneur Clay Faulkner for his wife, Mary.

Faulkner promised Mary that he would build her the finest house in Warren County if she would move next to their woolen mill, then 2.5 miles from town. She agreed, and a year later the couple moved in with their five children. In 1946 the 10,000-square-foot mansion was converted into a hospital and nursing home. By the mid-1950s the building had been added onto and named the Faulkner Springs Hospital. Today bloodstains can still be seen on the floor in a couple of spots, and the nursing station now houses some of the modern kitchen equipment.

In his tour of the house, George proudly points out that this was the first house built with central heat and air-conditioning in the county and that its foundation goes 17 feet belowground to solid bedrock. George was born and raised locally, and his sister was born in this house when it was a hospital. As a bed-and-breakfast, the mansion offers 4 guest rooms on the grounds of the mansion. Rooms are lavishly furnished with period antiques and private baths.

No guest rooms are inside the mansion. Rates start at $105 per room, per night, with a full breakfast. A honeymoon suite, complete with brass bed, has been built in the old kitchen. The house next door has been added to the complex and now serves as a visitor center with a large Victorian gift shop, a tearoom, a Jacuzzi suite, and a wedding chapel. Falcon Rest is off the US 70 bypass at 2645 Faulkner Springs Rd.

Warren County, for which McMinnville serves as county seat, is known as the *Nursery Capital of the World*. More than 500 commercial nurseries throughout the county produce trees, shrubs, and plants, many of which are located along the major highways and provide miles of flowering beauty for you to observe as you drive along. Several of the nurseries are open for tours; some have small retail outlets. For a listing of those open to the public, contact the chamber of commerce at (931) 473-6611 or warrentn.com.

Of Forests & Rivers

If you happen to be in this part of the state and are tired of beautiful, lush mountains and forests, trek on over to the *Ducktown* area, a portion of the state often referred to as *Tennessee's Badlands*. Here you won't be surrounded by lush, green vegetation. In fact, you'll be surrounded by a 56-square-mile area of barren red hills, stunted pine trees, and washed-out gullies. This area of raw landscape is similar in looks to the famed badlands area of the Dakotas.

The story about this area, known officially as the *Copper Basin* area of Tennessee, Georgia, and North Carolina, is a fascinating tale of hard work and inadvertent destruction of the environment. The area is steeped in the history of copper mining. Copper was first discovered in 1843 near Potato Creek, between Ducktown and Copperhill, and by 1860 copper mining was in full swing and dominated and dictated the lifestyle of the basin for generations until the last mine closed in 1987.

By the time the industry called it quits, there was a 56-square-mile area of denuded red hills shimmering with glowing colors ranging from soft pastels to dark copper hues. The area stood out because of the otherwise lush green of the Cherokee National Forest. From space, NASA photos show the area looking like a moonscape.

Through vigorous reforestation programs, most of the area now has some vegetation growing, and it will only be a matter of years before the Copper Basin blends in with the rest of the area. However, some historians are hoping to keep a part of the area barren as an example of their active copper mining heritage.

The copper mining story is told through numerous methods at the **Duck-town Basin Museum** (212 Burra Burra St.; 423-496-5778; ducktownbasin-museum.com) on the Burra Burra Mine site, now on the National Register of Historic Places. Founded in 1978, the museum sits on 17 acres that include the buildings, mining structures, and mechanical operations of the mine site just as they were when it went out of business. The state purchased the museum in 1988, making it the first state-owned historic industrial site.

This is a fascinating part of the state that few residents even know exists. It's also an industry that isn't much talked about in the state. Your visit here should begin at the museum. You'll learn about the industry, why the area looks as it does, why the social life was affected so drastically by the industry, and what part Native Americans played. You'll also get a chance to tour the mine site, but you are not permitted to go underground.

Hoist House held the equipment used to pull men and ore from the mines. This structure and the steam boiler building were two of the first edifices built at the turn of the 20th century by the Tennessee Copper Company. The museum is open Mon through Sat Apr through Dec; Tues through Sat Jan through Mar. Adults are charged $5; seniors, $4; children (ages 13 to 17) $2, and $1 for younger children (ages 12 and under).

In the quaint little village of Ducktown, around the corner from the museum is the **Company House Bed & Breakfast** (318 Main St.; 423-496-5634 or 800-343-2409; companyhousebandb.com). Built in 1850 by the mine company's doctor, the building has had a colorful past. After standing empty for nearly a decade, it was purchased by Margie Tonkin and Mike Fabian, who dove in and undertook 90 percent of the massive renovation project by themselves. That was 1994. "It took us two weeks just to figure out where to start, and we did it one room at a time," Fabian said. Now the structure is listed on the National Register of Historic Places.

Ask Tonkin and Fabian about the renovation and they'll pull out a volume of "before" and "after" photos that will astonish you. They'll also show you photos of the Italian Olympic whitewater team that stayed here during the Olympic trials that took place on the nearby **Ocoee River**.

The seven bedrooms, all with private baths, are named for area mines and are quite nice, as is the marvelous hearty breakfast the couple puts out every morning for their guests. All rooms are nonsmoking; well-behaved children over 12 years of age are welcome, Tonkin notes. Rates are from $99 to $109 plus tax per room for 2 adults.

A great many residential and industrial structures within the Copper Basin are listed on the National Register of Historic Places. More than 200 are listed as part of the **Copper Basin Historic District**. Along with Ocoee, **Copperhill**,

Rugged & Cool Counties

The **Tennessee Overhill Heritage Association** promotes the counties of McMinn, Monroe, and Polk, and there's plenty of cool stuff to promote in this southeast area of the state! This is where the best whitewater rafting and outdoor adventures take place. Plus, some of the most spectacular scenic drives in the state are here. The association has a great website at tennesseeoverhill.com where you can order all sorts of specialty brochures, or call (423) 263-7232.

across the Ocoee River from Georgia, was another major town during the copper days. It was the corporate headquarters for the Tennessee Copper Company in 1904 and still resembles the company town that it was.

The storefronts along Ocoee Street and the stone steps that lead to the houses on various levels of the hill above the town offer a glimpse of early life there. As in any company town, the workers lived at street level, closest to the factory or mine. Other employees lived farther up the hill in order of importance, most often with the president at the top so that he could overlook the entire operation. Many of those houses are still in use today and are a part of a walking tour of Copperhill's residential area. Maps are available throughout the town.

In 1911 the Grand Avenue Bridge was built across the Ocoee and connected the mining town of McCaysville, Georgia, with Copperhill. Take a walk across the bridge and look for the spot where you can stand with one foot in Tennessee and one in Georgia. Farther down US 64, between Ducktown and Cleveland, you'll find yourself driving along the Ocoee River, one of the top 10 whitewater rivers in the country. You'll also find numerous business establishments that will be more than happy to rent you a raft, canoe, or kayak so that you, too, can experience an adventure of a lifetime. The river is such a good area for whitewater events that it was chosen as the site of the whitewater competition in the 1996 Summer Olympics, held in nearby Atlanta.

The **Ocoee Whitewater Center** (423-496-0100; fs.usda.gov), a few miles northwest from Ducktown at 4400 US 64, was the site of the 1996 Olympic Slalom Canoe/Kayak events and following the games became a visitor center and a hub for both land- and water-based recreation activities in the Cherokee Forest and Ocoee River areas.

Now open to the public, the center houses a gift shop, the Olympic Legacy exhibit, and a conference center. Open daily 9 a.m. to 5 p.m. from mid-Mar to mid-Nov; from 8:30 a.m. to 4:30 p.m. Fri through Sun in Nov through mid-Mar.

Outdoor areas are open year-round. Parking in lower main area is $3. Administration parking lot is free but limited to 30 minutes.

Outside, a native flower garden and a magnificent pond have been created. A path has been built along the whitewater channel where the races took place, and you can hike or bike the Old Copper Road, a section of which has been restored adjacent to the center.

A walk along the 2.4-mile-long section of the *Old Copper Road* takes you across four footbridges from the 1850s era. Built in 1851, the 33-mile-long road was used to haul copper ore from the mines in Ducktown to the railhead in Cleveland. Most of the original section was destroyed when the adjacent US 64 was built in the 1930s, and this is the only original section still intact. Along the road you'll find an abundance of flora and fauna. Take time to go out on the deck overlooking a beaver pond. Neat place!

If you're not of the adventurous variety or don't have the time, there are several pull-offs where you can experience the danger and the excitement of the whitewater vicariously. The mostly 2-lane road is very busy here, so be careful to exit the road completely before you take in the beauty.

If you do choose to be adventurous (and you really should), a good place to stop is the *Ocoee Adventure Center* (4651 Hwy. 64; 888-723-8622; ocoee adventurecenter.com), 3 miles east of the Ocoee Whitewater Center. The proprietor of this outpost worked the river for decades for other people. When he decided to go off on his own, he brought along some of the best river guides in the area.

You'll get a lesson on how to best combat the whitewater adventure awaiting you, then you'll be told how you must respect the river itself. "It's a wild, unpredictable ride, and you must be ready to handle everything. This is not an amusement park ride," our guide told us.

With life jackets and helmets in place, you'll climb aboard a school bus for a 4-mile trip down to the river's entry point. There you'll be launched for one great ride through areas of the river with such ominous names as Grumpy's Ledge, Hell's Hole, Tablesaw, and Double Trouble. The cost here and at most outfitters along the river usually depends on the day of the week you choose for your trip, with Sat during peak season costing approximately $49 for a half-day journey. It's $45 per person Sun through Fri. No one under 12 years of age is permitted.

Look closely through the trees on the other side of the river and you'll see the largest wooden flume known to exist in the US. The *Ocoee Flume* is 5 miles long, 11 feet wide, and 14 feet tall. Originally built in 1912 by the Tennessee Valley Authority (TVA), it was closed for a few years in the late 1970s and then rebuilt.

Its major function is to divert water from the river to help produce hydro-electric power, but it has also been a savior of the river for the whitewater aficionados. With the diversion the flume creates, the TVA can produce their power and the river can still run to the point of whiteness.

The **Webb Bros. Float Service** in Reliance, along the Hiwassee Scenic River at 3708 TN 30, is not only a professional outfitter, but the **Webb Brothers Store** (423-338-2373 or 877-932-7238; webbros.com), in which it is located, is a fun and funky general store to visit.

If it's a peaceful, easy journey down a scenic river you're looking for, this is your place. They rent 1- or 2-passenger rubber "duckies" that are self-bailing and hard to flip over. Resembling a kayak, they rent for $27 per person, including the 5-mile trip up the river where you're dropped off. You then paddle and float the current back downriver and get out at the store, where you began your journey.

The trip can be direct, or you can stop and swim, rest, or just sit and watch the other boats go by. If you like, pack your lunch and take it along. This is a great first river adventure for smaller children and the weak at heart, and it's a beautiful journey as well. Rafts are $50 for 1 or 2 people, $22 each for 3 or more people. All rafts and duckies containing children 10 and under must have an adult in the boat at all times. Children younger than 10 receive half-price rate for duckie or raft rentals when accompanied by parents.

In addition to its river services, the store sells groceries, prepared foods, snacks, gasoline, and just about anything else you'll need while you're in the area. The store, built in 1955, also serves as the town museum and has photos and memorabilia of early **Reliance**. Entry is free.

The Webbs is a good starting place for your tour of the **Reliance Historic District**, listed on the National Register of Historic Places. You can pick up information and quite a few stories about the area that will make your visit a lot more fun. The district, off Highway 30 along the river, has five principal buildings, including a hotel and the first house to have indoor plumbing. None of the restored structures are open to the public on a regular basis, but they are beautiful to look at. The area is still quite underdeveloped, so a drive through can give you a good idea of what life was like along the river at the turn of the 20th century.

For a spectacular view of the Hiwassee River, you'll want to walk all or part of the **John Muir Trail**, a 20-mile-long path that meanders along the river. Not only are the views of the river fantastic, but you'll also see a tremendous amount of wildlife and native plants. Watch for the beaver activity all along the trail. In addition, you'll have the opportunity to view ruby-throated hummingbirds, mink, raccoons, and great blue herons.

The trail begins at Childers Creek, near Reliance (follow the signs), and ends near Highway 68 at Farner. If you have your entire family to watch out for, you might want to stick to the first 3-mile section of the trek; it has been designated as an easy walk but still covers some beautiful terrain.

Mention mountain forests and fantastic views, and most people think of the Smoky Mountains. That's why the 620,000-acre **Cherokee National Forest** (423-338-3300; fs.usda.gov/cherokee) here in the southeast portion of the state remains virtually untouched by crowds. An annual pass costs $30. Admission is $3 per vehicle.

More than 1,100 miles of roads have been cut through the dense forest, opening up all sorts of opportunities for outdoor enthusiasts or for those who simply enjoy driving and looking. Take your time; there's a real good chance that no one will be honking and trying to get around you. The Forest Service maintains 29 camping areas, horse trails (bring your own horse), and 105 hiking trails. This area is every bit as beautiful as the Smokies, making it a great alternative that most locals are hesitant to tell too many people about. The supervisor's office can give you more specifics; call (423) 476-9700.

When you're in **Cleveland**, you're deep in Cherokee country, and history abounds. This was the geographic center for Native American culture in the Southeast, and there are reminders of that fact throughout the city and county.

The historical area of Cleveland is known as the Downtown Historic Greenway. Johnson Park, in the heart of downtown, is a great place to start a walking tour of the city. There are 20 different historic sites on the tour, including restored churches and buildings. While in Johnson Park, stop by and marvel at the *Cherokee Chieftain,* a wonderful sculpture of an Indian chief carved from a tree by internationally known Native American artist Peter Toth.

To get a better idea of the role the county played in the everyday life of the Cherokee, two self-guided tours have been developed. Maps and additional information are available at the **Cleveland/Bradley Tourism Development** (225 Keith St.; 800-472-6588; visitclevelandtn.com). The Cherokee Heritage Wildlife Tour points out the best locations in the area to view wildlife and allows you to get a good feel for the Cherokee heritage. The Cherokee Scenic Loop Tour begins and ends in Cleveland and takes you throughout the county, where you'll visit many of the areas mentioned in this chapter, including Red Clay and the Ocoee River. Both maps offer a well-organized way to see the best the county and the region have to offer.

One of the state's most forward-looking historical museums is located in the 5ive Points area of downtown Cleveland. The **Museum Center at 5ive Points** (423-339-5745; museumcenter.org) incorporates the **Cleveland Bradley Regional Museum** and the **Amanda T. Gray Cultural Center**.

Unlike most historical museums included on our off-the-beaten-path journey through Tennessee, this one merits a few words because of its community-
minded, contemporary mission. It's really much more about today than it is
about yesterday, and it's way beyond your father's typical stuffy local museum.
Hats off to you folks in Cleveland.

The museum center was created to fill four distinct community needs: Create a place to preserve heritage in order to give residents, children, and visitors
a sense of the area's rich history; create a showcase for the entrepreneurial
spirit that continues to fuel the community; create a cultural center to showcase
the talents of residents; and create an anchor for the 5ive Points revitalization
project.

Located at 200 Inman St. East, the center opens Tues through Fri 10 a.m.
to 5 p.m., Sat 10 a.m. to 3 p.m. Admission is $5 for adults and $4 for seniors
and students; children under 5 are free.

If you're looking for some great food and want to have a little fun at the
same time, head out to the *Apple Valley Orchard* (351 Weese Rd.; 423-472-
3044 or 877-472-3044; applevalleyorchard.com), 10 miles southeast of Cleveland. There you'll visit a farmers' market and bakery that offers a variety of
foods. Fresh-baked apple goods don't get any better than this.

Apple Valley Orchard also has a lovely story about how it all began. During the early 1960s, Charles McSpadden planted two apple trees in the backyard. He was so pleased that the family added about 40 more trees. When Fay
McSpadden saw how much her husband loved his new hobby, she suggested
that he plant a few more trees. She had in mind about 40 more. But Charles
brought home 10 times that amount. Then even more—and more. Today, the
orchard has about 15,000 trees.

The McSpaddens sold their first apples in 1974. At the time, that was the
only product they sold. But, as the business grew, the family started adding
other items. They installed a cider mill in 1978. In 1987, they built a new
apple house complete with bakery. In 1996, a new strain of the Gala apple

Celebrating Ramps

The one-of-a-kind *Polk County Ramp Tramp Festival* takes place each year during
the fourth week of April at Camp McCroy 4-H Camp in Greasy Creek, on Highway
30 south of Reliance. The day begins with a trip to Big Frog Mountain to dig, and
then you come back to camp and cook and eat the ramps. A popular annual event
since 1958, the festival features local bluegrass music along with your ramps. Call
(423) 338-4503, or visit ramptrampfestival.com.

was discovered in the orchard. In honor of their daughter, the family named the new strain the "Caitlin Gala." In 2001, they enlarged the sales floor of the apple house and added a picnic pavilion. Today, son Chuck is in charge of the family business. Open daily; no admission charge. Wagon rides and tours are available Sept and Oct on Sat and Sun at 2 and 4 p.m. No wagon rides the 3rd weekend of Oct. Open 9 a.m. to 5 p.m. Mon through Sat, noon to 5 p.m. Sun.

About 12 miles south of Cleveland, via a series of back roads, you'll find the *Red Clay State Park* (1140 SW Red Clay Park Rd.; 423-478-0339; tnstate-parks.com/parks/red-clay). Red Clay was the site of the last council ground of the Cherokee nation before their forced removal in 1838. It was the site of 11 general councils, national affairs attended by up to 5,000 Native Americans each.

The US government wanted the Cherokees to surrender their eastern lands and move the entire tribe to lands in Oklahoma. The Cherokees fought it for quite a while, but controversial treaties resulted in their losing the land. The journey to Oklahoma, known today as the Trail of Tears, actually began here at Red Clay.

The march, often referred to as the Great Removal, was a wintertime cross-country journey that covered more than 1,000 miles. Reportedly, 4,000 of the 18,000 who were forced to leave perished during the trek. That was almost one-fourth of the entire Cherokee nation.

Today people can drive that same path across the state on the *Trail of Tears State Historic Route.* It's marked quite well, and maps that explain the various historical activities along the way are available at Red Clay. About 80 percent of the original trail is now covered by modern highways.

Here where it all began, a 275-acre state historic area has been developed. The only original part left is the council spring, locally known as the "blue hole." It was this pure running spring that probably attracted the Cherokees to this site in the first place.

Also on the grounds are various reproductions of early Native American homesteads and an interpretive center with displays and historical exhibits.

It's not an easy place to find. Take Highway 60 south out of Cleveland and follow the signs. They are good signs, but they are often understated in size and can be easily overlooked if you happen to be looking at the cows and horses along the way. If you see a sign that reads WELCOME TO GEORGIA, you've gone about a half mile too far. Open daily; admission is free.

For more information on the Cherokee Mountains, the Ocoee River, Cleveland, and the entire Bradley County area, call (800) 472-6587 or visit the Cleveland/Bradley Chamber of Commerce website at clevelandchamber.com.

Crossroads of Dixie

Chattanooga, the state's fourth-largest city, with a population of 180,557, is located along a 7-mile bend in the Tennessee River. The deep ravine along the river is often referred to as the *Grand Canyon of the South*.

Lookout Mountain is probably the best known of the three major "ledges" that loom over the city. As in any major tourist destination, the beaten path and the unbeaten path catch up with each other here, with the same attraction often offering different things to different people.

A lot of states have large public aquariums, but none can beat the *Tennessee Aquarium* (1 Broad St.; 800-262-0695; tnaqua.org) here in Chattanooga next to the Tennessee River. The location is quite appropriate for the theme of this beautiful facility.

Billed as the "world's largest major freshwater life center," the aquarium salutes the state that has more species of freshwater fish than any other. Few of us will ever have the chance to personally explore the entire length of the magnificent Tennessee River, but here's your chance, and it will take less than 2 hours. During that time you'll have the opportunity to see more than 9,000 creatures that swim, fly, and crawl—all in their natural habitats.

Through exhibits of live and luxuriant flora and fauna, you can take a journey from the river's source in the Appalachian High Country through its midstream and finally to the Mississippi Delta. A visit to the aquarium is an enjoyable experience for the entire family. Save time to enjoy the aquarium's IMAX 3D theater with its new laser projection system. The digital images are terrific. Open every day except Christmas and Thanksgiving. Admission is charged.

The *Chattanooga Visitors Center* (215 Broad St.; 800-322-3344; chattanoogafun.com) is a great place to start your visit here. The center is across the street from the Tennessee Aquarium. Open daily, the center offers a wide assortment of brochures on the area's attractions, accommodations, and restaurants. Information specialists are on hand and will be glad to point you in the right direction. Among the bright and shiny brochures is a set of historical and architectural tour brochures. Pick them up, as they offer a vast amount of information on various areas and neighborhoods of the city, places you might otherwise overlook. Inside the center are public restrooms, vending machines, a gift shop, and an ATM. Catch the free CARTA Electric Shuttle that comes through the breezeway every 10 to 15 minutes. The free shuttle runs continually in the downtown area weekdays from 6:30 a.m. to 9:30 p.m., until 11 on Sat, and from 9:30 a.m. to 8:30 p.m. on Sun. It goes along Broad Street from the Chattanooga Choo-Choo on the southside of

Coolidge and Renaissance parks and the trendy Frazier Avenue shopping area on the Northshore.

The city is obviously quite proud of its river heritage. To prove that point, the city founders have created the **Tennessee Riverpark** along the mighty Tennessee River, adjacent to the aquarium. Beware; there are some steep grades and a lot of steps, but it does appear to be wheelchair accessible via a series of ramps. The area includes parks, fishing piers, a riverside amphitheater carved out of the bluff under a highway overpass, and playgrounds.

Along the Riverwalk, which runs through the Riverpark, you'll come upon the 2,370-foot-long **Walnut Street Bridge** spanning the river. The circa 1891 bridge is considered the longest pedestrian walkway in the world. Once the only way across the river within the city, the structure underwent a $4 million renovation in 1993 and is now a fun place to walk, jog, or sit upon one of the benches and enjoy a fantastic view of the river far below and the Ross's Landing area of the city.

A fun event takes place on the Walnut Street Bridge in early October each year. The **Wine Over Water Festival** (423-265-2825; wineoverwater.org) is a wine-tasting event that offers a fine selection of wines, entertainment, and activities.

While tasting the fruit of the vine on the bridge, make sure you walk over to the north shore and visit Coolidge Park, located on the waterfront between the Walnut Street and Market Street Bridges. You'll find a historic carousel that operates most of the year, offering rides for $1.

A stroll farther up the Riverwalk takes you to the **Bluff View Art District** (411 E. 2nd St.; 800-725-8338 or 423-265-5033; bluffviewartdistrictchattanooga .com), where you'll uncover a classy little conclave of arts and dining. High on a bluff overlooking the Tennessee River, the area is definitely the hippest area in the city.

The **Bluff View Inn** consists of three turn-of-the-20th-century restored homes, all offering spectacular bird's-eye views of the river. Rates start at $125, including breakfast.

Once you've settled into a classy room, get out and walk around the area. It's amazing up here, with everything only a couple of steps away from everything else.

There are several restaurants to choose from. **Tony's Pasta Shop and Trattoria** (212 High St.) serves up a classic Italian menu specializing in fresh house-made pastas, sauces, and European-style breads. It's open daily year-round for lunch and dinner. The **Back Inn Cafe** offers upscale cuisine and scrumptious desserts and has extensive wine and beer lists. Open daily for dinner, it has terrace dining overlooking the river, weather permitting.

If it's good coffee and a fresh pastry or overstuffed sandwich you're looking for, **Rembrandt's Coffee House** (204 High St.) is open every day for breakfast, lunch, and dinner.

The newest addition to the Bluff View family is the **Bluff View Bakery**. The establishment is located in the renovated Powers & Condon building across from the River Gallery Sculpture Garden. Here you'll find the famous Bluff View Art District's signature breads, including the ciabatta and the country loaf, and of course a bunch of other really cool baked goods.

Among the tall shade trees at 10 Bluff View Ave., you'll find the **Hunter Museum of American Art** (423-267-0968; huntermuseum.org), housed in a restored classic revival mansion. It offers the most complete collection of American art in the Southeast. Nearby, the **Houston Museum of Decorative Arts** (201 High St.; 423-267-7176; thehoustonmuseum.org) houses the renowned decorative arts collection of Anna Safley Houston.

The **River Gallery** (423-265-5033; river-gallery.com) is housed in a turn-of-the-20th-century home at 400 E. Second St. and showcases an extensive collection of regional, national, and international fine art and crafts, including paintings, sculptures, and studio art glass.

The 2-acre **River Gallery Sculpture Garden** overlooks the Tennessee River and features 30 pieces of original art placed around a beautifully landscaped garden. All the art is for sale through the River Gallery.

whatadeal forabuck!

The first franchised Coca-Cola bottling plant in the world was built in Chattanooga in 1899 by two local attorneys, who bought the franchise bottling rights for $1 each.

The popular **Riverbend Festival** (423-756-2211; riverbendfestival.com) takes place along the river each May and usually attracts about a half million people during its 3-day run. It's so spread out, however, you don't usually feel crowded. Multiple musical artists perform on different stages, offering up everything from rock, country, and blues to jazz and folk. Of course, there are all kinds of food and drink and other festival-style activities as well.

Selected as one of the top 20 children's museums in the nation by *Child* magazine, the **Creative Discovery Museum** (321 Chestnut St.; 423-756-2738; cdmfun.org) in downtown Chattanooga is all about child's play. The museum is an awesome place to spend time playing and learning. Kids can climb up to a crow's nest, dig for dinosaur bones, see how bees make honey, spray jets of water to spin whirligigs, build robots, make a sculpture, and make music with all types of musical instruments.

The museum's Rooftop Fun Factory is designed to provide hours of fun and education—and it's only one of the choices at the Creative Discovery Museum. The Rooftop Fun Factory takes play outside and opens it up under a big sky. Explore the world of simple machines with sound, movement, and fun galore. Blow soap bubbles and watch as they gently sail through the sky. Turn a wheel to play a pretty tune. Use pulleys to lift yourself off the roof. Work a hand pump up and down to launch balls into the air and make them bounce through a cage. Crank a huge ball into the air and watch as it shakes the roof on its way back down.

In 1916, while steering a Tin Lizzie over a bumpy road, a Chattanooga motorist took a sharp right when he shouldn't have and helped create a major invention. When the dust cleared, John Wiley and his son found themselves unhurt. Their car, however, was submerged in the Chickamauga Creek. Only one wheel peeked above the water. When he got to the closest phone, Wiley called Ernest Holmes, a former student from his business college who now operated a garage and automobile repair shop. Holmes feared it was a hopeless cause, but the ingenious scheme he came up with worked. Using three poles, a pulley, and a chain hooked to the frame of a 1913 Cadillac, Holmes pulled the vehicle back up on the road. From that, the Wrecker King was born. With more and more horseless carriages chugging along the nation's roads, Holmes foresaw a need for handling wrecked and disabled vehicles. In fall 1917, the Chattanooga man created the first wrecker in the US. That tale is recounted at the *International Towing & Recovery Hall of Fame and Museum* (3315 Broad St.; 423-267-3132; internationaltowingmuseum.org).

At the museum, visitors can see all kinds of spiffy wreckers and towing equipment. A green 1929 Chrysler with a Weaver 3-ton auto crane sparkles everywhere, from its protruding headlights to its glistening black tow hook. Its gold-rimmed tires look as though they have never seen a spot of dirt. Then there's the 1936 Chevy truck emblazoned with the notice: IT'S A DIRTY JOB BUT SOMEONE HAS TO DO IT. The wrecker is waxed to the max. Opened in September 1995, the museum was built by the Friends of Towing, an organization boasting over 350 members throughout 21 counties. A Hall of Fame portion of the museum honors people who have in various ways significantly advanced the industry.

Children of all ages love a trip to the zoo and the *Chattanooga Zoo at Warner Park* (301 N. Holtzclaw Ave.; 423-697-1322; chattzoo.org) is a great place for walking around and animal watching. The small 7-acre zoo is ideal for a day's visit. One of its most popular exhibits is the Himalayan Passage, which houses the world's largest indoor red panda habitat. The Himalayan Passage includes habitats for snow leopards and Hanuman langurs (Asian primates).

safecave

Stocked with water and dehydrated food, **Ruby Falls** was a designated fallout shelter during the Cuban Missile Crisis in 1962. It could hold 720 people.

Children never seem to tire of visiting the Ranch Exhibit, where each day is a new adventure. Visitors are welcome to interact with "ranch" animals at a petting zoo. Animals making their home here include goats, sheep, Vietnamese potbellied pigs, miniature horses, Sicilian donkeys, dromedary camels, and man's best friend—dogs. The ranch also features tools used by ranchers and farmhands—saddles, bridles, saws, shovels, pitchforks, and more. Children will learn that before tractors and other farm machines were invented, farmers and ranchers used animals to prepare fields for planting, as well as for herding livestock and for transportation.

The zoo's Walkin' the Tracks showcases animals found in the US. The Gombe Forest features two waterfalls, a vine-draped indoor viewing area, and an outside play yard where critters can be seen at play. The Corcovado Jungle highlights the rainforest of Latin America.

Chattanooga is one of those cities where there is an abundance of off-the-beaten-path things to see and do. Everywhere you look there are unique and fun experiences. Unfortunately, we don't have room to cover them all here. Call the visitor bureau at (800) 322-3344 for a bevy of additional activities, or visit chattanoogafun.com. But we'll come back to the city after a brief detour up Lookout Mountain.

Up on **Lookout Mountain**, one of the Civil War's most famous battles was fought. Known today as the "Battle above the Clouds," the fight at Chickamauga Creek and the Battle of Chattanooga are immortalized in the nation's first and largest national military park. The huge **Chickamauga-Chattanooga National Park**, established in 1890, contains more than 400 markers on the battlefield that outline the series of events that claimed 34,000 casualties. The park also contains 666 monuments honoring the men who fought on the grounds.

As you continue to climb Lookout Mountain, you'll pass several other well-known attractions, including the incredible **Ruby Falls** (423-821-2544; rubyfalls .com). They are very much on the beaten path but shouldn't be overlooked just because you don't like crowds or don't want to visit a place where everyone else in the world has been first. Open every day but Christmas; admission is charged.

The **Mountain Memories** (423-821-6575) gift shop is located at 906 S. Scenic Highway, less than a mile up the mountain from Ruby Falls, and if you're looking for some funky stuff, this is the place to stop. The outside of the building is covered with advertising signs, and the porches are overflowing with rustic crafts. They offer the best price around on "See Rock City" birdhouses and bird feeders, and they have one entire area dedicated to beautiful handmade quilts. Located next to the incline tracks, the store is open daily year-round.

Many Tennessee natives don't realize that one of the most popular attractions on Lookout Mountain, *Rock City* (706-820-2531 or 800-854-0675; seerockcity.com), is actually across the state line in Georgia at 1400 Patten Rd.

"See Rock City" birdhouses and painted barn roofs throughout the Southeast have made this attraction a genuine piece of Americana. There's nothing like it anywhere else. Ten acres of natural rock gardens, some with formations looming 20 stories high, and a barren spot called *Lover's Leap*, from which seven states can be seen, are the highlights of the attraction. Twisting paths take you through wonderfully landscaped gardens and narrow crevices. One such crack is thoughtfully named "Fat Man's Squeeze."

The founder, Garnet Carter, first built a hotel on the property and in early 1928 developed a recreational outlet that changed leisure-time activities from coast to coast. Using the natural hills, rocks, hollow logs, and pools of water as hazards, he created a miniature golf course for his guests who didn't want to take the time to play a complete round of regulation golf.

Within a short time, various other hotels in the country asked him to design courses for them, and *Tom Thumb Golf* took the country by storm. By 1930 about 25,000 miniature golf courses were operating in the US, many of which were Carter's courses.

The original course and the hotel are now gone, but several of the small characters that were placed around the course are a part of the Fairyland portion of Rock City. Admission is $21.95 for adults and $12.95 for children (ages 3 to 12). Prices vary on date of visit and events planned. Combo tickets for Rock City, Ruby Falls, Incline Railway, and zipline also are available. Parking is free.

See Rock City

That's a phrase you've seen painted on the roofs and the sides of barns throughout America. Have you ever wondered who painted most of those barns? Clark Byers can be given that credit. As the Depression drew to a close in the 1930s and more and more tourists began hitting the nation's highways once again, *Rock City* Garden's owner, Garnet Carter, enlisted Byers to paint the barns as unique billboards. Legend has it that when Byers asked what he was supposed to paint, Carter gave him a slip of paper with three words: See Rock City.

Farmers welcomed the new paint jobs on their barns, and Carter enjoyed the increased business the signs brought to him. Being a creative person, Byers often added mileage and the best route to the attraction on his own. The barns can still be seen as far north as Michigan and as far west as Texas. The barns became legendary, and today birdhouses can be purchased with "See Rock City" on their roofs, and modern billboards for the attraction are in the shape of a barn (or birdhouse) with the famous words on top. There are also several new books that feature the barn art. For more information visit seerockcity .com.

Less than a mile from Rock City, at the very top of the mountain, the **Castle in the Clouds Resort Hotel** was built in 1928. Today the old hotel, since restored, is the main building for **Covenant College** (706-820-1560; covenant.edu), a small liberal arts school. Other buildings on the campus also have historical as well as nostalgic appeal. Call ahead of time and school officials or students will be glad to give you a tour.

If you're a little leery about driving up the mountain, there's a solution. Built in 1895, the **Lookout Mountain Incline Railway** (423-821-4224; ride-theincline.com) is now a part of the city's transit system. Billed as the "World's Steepest and Safest Incline Railway," it has a 72.7 percent grade near the top. At the top of the mile-long ride, the upper station has been developed into a small retail village, which happens to have some of the best ice cream in the Chattanooga area. A round-trip costs $15 for adults and $7 for children (ages 3 to 12). The Lookout Mountain Station is open daily 10 a.m. to 6 p.m. At the bottom of the incline, the St. Elmo Station is located at 3917 St. Elmo Ave. Free bus and RV parking is available at St. Elmo Station. At the top of the incline, the Lookout Mountain Station is located at 827 E. Brow Rd.

At the foot of the "other side" of the mountain, the west side, in Lookout Valley, the **Reflection Riding Arboretum & Nature Center** (400 Garden Rd.; 423-821-1160; reflectionriding.org) is an environmental education facility. This is a great place for your family to learn about the wonders of nature through interpretive activities. It features passive solar-design buildings that house a wildlife diorama, a touch-and-feel discovery room, and interactive exhibits. There's a 1,200-foot boardwalk out over the wetlands, with interpretive signs along the way.

The 300-acre nature preserve and botanical garden are absolutely beautiful during the spring. That's when all the wildflowers are in bloom. A 3-mile loop meanders through the area, and you can drive, walk, or ride a bike along the path. You might spot some deer or wild turkeys as you enjoy the flora of the park, open year-round. Admission is free but guests are asked to donate $10 for adults and $7 for seniors and children.

Pardon me, boy, is that the **Chattanooga Choo Choo**? Down in the city, the **Choo Choo** (1400 Market St.; 423-266-5000; choochoo.com) is one of the most unusual shopping areas in the state. Located at the old Terminal Station, the complex features 111 guest rooms aboard passenger cars plus standard rooms. The complex also has landscaped gardens, and myriad Victorian-era shops and restaurants. It's a train, it's a song, and, yes, it's a hotel. All play on the train theme.

If sleeping in a vintage railroad car sounds romantic to you, here's an opportunity to give it a shot. The 20 sleeper cars offer a nice nostalgic touch to the journey of an off-the-beaten-path road warrior. Several of the cars overlook a formal garden area, which offers a nice selection of plants and shrubs. In early summer the roses are wonderful.

The hotel's lobby, the original railroad terminal, was built in 1909 and is considered an architectural wonder. The 85-foot-tall freestanding brick dome is the largest of its type in the world.

The city was one of the country's earliest and largest railroad centers, and this station was the hub of that activity. On the top floor of one of the terminal buildings, one of the world's largest model railroad layouts showing the area as it was during its heyday has been created by a local model railroad club. During the week it can be seen running under automated control, but on weekends members of the club come out and "play" with their creation.

Several stores sell copies of Glenn Miller's version of the "Chattanooga Choo Choo" song. The phrase itself was coined in 1880 when a reporter took the first train ride out of Cincinnati on the new Cincinnati-Southern Line. Since the tracks went only as far as this city, he called the train the "Chattanooga Choo Choo." The original recording is framed and hanging in the old terminal, now the hotel lobby.

Climb aboard a train at the **Tennessee Valley Railroad Museum** (423-894-8028; tvrail.com) and see what all the choo-choo excitement is about. Located at 4119 Cromwell Rd., the museum helps relive the golden age of railroading. The museum offers a wide variety of trips, such as the 55-minute Missionary Ride Local. It's quick, but it packs in all sorts of entertainment, from a ride through a Civil War–era tunnel to a guided tour of the restoration shop, as well as a chance to witness how a locomotive is turned around using a turntable. Looking for something a little longer? Try the Chickamauga Turn, a 5.5-hour round-trip journey to historic Chickamauga. For true rail enthusiasts, multiple Dixie Land Excursions are offered throughout the year. Among the most popular is the North Pole Limited with refreshments, storytelling, and sing-alongs. As the train gently rolls down the rails, a number of lighted holiday displays can be seen outside. Once the train pulls into the "North Pole," a special guest boards for a visit. During the return ride, Santa makes his way through the train cars to greet every child and present a keepsake item to each one.

In downtown Chattanooga at the corner of Martin Luther King Boulevard and Broad Street, the historic *Sheraton Read House Hotel* (423-266-4121) has much of the same charm it possessed through the years when five US presidents, Winston Churchill, and Eleanor Roosevelt were numbered among its guests. In 2016, Read House was purchased by Avocet Hospitality Group and underwent a $25 million renovation. In October 2018, the hotel reopened to welcome guests to the grandeur of the *Great Gatsby* era. The building is listed on the National Register of Historic Places.

Bessie Smith, the First Lady of the Blues, was born in Chattanooga in 1894 and is today immortalized in the city's *Bessie Smith Cultural Center* (423-266-8658; caamhistory.com). There the *Bessie Smith Performance Hall* features concerts, lectures, and seminars. There are several exhibits about her life and plenty of samples of her music. Her death certificate and piano are on display and among the museum's permanent collection. Elsewhere in the museum, there's a fun, interactive wall map of Africa before there was an America and several exhibits of local African American history. There's a nice display of African art as well. Located at 200 E. Martin Luther King Blvd., the museum is open Mon through Fri 10 a.m. to 5 p.m.; Sat from Feb 1 to Sept 30 from noon to 4 p.m.; Sat from Oct 1 to Jan 31 by appointment only. Admission is $7 for adults, $5 for students and seniors, and $3 for children (ages 6 to 12).

Leave Chattanooga via US 41/64/72, also known as Will Cummings Highway, and you'll be in the Raccoon Mountain area, on the "other" side of the city. Follow the signs to the *Raccoon Mountain Caverns & Campground* (423-821-9403; raccoonmountain.com), quite a fun complex tucked away in the mountains.

Outside the entrance to the Raccoon Mountain Caverns, you can pan for your own gemstones just like the old-timers did. Entrance to the caves is through the gift shop. During the 45-minute guided Crystal Palace Walking Tour, you'll meander past many beautiful formations and squeeze and duck through many small passages.

Don't miss the unique shield formation toward the end of the tour. There are only 20 such formations known to exist throughout the world, our guide told us. A map of Tennessee can also be seen outlined by formations on the ceiling in one of the rooms. On a hot day, the wonderfully cool cave can be a fun treat.

A Wild Cave Expedition Tour also is offered for the adventurous. Lasting from 2 to 4 hours, these tours visit the deeper undeveloped sections of the cave. Participants are required to wear gloves, pads, lights, and helmets, all of which are provided for use. Participants are guaranteed to get muddy as they crawl, climb, slide, and squeeze through the cave. Reservations are required for Wild Cave Expedition Tours. Admission is charged; open daily. The campground has a full-service RV camp as well as tent camping sites and cabins. The complex is located 1.25 miles north from I-24 at exit 174 at 319 W. Hills Dr.

Pickers and singers have been gathering together each Friday night since 1979 for the **Mountain Opry** (2501 Fairmount Pike; 423-886-3252) in the old schoolhouse at the top of Signal Mountain, just north of Chattanooga.

Specializing in acoustic Appalachian-style bluegrass and country music, the Opry features a half dozen or so different groups each Friday night. Whoever shows up usually gets to play. It's free to get in, but the 325 seats usually fill up, so get there a bit early if you can. The schoolhouse is located just off US 127 on Fairmount Parkway, at the top of the mountain in the little village of Walden. They'd appreciate a donation to help pay the rent and utilities, but pay as you please.

In **Dunlap**, there's a developing historic site that most overlook mainly because it was the illegal town dump for decades. Through the dedication of volunteers, history is being uncovered on the 62-acre **Coke Ovens Historic Site** (423-949-3483; cokeovens.com).

A huge coal industry was present in this area at the turn of the 20th century, and in this Dunlap industrial complex, coal was turned into coke for use in the iron and steel foundries in nearby Chattanooga.

When the company went out of business in 1917, there were 268 beehive-shaped coke ovens in operation. Through the years, the ovens were forgotten, covered up, and neglected. During the past few years, Carson Camp and members of the Sequatchie Valley Historical Association have uncovered a lot of the area's heritage that had almost been forgotten.

During 2001, Camp discovered that the land upon which the ovens were built was the site of an overnight encampment of the Cherokee Indians during their Trail of Tears trek to Oklahoma. Camp figures the Indians stayed here for the same reason the ovens were built: flat land and closeness to a spring.

The 77-acre park has been listed on the National Register of Historic Places, and a replica of the original coal company store commissary has been built on the original foundation of the old structure. That building now serves as a museum, which houses the largest collection of regional historic coal mining photographs in the state. Hundreds of donated mining artifacts are on display in the museum, and one room has been set aside as a local history museum for Sequatchie County and Dunlap.

Outside, the excavation is continuing. The museum is open Sun through Wed year-round. During peak summer months, it's also open on Sat. Dunlap is 50 miles north of Chattanooga on US 127, and the Coke Ovens Historic Site is 0.75 mile west of downtown, just off US 127 on Walnut Street. A *Bluegrass Festival* takes place on the grounds the first Fri and Sat in June.

Farther up US 41, just across the county line, you'll see the sign for the TVA's *Raccoon Mountain Pumped Storage Facility* (423-825-3100) on your right. It is the most unusual of all the Tennessee Valley Authority's operations. This hydroelectric plant uses more power than it generates. The safety officers on duty will usually agree with that arguable fact, but they will quickly tell you that the plant is very cost-effective.

The visitor center is located at the top of the mountain, about 9 miles from the front entrance, and what a view of the Tennessee River Valley it offers. Also at the top is a 528-acre lake. Deep inside the mountain is the mammoth power plant, totally protected from the elements and enemy attack.

At night, during off-peak hours, the extra energy produced at TVA coal-burning plants is used here to pump water from the Tennessee River up a 1,100-foot pipeline to fill the reservoir above. This is cheaper than shutting down and restarting those plants, and the electricity that would have been wasted is now used to stockpile water that will, in turn, create more power.

During the day, when the demand for electricity is greatest, the water is released from the reservoir and tumbles down the 35-foot-diameter intake tunnels to turn the four large generators, thereby producing electricity.

There are fewer than two dozen pumped storage facilities in the US, and this is the only one that is completely underground. There are several scenic pull-offs on the drive to the top and quite a few picnic areas. At the foot of the mountain, there are fishing areas along the river, all courtesy of the federal government. Admission is free.

When it comes to southern cooking, few meals can be complete without fresh corn bread, dripping with real butter. The folks in South Pittsburg loved their corn bread so much that they created another reason to eat more of it. The annual *National Cornbread Festival & World Championship Cornbread Cook-off* (423-837-0022; nationalcornbread.com) is held in late April, with a 2-day party to remember.

Main Street is closed off and lined with food vendors and exhibits, a carnival comes to town, and a juried show for artisans and crafters takes place. Usually there will be 50 or so crafters working, showing, and selling their wares. *South Pittsburg* is located a few miles west of I-24. Take exit 152 to US 72 West. Don't miss this festive event. The website also has winning corn bread recipes from past years that you can make yourself. Yummy!

Places to Stay in Plateaus & Valleys

CELINA

Horse Creek Resort
1150 Horse Creek Rd.
(931) 243-2125 or (800) 545-2595
horsecreek-resort.com

CHATTANOOGA

Bluff View Inn
411 E. Second St.
(423) 265-5033 or (800) 725-8338
bluffviewartdistrict chattanooga.com

Bode Chattanooga
730 Chestnut St.
(865) 290-2633
bode.co

Chattanooga Choo Choo
1400 Market St.
(423) 266-5000
choochoo.com

Chattanoogan
1201 Broad St.
(423) 756-3400
chattanooganhotel.com

Dwell Hotel
120 E. 10th St.
(888) 945-7866
thedwellhotel.com

Edwin Hotel, Autograph Collection
102 Walnut St.
(423) 713-5900
Marriott.com

Mayor's Mansion Inn B&B
801 Vine St.
(423) 265-5000
mayorsmansioninn.com

Read House Hotel
107 W. MLK Blvd.
(423) 266-4121
thereadhousehotel.com

RiverView Inn
2159 Old Wauhatchie Pike
(423) 821-8619
stayatriverviewinn.com

St. Francis Cottage
1349 Gunbarrel Rd.
(423) 400-4177
stfranciscottage.com

CLEVELAND

Clarion Inn
185 James Asbury Dr.
(423) 244-0331
choicehotels.com

Mountain View Inn
2400 Executive Park Dr. NW
(423) 472-1500
Mountainviewinn.us

DUCKTOWN

Company House Bed & Breakfast
318 Main St.
(423) 496-5634
companyhousebandb.com

GORDONSVILLE

Butterfly Hollow B&B
28 Russell Rd.
(615) 784-8551
butterflyhollow.com

MCMINNVILLE

Bonnie Blue Inn
2317 Old Smithville Rd.
(931) 815-3838
bonnieblueinn.com

Falcon Rest Mansion & Gardens
85 Bluff Springs Rd.
(931) 668-4444
falconrest.com

MONTEAGLE

Edgeworth Inn
19 Wilkins Ave.
(931) 924-4000
edgeworthinn.com

Jim Oliver's Smokehouse
850 W. Main St.
(800) 489-2091
thesmokehouse.com

Monteagle Inn & Retreat Center
204 W. Main St.
(931) 924-3869

MONTEREY

The Garden Inn B&B at Bee Rock
1400 Bee Rock Rd.
(931) 839-1400
thegardeninnbb.com

RACCOON MOUNTAIN

Raccoon Mountain Caverns & Campground
319 W. Hills Rd.
(423) 821-9403
raccoonmountain.com

RED BOILING SPRINGS

Armour's Red Boiling Springs Hotel
321 E. Main St.
(615) 699-2180
armourshotel.com

Donoho Hotel
500 E. Main St.
(615) 699-3141
thedonoho.com

Thomas House
520 E. Main St.
(615) 699-3006
thomashousehotel.com

SMITHVILLE

Bright Hill Bed & Barn
1586 Bright Hill Rd.
(615) 438-6062
brighthilltn.com

Evins Mill
1535 Evins Mill Rd.
(615) 269-3740
evinsmill.com

WATERTOWN

Watertown Bed & Breakfast
116 Depot Ave.
(615) 237-9999

Places to Eat in Plateaus & Valleys

CHATTANOOGA

Alleia
26 Main St.
(423) 305-6990
alleiarestaurant.com

Big River Grille & Brewing Works
222 Broad St.
(423) 267-2739
bigrivergrille.com

The Blue Plate
191 Chestnut St.
(423) 648-6767
theblueplate.info

Bluegrass Grill
55 E. Main St.
(423) 752-4020
bluegrassgrillchattanooga.com

Easy Bistro & Bar
203 Broad St.
(423) 266-1121
easybistro.com

Hennen's
193 Chestnut St.
(423) 634-5160
hennens.net

Public House Restaurant
1110 Market St.
(423) 266-3366
publichousechattanooga.com

Rib & Loin
5946 Brainerd Rd.
(423) 499-6465
ribandloin.com

St. John's Restaurant
1278 Market St.
(423) 266-4400
stjohnsrestaurant.com

Stir
1444 Market St.
(423) 531-7847
stirchattanooga.com

Urban Stack
12 W. 13th St.
(423) 475-5350
urbanstack.com

CLEVELAND

The Gondolier
3300 Keith St. Northwest
(423) 472-4998
Mygondolier.com

Stadium BBQ
773 Keith St. Northwest
(423) 790-0002
stadiumbbq.com

DECATUR

Cottonport Marina Restaurant
797 Cottonport Ferry Rd.
(423) 454-4110
cottonport.wixsite.com

Uncle Gus's Mountain Pit Bar B Que
810 Peakland Rd.
(423) 334-2487
unclegusbarbque.com

LIVINGSTON

Steel Coop
209 S. Spring St.
(931) 403-2667
steel-coop.com

Tennessee Barbeque
407 E. Main St.
(931) 823-8227
tennesseebarbeque.org

MCMINNVILLE

Collins River BBQ & Café
117 E. Main St.
(931) 507-3663
collinsriverbbq.com

Cumberland Biscuit Company
114 W. Main St.
(931) 474-8670
cumberlandbiscuitcompany.com

Prater's BBQ
9576 Manchester Hwy.
(931) 635-2259
Pratersbbq.com

MONTEAGLE

Big Porch
740 W. Main St.
(931) 924-9241
thebigporch.com

High Point Restaurant
224 Main St.
(931) 924-4600
highpointrestaurant.net

**Jim Oliver's Smoke
House Restaurant**
850 W. Main St.
(800) 489-2091
thesmokehouse.com

Mountain Goat Market
109 Main St.
(931) 924-2727
mtngoatmarket.com

The Heartland

Heart of the Heartland

Nashville. It very well could be the smallest city with the biggest reputation in the world. Anyone who has ever listened to a radio knows that Nashville is the country music capital of the world.

What a lot of people don't realize, however, is that the city's nickname is Music City, not Country Music City. It has some of the best recording studios in the world and absolutely the best studio musicians in the business. Everyone from Paul McCartney to Pearl Jam to Garth Brooks has recorded in Nashville. They come for the quality of the city as much as for the state-of-the-art studios.

There is an active jazz and blues culture, as well as rock and rap cultures. Clubs all over town offer a wide variety of music. The Tennessee Performing Arts Center in downtown Nashville has a Broadway Series that's second to none, and the Bridgestone Arena, home of the Nashville Predators NHL club, hosts some of the world's biggest stars, from Luciano Pavarotti to Shania Twain to the Rolling Stones.

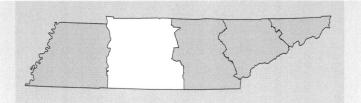

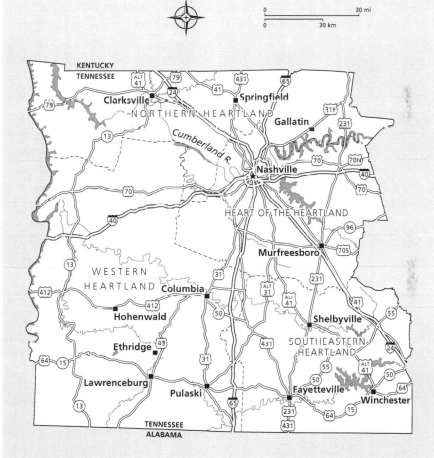

The National Football League's Tennessee Titans play in Nissan Stadium across the Cumberland River from downtown, and on Football Sundays the action is definitely in the various downtown districts.

Nashville is far from a mainstream city. It's one of those unique areas where the unbeaten path crosses the well-traveled path and merges for a few miles and dozens of experiences. The city's maternal relationship to country music has created quite a few one-of-a-kind attractions and events.

Music City is not only a place where musicians record—it's also the place they call home. While you won't find Vince Gill or Keith Urban listed in the phone book, it's not hard to find their homes. It's also not unusual to see the stars at the local supermarket, or at a gas station or musical event.

With all that Nashville has going for it, the majority of the visitors to the city still come to see the music-associated attractions—and that's good news for those who don't visit those attractions. The crowds are smaller (and sometimes nonexistent) at the doors of many of the city's other fun experiences.

The city of Nashville and the county of Davidson are one and the same, with a metropolitan government running the place. The 2017 census showed the area with a population of 691,243, a growth of nearly 10 percent over 2010.

There's plenty to do in downtown Nashville, but let's start our journey in the northwest quadrant of the city, where you'll find the mammoth Gaylord Opryland Resort & Convention Center approximately 13 miles from downtown.

Across from the Opryland complex and the world-famous WSM-AM radio station, the broadcast station of the Grand Ole Opry for more than 60 years, is the Music Valley Area and its complex of shops and activities. That's where you'll find the *Nashville Palace* (2611 McGavock Pike; 615-889-1541; nashville-palace.com) . The Palace is where country superstar Randy Travis was discovered while working as a dishwasher. Live music nightly and a delicious menu that includes "the best catfish in town" are featured.

AUTHOR'S TOP TEN PICKS

Bell Witch Cave	Jack Daniel Distillery
Cannonsburgh Pioneer Village	Mule Day Festival & Parade
Elephant Sanctuary	Nash Trash Tour
Ernest Tubb Record Shop	Nashville Cowboy Church
Hatch Show Print	Schermerhorn Symphony Center

The ***Ernest Tubb Midnight Jamboree*** (615-889-2474; etrecordshop.com), the second-oldest live country music radio show in America, is broadcast each Saturday night from the Texas Troubadour Theater (2416 Music Valley Dr.), a few blocks behind the Nashville Palace. The show is broadcast on WSM-AM 650 and features top-name country talent, many of whom may have played the Grand Ole Opry earlier that night across the street at the Opryland complex. Be there by 11:30 to get a good seat. Admission is free. Check the website late in the week to see who's booked for the Saturday show. If you're looking for vintage country music, the Ernest Tubb Record Shop next door is the place to search.

The Texas Troubadour Theater is also the site of the famous ***Nashville Cowboy Church*** (615-889-2474). It's a unique Nashville experience. Where else can you hear top-shelf southern gospel music while a genuine Stetson hat is passed for the offering? Services are held each Sun at 10 a.m.

The ***Gaylord Opryland Resort & Convention Center*** (2800 Gaylord Dr.; 615-889-1000; marriott.com), formerly known as Opryland Hotel, is a huge, amazing place. With 2,711 guest rooms, 171 suites, 776 atrium garden-view rooms, 12 restaurants, 10 lounges, and 30 retail stores, all inside, you can start to realize why this place is so amazing. Add to that 5 ballrooms, 152 meeting rooms, and nearly 1 million square feet of exhibit space, and you have quite a unique hotel. It's worth a visit, but make sure you wear your tennies; you'll be doing a lot of walking.

The fun thing to see and do here is to visit the three different atrium areas, which are under nearly 9 acres of skylights. The Conservatory and the Cascades are each 2-acre atriums featuring tropical gardens, running streams, and multilevel viewing areas. The newest area, the Delta, is a 4.5-acre interiorscape with a flowing river and 25-passenger flatboats that take guests on a voyage through the area.

Christmas at the hotel is especially fun. Nearly 2 million lights decorate the exterior of the hotel, and inside there are holiday-themed dinner shows, an arts and antiques show, and other seasonal activities.

The new concept of "shopper-tainment" has come to Nashville via the 1.2-million-square-foot ***Opry Mills*** (615-514-1100; simon.com) next to the resort at 433 Opry Mills Dr. The 200-plus retailers offer up a bevy of fun experiences, shopping opportunities, and dining facilities. Among the tenants: Bass Pro Shop, Rainforest Cafe, and an IMAX Theater.

The ***Grand Ole Opry*** is the show that started it all. And this is the place the Opry has called home since moving from the Ryman Auditorium in 1974. Located at 2804 Opryland Dr., the Grand Ole Opry is known for its mix of music and stars. A typical Opry performance might feature traditional country,

OTHER ATTRACTIONS WORTH SEEING

Adventure Science Center
Sudekum Planetarium
800 Fort Negley Blvd., Nashville
(615) 862-5160
adventuresci.com

Cheekwood Gardens & Art Museum
1200 Forrest Park Dr., Nashville
(615) 356-8000
cheekwood.org

Frist Center for the Visual Arts
919 Broadway, Nashville
(615) 244-3340
fristcenter.org

George Jones Museum
128 2nd Ave. N, Nashville
(615) 818-0128
georgejones.com

The Hermitage
4580 Rachel's Ln., Hermitage
(615) 889-2941
thehermitage.com

Johnny Cash Museum & Café
119 3rd Ave. S, Nashville
(615) 256-1777
johnnycashmuseum.com

Ryman Auditorium
116 Fifth Ave. North, Nashville
(615) 889-3060
ryman.com

Smith-Trahern Mansion
101 McClure St., Clarksville
(931) 648-9998
Fceclarksville.org

Tootsie's Orchid Lounge
422 Broadway, Nashville
(615) 726-0463
tootsies.net

bluegrass, comedy, Cajun, new country, gospel, and more. Performers include country legends as well as up-and-coming artists. The lineup is released a couple of days before showtime, but you never know who might turn up. It's not unusual for a special guest to drop by for a duet or surprise appearance during these unrehearsed performances. Tickets start at $25.

For a better understanding of the show, take a backstage tour of the **Grand Ole Opry House** (615-871-6779; opry.com) to get an authentic look behind the scenes. Tour guides have a wealth of fascinating stories about the Opry and about country music greats past and present.

Tours include a visit to the Opry House artist entrance as well as a stop in Studio A, a live television studio and former home of *Hee Haw*. A custom-built theater features music, state-of-the-art special effects, 3D film images, archival footage, and superstar hosts Trish Yearwood and Garth Brooks. Also showcased during the tour are artist dressing rooms, newly refurbished following the Nashville flood of 2010, and the world-famous Opry stage. Look for a circle of wood in a prime spot on the floor. It was cut from the original Ryman Auditorium as a reminder of the greats who once stood there.

TOP ANNUAL EVENTS

FEBRUARY
Antiques & Garden Show of Nashville
Music City Center
Nashville
(615) 352-1282
antiquesandgardenshow.com

APRIL
Main Street Festival
Franklin
(615) 591-8500
downtownfranklintn.com
Crafts, food, entertainment

Mule Day
Columbia
(931) 381-9557
muleday.org
Old-time festival with mule shows, mule pulling, flea market, clogging contest

Nashville Earth Day Festival
Nashville
Nashvilleearthday.org

MAY
Old Timers Day
Dickson
dicksoncountyoldtimersday.com
Crafts, flea market, quilt show

Tennessee Crafts Fair
Nashville
(615) 385-1904
tennesseecraft.org

Tennessee Renaissance Festival
Arlington
(615) 395-9950
tnrenfest.com

JUNE
CMA Music Festival/Fan Fair
Nashville
(615) 244-2840
cmaworld.com
Attracts fans from around the world

RC Cola and Moon Pie Festival
Bell Buckle
Bellbucklechamber.com

JULY
Annual Irish Picnic
St. Patrick's Church
McEwen
(931) 582- 3493

Independence Day Celebration
Nashville
(800) 657-6910
visitmusiccity.com

SEPTEMBER
African Street Festival
American Cultural Alliance
Nashville
(615) 942-0706
Aacanashville.org

Fall Tennessee Craft Fair
Nashville
(615) 736-7600
tennesseecraft.org

Living History Tour
Nashville
(615) 862-7970
thenashvillecitycemetery.org

Tennessee State Fair
Nashville
(615) 582-8997
tnstatefair.org

Uncle Dave Macon Days
Murfreesboro
(800) 716-7560
uncledavemacondays.com

OCTOBER
Celebration of Cultures
Nashville
Celebratenashville.org

TOP ANNUAL EVENTS (CONTINUED)

Grand Ole Opry Birthday Celebration
Nashville
(615) 871-6779
opry.com

NOVEMBER

Christmas Village
Nashville
(615) 256-2726
christmasvillage.org

Country Christmas
Gaylord Opryland Resort
Nashville
(615) 889-1000
Marriott.com

DECEMBER

Dickens of a Christmas
Franklin
(615) 905-8937
Downtownfranklintn.com

Nashville Ballet *Nutcracker*
Nashville
(615) 297-2966
nashvilleballet.com

Yulefest: A 1780s Christmas
at Mansker's Station Frontier Life Center
Goodlettsville
(615) 859-3678

Daytime tours are available 7 days a week Jan through Oct. On evenings on which there is only one Opry performance, tours are also available immediately after the show. Opry House Backstage Pass Tours can be booked up to two weeks in advance. Tour schedules and times vary based on Opry House availability. Tours cost about $25 per person. A Behind the Curtain Star Experience lets visitors be backstage during a performance of the Opry.

In downtown Nashville, an area called **The District** is centered on Second Avenue, running north off Broadway to the county courthouse. It's where you'll find the typical tourist traps, but it's also where you'll find some great restaurants and drinking emporiums. All the businesses are in restored turn-of-the-20th-century buildings and warehouses.

Country music wasn't always as slick as it is today, and that wonderful old-time sound is still alive and well and being played daily in the honky-tonks of Lower Broadway, just around the corner from The District.

There's a big difference between a honky-tonk and a country music club. First of all, honky-tonks are real beer joints with small, crowded dance floors and live music from great musicians you've probably never heard of—and if you order a glass of wine or a fancy drink, you'll probably be laughed right out the back door.

Lower Broadway's honky-tonk neighbors are the genuine articles, left virtually untouched through the years. Most keep their doors open so that you

Patsy Cline Museum

Patsy Cline saved the memories of her life. After the singer's death, her husband Charlie Dick kept his wife's memorabilia safe without telling even their daughters. Locked away for more than half a century, Patsy Cline's collection is now being shared with the public at a new museum opened in downtown Nashville on April 7, 2017, at 119 Third Ave. South; (615) 454-4722; patsymuseum.com.

"Patsy Cline was very sentimental," said museum founder Bill Miller. "I think people will be really surprised at what we have in the museum."

Arranged in chronological order, exhibits trace Patsy Cline's life from her birth on September 8, 1932, in Winchester, Va., to her death in a plane crash near Camden, Tenn., on March 5, 1963. She was 30 years old. Artifacts are displayed from every stage of Cline's life, including a porch seat from her childhood home and a booth from Gaunt's Drug Store where she used to work. After her father deserted them, Cline dropped out of school at 15 to help support the family.

She sang in juke joints, amateur musicals, and talent shows. It was at a local club where Cline met Charlie Dick. The two married in 1957 and had two children: Julie, born in 1958, and Randy, born in 1961. Dick died November 8, 2015, at age 81 and was buried next to Cline in Winchester, Virginia. Some of the surprising exhibits are furniture, ashtrays, and a still-running Norge refrigerator Cline had in her Nashville home. A carefully arranged photo album commemorates her wedding to Charlie Dick. And the front door key to her "dream home" still dangles from a tattered string.

Among the most poignant items are those recovered at the site of the plane crash that took Cline's life, as well as the lives of singers Hawkshaw Hawkins and Cowboy Copas and Cline's manager Randy Hughes who was piloting the plane. The group was returning from a benefit show in Kansas City. Displayed is the silver Elgin watch Cline was wearing when she died.

The final exhibit showcases outfits that Cline had designed and wanted famed tailor Nudie Cohn to create for her. "When an artist wore Nudie, it was their way of saying, 'I've arrived,'" the exhibit notes.

Cline wrote to Cohn on February 28, 1963, including her instructions and measurements. Nudie responded to Cline that he would take on the work. But his letter arrived too late. Cline was dead.

"We didn't want to leave people with the somber exhibit of Patsy's death so this year we had Nudie's granddaughter make the outfits from Patsy's designs," Miller said. "When the family found all of Patsy's things that Charlie Dick had saved, it makes me believe that this museum was meant to be. Patsy Cline was an icon, the best loved female singer of all time."

can hear the music from the sidewalk, and most have the bands up front so that you can watch the performers through the large windows.

Sitting on the corner of Fifth and Broadway, *Legends Corner* (428 Broadway; 615-248-6334; legendscorner.com) guards the entrance to the strip known as Honky Tonk Highway. You might not find it on a map, but Honky Tonk Highway is one of the most popular destinations in Nashville. It's the affectionate nickname for downtown Broadway's row of iconic bars.

Hillbilly heaven is anchored by the grandmother of all Nashville honky-tonks, *Tootsie's Orchid Lounge* (422 Broadway; 615-726-0463; tootsies.net). The back door of Tootsie's is across the alley from the back door of the Ryman Auditorium, where the Grand Ole Opry took place for years. Hattie Louise "Tootsie" Bess ran the joint from 1960 to 1978 and during that time welcomed some of the greatest Opry performers through the back door while they waited for their turn to perform on the stage. When Tootsie bought the club, she hired a painter who mistakenly painted the exterior purple. She kept the color, and today the purple facade stands out from the rest. Legend says that Willie Nelson got his first songwriting job after singing at Tootsie's. Kris Kristofferson was known to spend hours at Tootsie's soaking up vibes for the treasured tunes he wrote. That great band or young singer you see performing free in a Honky Tonk Highway bar might be the next big star.

While Tootsie's has the history, it also attracts more of a tourist crowd; it's the place many locals take visitors from out of town. Try a few of the others that will probably be less crowded: *Roberts Western World* (416 Broadway; 615-244-9552; robertswesternworld.com); *Layla's* (418 Broadway; 615-726-2799; laylasnashville.com); and the *Second Fiddle* (420 Broadway; 615-251-6812; thesecondfiddle.com).

Across Broadway from these honky-tonks at 417 Broadway is the *Ernest Tubb Record Shops* (615-255-7503; etrecordshop.com), opened by the country star himself in 1950 and the former location of the Midnite Jamboree, now held at the Music Valley location, every Saturday night for many years. During those years, Tubb featured many of the top Opry stars on his stage. Today the shop's walls are lined with autographed pictures and album covers. The shop is a good place to find a huge selection of bluegrass and country music. They specialize in the older, harder-to-find artists on CDs.

The Stage on Broadway (412 Broadway; 615-726-0504; thestageonbroadway.com) is exactly that—the biggest stage on Broadway. Offering two floors with seating, the Stage is said to have had famous musicians drop in for a drink and a jam session, including Toby Keith and Joe Diffie.

Country music stars also are opening new places on Honky Tonk Highway— *Jason Aldean's Kitchen & Rooftop Bar* (307 Broadway; jasonaldeansnashville

.com); ***John Rich's Redneck Riviera Bar & BBQ*** (208 Broadway; 615-436-4070; redneckrivieranashville.com); ***Luke Bryan's 32 Bridge*** (301 Broadway; 740-341-6205; lukes32bridge.com); ***Dierks Bentley's Whiskey Row*** (400 Broadway; 629-203-7822; dierkswhiskeyrow.com); ***FGL (Florida Georgia Line) House*** (120 3rd St. S; 615-961-5460; fglhouse.com); ***Blake Shelton's Ole Red*** (300 Broadway; 615-780-0900; olered.com); and ***AJ's (Alan Jackson) Good Time Bar*** (421 Broadway; 615-678-4808; ajsgoodtimebar.com).

Situated among the honky-tonks and shops is ***Hatch Show Print*** (224 Fifth Ave. S.; 615-256-2805; hatchshowprint.com). Open to the public, this is

Structurally Sound

The home of the **Country Music Hall of Fame & Museum** is not just a building. It is an architectural salute to the history of the beloved form of music. It's no accident that the dark, narrow windows on the swooping facade resemble piano keys. That's just one of many elements that the Hall of Fame's designers incorporated into the modern building as symbols of country music.

Recognizing that country music is an art form whose roots stretch from farms and factories to churches and prisons to country stores and urban bars, the designers, Tuck Hinton Architects, used a variety of materials and included many symbolic representations throughout the attractions. Some symbols, like the windows, are obvious. Others are more subtle. Seen from above, the building's curved facade and drum-shaped segment resemble a bass clef, while the front wall's slanted end is a nod to late-1950s Cadillac tail fins.

A not-so-obvious symbol is the hall's riveted-steel structure and Mississippi yellow pine flooring in the conservatory, which allude to early-20th-century bridges and factories. Suggesting an Appalachian stream, or perhaps the flow of artistic inspiration from the Hall of Fame's legendary members, water from a fountain cascades alongside a long staircase. At the bottom, the stream ends in a "wishing well" pool in the spacious conservatory, a space designed to symbolize the "front-porch" origins of country music.

There are several other symbols, but perhaps the most apparent architectural expression of county music is the building's Hall of Fame rotunda, which acknowledges the beloved anthem "Will the Circle Be Unbroken." Around the exterior circumference of the silo-like space are slabs of Crab Orchard stone, designed to represent notes from the famous Carter Family song.

Atop the rotunda is a tower/steeple/chandelier modeled after the WSM-AM 650 radio tower, a tribute to the station's role in the creation of the Grand Ole Opry and the popularization of country music worldwide. Inside the rotunda, which has an almost sacred feel, are additional reminders of the unbroken circle or continuity of country music, from its earliest days to the present.

abitofnashville
tennesseetrivia

The world's first nighttime airplane flight took off from Cumberland Park on June 22, 1910.

President Theodore Roosevelt coined the phrase "good to the last drop" while drinking coffee at the old Maxwell House Hotel.

The Grand Ole Opry House is the world's largest broadcast studio.

Iroquois, a Nashville horse, was the first American horse to win the English Derby. The Iroquois Steeplechase race held here each May is named for him.

While visiting the Belle Meade Plantation, President William Howard Taft got stuck in the bathtub. The owners then installed a stand-up shower for his next visit.

With more than 800 churches, synagogues, and temples, the city is known as the "buckle of the Bible belt."

The driveway at the Hermitage, home of President Andrew Jackson, is shaped like a guitar.

Elvis Presley recorded more than 200 songs at RCA's Studio B.

one of America's oldest surviving show poster printers. Founded in 1879 by two brothers, the business printed posters for the circus, sporting events, and vaudeville shows. It won the Grand Ole Opry account and printed not only the Opry's posters but also the show posters for most of country music's greatest legends. Thousands of posters printed from the original cuts are available for purchase. Tours show how the posters are made, then visitors can make their own keepsake poster. Tours are $18 for adults, $15 for children.

The *Country Music Hall of Fame and Museum* (615-416-2001 or 800-852-6437; countrymusichalloffame.org) opened in 2001 to much ballyhoo in Nashville and the world's country music circles. The place is a classy celebration of the musical genre that made Nashville famous worldwide.

The building takes up an entire block at the corner of Fifth and Demonbreun Avenues and houses an extensive collection of memorabilia, gold records, the Hall of Fame, and Elvis's solid-gold 1960 Cadillac. Even if you're not into country music, this is a fun and quite educational place to visit.

The *SoBro Grill and SoBro2Go* are located in the conservatory and do not require an admission fee to visit. Live performances are a part of the museum experience, and Country Music Television broadcasts a live daily show from the conservatory. Everyone is invited to be a part of the live audience. The museum opens daily at 9 a.m. and closes at 5 p.m. Admission is charged.

One beautiful Nashville landmark, comparable to the greatest music halls in the world, is the $120 million *Schermerhorn Symphony Center* (615-687-6400; nashvillesymphony.org), designed to be an acoustic masterpiece. Located at One Symphony Place, the center is home to the *Nashville Symphony*

Orchestra. Designed by architect David M. Schwarz, the 197,000-square-foot center has 30 soundproof windows above the hall, making it one of the only major concert halls in North America with natural light. Named in honor of the late orchestra conductor Kenneth Schermerhorn, the center is a sophisticated modern building that is neoclassically inspired, with a classic limestone exterior and columns. A garden is open to the public throughout the day and during concerts.

In May 2010, severe flooding caused significant damage in and around Nashville, including about $40 million in damages to Schermerhorn Symphony Center. At the height of the flood, the lower reaches of the building were filled with 24 feet of water. Among the losses were electrical and mechanical equipment, a large kitchen, and numerous instruments. Significant instrument losses included two Steinway & Sons pianos and the blower and console units of the Schoenstein pipe organ. Repairs to the center began almost immediately, and it reopened less than 8 months later with a concert featuring Itzhak Perlman on New Year's Eve 2010. The organ restoration was completed in time for a May 2011 concert by organist Cameron Carpenter.

The **Music City Center** (nashvillemusiccitycenter.com) is an impressive $585 million facility that totals 2.1 million square feet. That includes 1.2 million square feet of public spaces and a 900,000-square-foot garage with 1,800 parking spaces.

Major features include a public art collection comprised of more than 80 pieces. The center is so massive that Sixth Avenue runs through the building. It has a 57,500 square foot Grand Ballroom that seats 6,000 people. Green features include solar panels and a green roof. The building is on track to receive LEED Silver certification.

The new center is designed to serve as the city's "front porch," located in the heart of downtown Nashville, just steps from the Ryman Auditorium and the Broadway honky-tonks. It also is able to host 75 percent of the conventions in the country, compared to the 25 percent that could be accommodated at the old Nashville Convention Center.

Along with being a place to host visitors, the Music City Center also serves as a central meeting point for Nashville residents. A wide green pavilion circles the building on all sides, designed to serve as public space for art, music, and just sitting a spell and visiting.

The Music City Center sits just south of Broadway on a 16-acre site that runs from Fifth Avenue to Eighth Avenue, west to east, and from Demonbreun Street to Franklin Street, north to south. It is adjacent to both the Bridgestone Arena and the Country Music Hall of Fame.

Goo Goo

If there were a candy hall of fame, Nashville would have a place in it. Music City is where the first combination candy bar was invented, and it's still made right in Nashville at the **Standard Candy Company.**

The historic candy—the Goo Goo—has been satisfying sweet tooths for more than 8 decades. As they say on the *Grand Ole Opry* radio show, which Standard has sponsored since the early 1960s, "Generations of Southerners have grown up on them." Southerners as well as non-Southerners from as far away as California and Canada are gaga over Goo Goos. They write the company each week requesting orders of the chewy, gooey candy. But you don't have to write for it; you can find Goo Goos in just about every part of the country in well-known grocery stores and markets. They are most plentiful in Music City, however, and tourist attractions and gift stores usually keep a good supply on hand for visitors who want to take home a taste of Nashville.

Standard, today operated by Jimmy Spradley, sells about 25 million Goo Goos (approximately $8.5 million worth) each year. The Goo Goo was invented by Howell Campbell, who, in 1901 at the age of 19, founded the Standard Candy Company. The company's first products were hard candies and chocolates, but Howell and original plant superintendent Porter Moore developed a recipe combining fresh roasted peanuts, caramel, marshmallows, and milk chocolate. The recipe became a classic. Today, the Goo Goo comes in three varieties—the original Goo Goo Cluster, the Peanut Butter Goo Goo, and the Goo Goo Supreme.

The candy bar didn't have a name at first because no one could decide what to call it. Stories of how the candy got its name vary. One tale says that Campbell's son, Howell Campbell Jr., says his father took a streetcar to work each morning and would discuss the matter with fellow passengers. One passenger, a schoolteacher, was said to have suggested Goo Goo. But some people say the candy was given the name because it's the first thing a baby says.

In its early days, the candy bar's circular shape made it difficult to wrap, so it was sold unwrapped from glass containers. Later, the Goo Goo was hand-wrapped in foil and advertised as a "Nourishing Lunch for a Nickel." While it wouldn't pass for a nourishing lunch today (the Goo Goo Cluster in the silver package has 240 calories, 11 grams of fat, and just a smidgen of calcium, protein, and iron), the candy is still a delicious treat.

If your hunger can't wait, go to the **Goo Goo Shop & Dessert Bar** (116 Third Ave. S.) in downtown Nashville. Open daily, the shop is no ordinary retail store. It is also a museum where visitors can walk though Goo Goo history by reading more than a century of time lines complete with Goo Goo memorabilia. Visitors can also watch Goo Goos being made by hand in a glass-enclosed confectionary kitchen. The Dessert Bar serves up all sorts of sweet treats, sundaes, sodas, and milkshakes. Slide into a retro red booth and enjoy. Or for hands-on fun with chocolate, join in a chocolate class. For fans of *The Walking Dead* television show, in an episode's closing scenes, a series character takes a Goo Goo Cluster from his pocket and places it on the altar of a church littered with dead bodies.

Symbolism? Regular viewers can probably figure that out.

The building features a 350,000-square-foot exhibit hall. It also offers 90,000 square feet of meeting room space—approximately 60 meeting rooms— and 32 loading docks that provide ultimate flexibility and ease of loading for convention planners. The center was designed by Atlanta-based Thompson, Ventulett, Stainback & Associates and Nashville-based Tuck Hinton Architects and Moody-Nolan Architects.

Have a favorite song or two? Know who wrote those lovely words and music? Stop by the ***Nashville Songwriters Hall of Fame*** to see some famous songwriters and their creations. Located in the lobby of the Music City Center, the Hall of Fame features songwriting artifacts as well as three 55-inch touch screens. The screens allow visitors to access sound, video, and other digital information about the history of Nashville-connected songwriting and the more than 200 members of the Hall of Fame.

From every genre of music, the names of Hall of Fame members are engraved in a special outdoor Songwriters Square at the corner of Fifth Avenue and Demonbreun, as well as on the stone steps leading from Fifth Avenue up to the interior display.

"The music industry is a vital part of Nashville's unique culture, and song- writers are often the 'unsung heroes' of the business," former Nashville Mayor Karl Dean said at a dedication ceremony. "This location at the Music City Cen- ter is a fitting space to honor songwriters and their creativity, and it gives both local residents and visitors from out of town yet another reason to stop by our new convention center."

Songwriting is a revered occupation in Nashville. No other city pays atten tion to its writers the way ***Music City*** does, and radio announcers are just as apt to say who wrote a song as who performed it. Writers' nights are held in various locations on a regular basis and are great places to get right down to the basics of country music. Hearing a popular writer singing his or her list of hits that others made into million-sellers is like listening to an oldies jukebox.

Perhaps the best-known cafe in the city, the ***Bluebird Cafe*** (4104 Hills- boro Pike; 615-383-1461; bluebirdcafe.com), is also one of the best places to attend a writers' night. The food is good, the talent is excellent, and chances are that you might be sitting next to a country superstar. They hang out here a lot, especially during writers' shows. Several of today's superstars were regulars here on their way up the ladder, including Garth Brooks and Kathy Mattea. If you want to talk, dance, or be rowdy, the Bluebird is not the place to go, however. Music lovers will politely tell you to "Shush!" so they can hear what they came to hear. The Bluebird is located in the Green Hills area of the city, about 15 minutes from downtown.

Immaculate Confection

The **Bongo Java Coffeehouse** was birthplace of the world-famous **NunBun**. Baker Ryan Finney decided to eat one of the rolls he was baking one morning, and he caught a divine image just before taking a bite. The roll possessed an uncanny likeness to Mother Teresa. It was indeed the immaculate confection, Finney said. "I was horrified because I almost ate this religious piece of dough," he was heard to say. It was stored in a freezer for a week and then became the center of a 9-minute video documentary titled *A Music City Miracle: The Story of the NunBun*. Local papers and television stations ran stories, and before long it appeared on David Letterman, Paul Harvey, *Hard Copy,* in the *Calcutta Times,* on the BBC, and other media worldwide.

Properly preserved, the NunBun was on display at the coffeehouse so the masses could take a look for themselves. On Christmas Day 2005, the unthinkable happened. The NunBun was stolen and has never been seen since. Go online to read the saga for yourself at bongojava.com. Located at 2007 Belmont Blvd., across from Belmont University; call them at (615) 385-5282.

Remember when coffee was just another cuppa joe? Those days are now gone forever. On 21st Avenue, down in Hillsboro Village, the **Bongo Java Roasting Co.** shares the old Jones Pet Shop with **Fido**, a cafe named for the dog who discovered coffee (615-777-3436; bongojava.com). The cafe opened when the pet shop closed in 1996, after 50 years in business. The funky neon pet shop sign has been restored and sits upon the roof.

Fido features a breakfast menu served all day, with such items as the McFido eggs and cheese on a bagel. During the rest of the day for lunch and dinner, there's a full menu of sandwiches, soups, snacks, bagels, and full meals, including grilled salmon, fish tacos, steak and hash, and the popular green chile mac and cheese.

There are plenty of specialty coffee drinks, and the desserts are great. P.S. Don't forget to eat while you're there; they have some great nontraditional food items. But take a look before you bite and you may discover something cool. Open daily for all three meals.

They open Mon through Fri at 7 a.m. and on Sat and Sun at 8 a.m., and they stay that way until 11 p.m. daily. Their address is 1812 21st Ave. South. Upstairs at Bongo is an intimate theater and music venue, the **Bongo After Hours Theater** (615 385-5282; bongoafterhours.com). Check the schedule to see the newest programs.

When a country music record company executive or a group of songwriters want to meet for a "power breakfast," there is usually no discussion of where that meeting will take place.

The **Pancake Pantry** (1796 21st Ave. South; 615-383-9333; thepancakepantry.com) has served the Music Row area for more than 4 decades now, and it's a great place for breakfast at any time of the day, even if you aren't in the music business. The wild blueberry pancakes, sweet potato cakes, buttermilk stacks, and myriad other choices are all quickly served by waitresses who have been here so long, they probably have seen it all. But they don't usually have time to tell it all because they are busy taking care of the constant crowds that frequent the pancake fixture in Hillsboro Village, a few doors down from Fido's. Open daily for breakfast and lunch. Parking behind the Pancake Pantry is free, but you must obtain and place a receipt on the vehicle dashboard. A receipt can be obtained from the machine at the lot entrance. Press 1 for 1.5 hours of free parking to dine at the Pancake Pantry.

The state of Tennessee turned 200 years old in 1996, and as a present to itself, officials created the **Bicentennial Capitol Mall State Park** (600 James Robertson Pkwy.; 615-741-5280; tnstateparks.com/parks/bicentennial-mall), down the steps and across the parkway from the state capitol. In addition to being a nicely appointed park and gathering place, the mall has permanent state historical exhibits and a great view of Capitol Hill.

The 19-acre state park and outdoor history museum feature an amphitheater, a 200-foot-long granite map depicting every city in the state, 31 fountains representing each of the state's rivers, a botanical garden, and a 1,400-foot wall engraved with images of Tennessee's historic events. Free; open 6 a.m. to 10 p.m. daily. Visitor Center hours are 8 a.m. to 4:30 p.m. Mon through Fri.

The more than 360,000 Tennesseans who served their country in World War II are honored here in the **World War II Memorial**, located on the west side of the mall. We've all seen war memorials before, but we think this one is quite impressive and well worth a visit. There are 10 granite pylons, which feature interesting information about the major events that took place during the war.

The prominent single landmark of the memorial is an 8-ton solid granite globe, the largest of its type ever made. The 1940s-world globe pinpoints major battle sites to illustrate how far Tennesseans traveled during the conflict. The sphere rotates on a thin cushion of water and can be turned by hand. Take time to study, learn, and appreciate. A free park tour is conducted every Wed at 2 p.m. Additional times are at 10 a.m., 1 p.m., and 3 p.m. on the first Mon of each month. The tour meets under the train trestle outside the Visitor Center. The tour lasts about an hour and discusses the significance of the park and the history of Tennessee. No sign-up necessary, except for groups of 25 people or more. The mall is open daily, year round.

Adjacent to the Bicentennial Mall is the ***Farmers' Market*** (900 Rosa L. Parks Blvd.; 615-880-2001; nashvillefarmersmarket.org) covering 16 acres of urban land. Here, you'll find fresh Tennessee-grown produce, from apples to zucchini, plants, flowers, and trees. On the inside are two restaurants, an international market, a hot sauce vendor, and fresh fish and meat peddlers. Early-morning crowds consist mostly of buyers from local restaurants coming in for their fresh-picked produce. Open year-round, with peak operating hours during the summer growing season from 5 a.m. to 9 p.m., but with shorter hours during the winter months. A flea and crafts market takes place here each weekend, year-round, and there are various festivals on the grounds every second Sat of the month, May through Nov. The ***Grow Local Kitchen*** offers a dynamic culinary class and event schedule.

Also in the heart of downtown Nashville lies the ***Tennessee State Capitol*** (600 Dr. MLK Jr. Blvd.; 615-741-2001; tnmuseum.org). Finished in 1859, it was designed by William Strickland, who also helped design the US Capitol. The beautiful building was recently renovated and should not be undervalued by tourists. Strickland loved the place so much that he requested to be interred in its walls. President James K. Polk is also buried there. Admission is free. Guided tours are offered Mon through Fri at 9 a.m., 10 a.m., 11 a.m., 1 p.m., 2 p.m., and 3 p.m. Tours begin at the Information Desk on the first floor.

The city has its own ***Arcade*** (615-244-8060; onepaper.com/nashville arcade), and it has been restored to its finest. It was built in 1903 as a two-tiered shopping mall, an identical copy of the Galleria Vittorio Emmanuele II arcade in Milan, Italy. Today it is occupied by specialty shops, including several restaurants and the mandatory roasted-nut store, whose aroma pervades the entire complex. The arcade runs 350 feet long to connect Fourth and Fifth Avenues, between Church and Union Streets. Check out their great website for a history of the Arcade as well as a listing of its current tenants.

Across the street and down a few storefronts from the Arcade's Fifth Avenue entrance is Nashville's funkiest art gallery, the ***Arts Company*** (215 Fifth Ave. North; 615-254-2040; theartscompany.com). Headed up by one of the city's great arts cheerleaders, Anne Brown, the full-service art gallery represents regional, national, and international artists in photography, painting, sculpture, and contemporary folk art. The latter category is what sets this fun place apart from the rest of the great galleries in the city. If you're looking for eclectic art, from fine Parisian art to rusted tin monkeys, this is the place. Open Tues through Sat 11 a.m. to 5 p.m. Their website offers links and calendars for other cultural events in Nashville as well as a photographic inventory of their own offerings.

Wackiest Tour in Town

The Jugg Sisters, Sheri Lynn and Brenda Kay, wear boots and tight pants and have some of the biggest hair around. They also promise to take you on a country music tour of Nashville you'll never forget. In fact, you probably won't even pay attention to what the girls are talking about outside the bright pink bus you'll be riding on because there's so much going on inside the bus.

The **Nash Trash Tour** is the wackiest tour in the state, no doubt. It's truly tacky and tasteless, and if you're into political correctness, stay off their bus! A journey with the Juggs is comedy kitsch at its best. They point out the underbelly of the city's music industry. They dig up the dirt on countless notables. Bubba, or Bubbette, depending on who's available to drive the bus, takes you past the county jail, and the girls roll off a roster of famous names who have slept there. The sisters sing original songs about the seamier side of Music City, and they even have a bit of choreography to go with it. They point out the pool where Elvis went skinnydipping and the bar where Tanya Tucker took off her shirt for a national reporter.

Other highlights of the tour include celebrity sightings. You might see Garth Brooks, Trisha Yearwood, Keith Urban, Dolly Parton, or Willie Nelson. "Of course, the stars all look different without their hair and makeup on," the girls are quick to point out.

The Juggs offer makeup and styling tips, casserole recipes, and fancy cracker-and-cheese hors d'oeuvres. They make sure all their passengers are aware that the major tour operators in the city don't have snacks aboard. "No cheese, no crackers," they sing.

This is a fun and very, very entertaining 90 minutes, and it's cheaper than a ticket to a comedy club. The bus loads at the north end of the Farmers' Market, next to the Bicentennial Mall, downtown. Get there at least 30 minutes early, because the fun and jokes begin as soon as you arrive. And if you aren't there at least 15 minutes before the tour's starting time, you will be considered a "noshow." Guests are encouraged to bring coolers with drinks but not food inside. Tours leave at 10:30 a.m. on Thurs and Fri and at 11 a.m. and 2 p.m. on Sat and Sun. Rates for the Jugg Sisters Tour are $40 per person. Pip's Music Row Confidential and The Ben Tour are $35 per person. The tours are quite different, so read the website to be sure you pick the one you want. Fair warning—"No bachelorette parties are allowed on any tour," the Juggs note. "And if your group behaves like a bachelorette party, you will be charged a $20-per-head nuisance fee." Children under 15 (including infants) are not allowed on the adult-oriented tours. Find out more by calling (615) 226-7300 or (800) 342-2132 or go online at nashtrash.com.

Look! Up in the sky! At 632 feet, the AT&T Building, fondly known locally as the **Batman Building** because of its uncanny resemblance to the caped crusader, is the tallest building in the state. It has 27 floors of office space and above that several other storage, mechanical, and open floors. At the very top,

civilwarfacts

More battles were fought in Tennessee than in any other state except Virginia.

Tennessee was the last state to secede from the Union and the first state to be readmitted after the war.

East Tennesseans were primarily on the side of the Confederacy.

The free booklet *A Path Divided: Tennessee's Civil War Years* provides a thumbnail history of the war and a list of related events and attractions throughout the state.

two spirals go heavenward from either side, hinting of Batman's pointed ears. The behemoth makes quite a statement.

"That's what the architect wanted to do," said an AT&T official. "The design philosophy was to be unique, be distinctive in the Nashville skyline, and avoid being another boxy skyscraper." He noted that while not planning to make it look like Batman, the design "does evoke that image, and others as well. Many people think it looks like a phone receiver and handset at the top," he said, adding that he has been told the 9-level underground parking garage was the largest building construction excavation ever in the state.

When the **Frist Art Museum** (919 Broadway; 615-244-3340; fristartmuseum.org) opened its doors in 2001, the fine art museum set the stage for a new city cultural landscape. The Frist is located in Nashville's historic downtown post office, which was built in 1933–34. The beautiful art deco structure is listed on the National Register of Historic Places. The Frist has no permanent collection but showcases changing exhibits, always a new reason to return. Since opening, the Frist has brought world-class exhibits to the city, contributing to a vibrant arts scene. The Frist has a 250-seat auditorium, gift shop, and the Frist Center Cafe. Be sure to visit the gift shop. I have bought some lovely jewelry, scarves, and gifts there every time I visit. Open Mon through Wed 10 a.m. to 5:30 p.m.; Thurs and Fri 10 a.m. to 9 p.m.; Sat 10 a.m. to 5:30 p.m.; and Sun 1 to 5:30 p.m. Admission is $15 for adults, $10 for senior citizens and college students, free for under 18.

When the **Hermitage Hotel** (615-244-3121; thehermitagehotel.com) was built in 1910, it was the city's first million-dollar hotel, and it became a symbol of Nashville's emergence as a major southern city. It flourished for more than 50 years, only to start deteriorating with the rest of the downtown area in the 1960s. Now, as the downtown area has gained a new life, so has the Hermitage Hotel. From its Beaux Arts design—the only commercial example of it in Tennessee—to its magnificently ornate lobby, the hotel is once again a symbol of pride for downtown Nashville.

Make sure you check out the men's room, next to the Capitol Grille on the lower level. It is the coolest restroom in the city. A bronze plaque mounted next to the door reads "Once the site of many business transactions, this unique art deco bathroom has been the selected location of several interviews, music videos, and fashion photography. It has been said that more women have toured this men's room than any other in the country." Ladies, make sure you announce yourself before entering.

The Hermitage, owned by Historic Hotels, received a $15 million renovation in late 2002 and early 2003, and within a short time of reopening on Valentine's Day 2003, it received a five-diamond ranking, followed by a five-star listing as well. It is now the only five-diamond, five-star hotel within a 9-state area.

Located across from the Tennessee Performing Arts Center and the State Capitol, at 231 Sixth Ave. North, the hotel is a comfortable, classy place to call home while exploring Music City.

The Plant That's Eatin' Tennessee

That's *kudzu* (pronounced cudzoo) you see growing all over the roadsides throughout Tennessee. The large hairy leafed, bright green invasive vine is also known as the mile-a-minute vine and "The Vine That Ate the South." It grows as much as a foot a day or 60 feet a summer in good weather and can take up to a decade to kill. It is said that southerners keep their windows shut at night to keep out the kudzu.

Kudzu was introduced to the US in 1876 at the Centennial Exposition in Philadelphia by the Japanese. During the Great Depression of the 1930s, the Soil Conservation Service promoted kudzu for erosion control, and hundreds of men planted it on roadsides throughout the South. Farmers were paid by the government to plant fields of the vines in the 1940s.

It does control erosion, but it also runs rampant and kills virtually everything in its path and climbs anything it contacts, including telephone poles and trees. Where it grows, kudzu has the ability to outcompete and eliminate native plant species and upset the natural diversity of plant and animal communities.

The vine has been known to kill entire forests by preventing the trees from getting light. During warm weather, the plant, classified a weed by the government in 1970, bears 6- to 10-inch spikes of small, fragrant purple flowers. The state has been having some success eradicating the vine by using various tools available. Methods include mechanical treatment (usually brush-hogs and shredder mulchers), prescribed burning, herbicides, and biological control. The emphasis is on persistent and consistent attempts to eradicate kudzu.

Don't be tempted to dig up any of the plants to take home with you. They will soon become a nuisance, and you'll spend the rest of your life trying to get rid of them.

Several decades before the city was known for its music, it had a reputation as a regional center of culture and education. Numerous colleges advanced the learning of the classics, and it wasn't long before the city was known as the *Athens of the South*. In 1896 it was only natural for planners of the state's centennial celebrations to elaborate on this classic theme.

An exact replica of the *Greek Parthenon* (615-862-8431; nashville.gov), with a tolerance of less than one-tenth of an inch, was built for the huge exposition, held in what is now known as Centennial Park, just a few miles out West End Avenue from downtown at 2500 West End Ave. Now fully restored and still the world's only full-size replica, the Parthenon houses art exhibits and serves as a backdrop for various cultural events in the park. A 42-foot replica of Athena Parthenos has been sculpted and is on display in the main hall. Open Tues through Sat 9 a.m. to 4:30 p.m.; Sun 12:30 p.m. to 4:30 p.m. Admission is $6 for adults and $4 for senior citizens and children (ages 4 to 17).

Next to the Parthenon, the neatest structure in the park is the concrete ship's prow, near the 25th Avenue North entrance. Now more than 100 years old, the reinforced concrete replica of the front end of a ship has an ornate metal figurehead, the original cast that was used to make the one on the *Tennessee,* a US cruiser that plied the waters during the 1898 Spanish-American War. The decorative metalwork was exhibited at the 1909 Seattle Exposition, and when that event was over, the metalwork was shipped here by request of Nashville-raised Navy admiral Albert Gleaves. The concrete prow was built and the metalwork mounted, making the structure look like "a ship that had been driven ashore in the shrubbery," as one Nashville journalist described it at the time.

Centennial Park is the site of many events during the year, including three quality arts and crafts fairs. In May *Tennessee Craft* (615-736-7600; tennesseecraft.org) produces a juried crafts festival that is one of the largest marketplaces for quality crafts anywhere in the state. Nearly 200 Tennessee craftspeople show up to peddle their wares.

In June the *American Artisan Festival* (americanartisanfestival.com) takes place over Father's Day weekend. More than 150 craftspeople from 35 states show up for the weekend. The food at this particular festival could be considered the best of any food at any festival in the state. It's eclectic, with an emphasis on the unusual and the healthy. This show is sponsored by the American Artisan Crafts Gallery, just down the road from Centennial Park.

Held in October, the *Fall Tennessee Craft Fair* (tennesseecraft.org) is a juried show for all craftspeople, not just those from Tennessee (as is the May festival). Again, quality crafts are abundant, and the show comes at a perfect time to start Christmas shopping.

There are notables buried in just about every cemetery in the world, and Nashville is no exception—except that we have more than our share of country crooners interred.

At the huge **Woodlawn Memorial Park** (615-383-4754), between I-65 and Nolensville Road just south of downtown at 660 Thompson Ln., several country and music legends are buried, including Roy Orbison, Webb Pierce, Marty Robbins, Red Sovine, George Jones, Eddy Arnold, Webb Pierce, Porter Wagoner, and Tammy Wynette. To find exact locations, go to the office; someone there will provide you with a map.

Roy Acuff, Floyd Cramer, John Hartford, Kitty Wells, Keith Whitley, and Hank Snow are among the country notables buried at the **Spring Hill Cemetery** (5110 Gallatin Pike South; 615-865-1101). Also there is Beth Slater Whitson, who wrote the lyrics to "Let Me Call You Sweetheart."

Nashville City Cemetery (1001 Fourth Ave. South; 615-862-7970; nashvillecitycemetery.org) is the oldest public cemetery in the city, and with 23,000 graves dating back to 1822, you can imagine the scope of the historical figures buried here, including three Civil War generals—Bushrod Johnson, Richard Ewell, and Felix Zollicoffer; William Carroll, who served as Tennessee governor from 1788 to 1844; and James Robertson, the founder of Nashville. Also here is Captain William Driver, who first called the American flag "Old Glory."

The cemetery is run by the Metro Historical Commission and is listed on the National Register of Historic Places. Historical markers are placed throughout with specific information. This historic site is open daily until dusk.

Over at the **Tennessee State Fairgrounds** (500 Wedgewood Ave.; 615-862-8980; thefairgrounds.com), the state's largest flea market takes place the fourth weekend of each month. There are nearly 2,200 vendors on any particular weekend, with 600 of them located indoors. They are open 6 a.m. to 6 p.m. Sat and 7 a.m. to 4 p.m. on Sun. *Hint:* Vendors can set up any time after 3 p.m. on Fri, and most will sell to you if you drop by while they are at it. That's when they all wheel and deal with one another, and it's when you'll definitely get the best choice. Admission is free.

The **Tennessee State Fair** (615-800-3675; tnstatefair.org) is held on these same grounds the second week of September. Lots of carnival rides, great-tasting (albeit fatty) foods, and plenty of farm animals are on hand for the entertainment and education of guests. There's usually a circus and a major country concert held during the event. A village with log cabins and working craftspeople provides a glimpse into the early days of the state.

Two close-by, fun, and delicious places to eat can be found on Elliston Place. **Rotier's** (2413 Elliston Place; 615-327-9892; rotiersrestaurant.com) is located just east of Centennial Park, behind Eckerd's Drugs. Year in and year

Johnny Cash Museum

When Bill Miller was 13 years old, he went to a Johnny Cash concert that changed the course of his life. "*Johnny Cash* played a harmonica and tossed it into the audience when he was done," Miller said. "I caught it."

That was just the beginning. Over the years, Miller collected a treasure trove of Johnny Cash memorabilia and became friends with the legendary entertainer. After Cash's death, Miller decided to share his collection with the public as a tribute to "The Man in Black." The *Johnny Cash Museum* (119 Third Ave. South; 615-256-1777; johnnycashmuseum .com) opened in downtown Nashville in 2013 and has been drawing visitors ever since.

Walking in the footsteps of Johnny Cash, visitors to his museum traverse exhibits from the singer's life, including his hardscrabble childhood days in Dyess, Ark., his Air Force years, his famous prison concert tour, his TV and movie career, his marriage to June Carter, and his final days.

Johnny Cash's youngest sister, Joanne Cash Yates, remembers that her brother was determined to become a singer, despite the odds against him. "He said, 'Baby, one day you're going to hear me singing on the radio.' I laughed at that. He always called me 'Baby' because I was the youngest girl."

To Yates, however, her big brother was always J.R. "That was the name on his birth certificate. That's what we always called him," she said. "Mommy wanted to name him John after her father. Daddy wanted to name him Ray after himself. They couldn't decide so they named him J.R."

When Cash went in the Air Force, the government wasn't going to allow a serviceman to have two initials for his name. "They told him that wouldn't do. So J.R. said his name was John and that's what people started calling him. I guess Mom won after all," his sister says.

Items include four glass marbles that were among Cash's few childhood toys and a guitar with a dollar bill stuffed into the upper strings. Because Cash's band did not have a drummer until later, the dollar bill was used to simulate the sound of drums keeping a beat. You can hear this most in the original recording of "I Walk the Line." Visitors also can put on headphones and listen to Cash music from various decades, including one of his final hit releases before his death—the heart-rending video for "Hurt." In it, the tormented still-powerful voice intones: "Everyone I know goes away in the end."

Cash was 71 years old when the video was filmed in February 2003. Seen in the video sadly gazing at her husband, June Carter Cash died May 15, three months after filming. Johnny Cash lived only four months after his wife died. What he wrote on a box of Valentine candy he gave her in 1998 seems to say it all—"My Love, My Life, For Life."

For Miller, the museum was a labor of love, a tribute to the man he called a friend. "I was with Johnny about a week before he passed. I know he would love the museum."

Cash's sister agrees. "Not long before J.R. passed away, he said to me, 'Baby, when I'm gone, I wonder if anybody will really care,'" she said. "So, I think he'd be real proud that this museum is here where people can come and remember him."

out, "Mama" Rotier's comes in at the top, or very close to the top, in the best-hamburger-in-town competition. Served on French bread, the burgers and all the fixings are held together with a toothpick when they reach you. It seems like everyone comes here, and at times it also seems like all the waitresses know everyone. I've seen some of country music's top stars here enjoying a burger and a chocolate milkshake. The popular spot also has daily luncheon specials, including some very good meat loaf and a big variety of bottled beers.

Continue east on Elliston to find the ***Elliston Place Soda Shop*** (2111 Elliston Place; 615-327-1090; ellistonplacesodashop.com) on your right, just before you get to the Krispy Kreme, the doughnut den of heaven. Virtually unchanged from when it opened in the 1940s, the shop has turned into much more than a funky soda shop. The milkshakes are the best in town, and it's fun sitting there sipping your shake in your own booth, choosing music on your personal jukebox. Country ham, fresh biscuits, a bevy of vegetables including black-eyed peas, and plenty of other "meat-and-three" offerings can be found on the menu. Breakfast is served daily. Check the website for hours.

Another classic blast from the past is ***Bobbie's Dairy Dip*** (5301 Charlotte Ave.; 615-463-8088), at the corner of 53rd Street. It's an old-fashioned, walk-up ice-cream stand, which also serves a great burger and fries. They sell soft serve and real, premium ice cream and are great at piling it together to create some wonderful concoctions.

On Charlotte, between Bobbie's and 49th Street, there are a bunch of other notable places to spend a bit of your time. The ***Southern Thrift Store*** (5010 Charlotte Ave.; 615-292-1807; southernthriftstore.com) is the best-stocked thrift shop in Nashville. It is constantly getting new (old) stuff, and it has some of the best deals. If you're looking for a country star T-shirt, you'll find a huge selection here, hung neatly on hangers, for as little as 99 cents. There is also plenty of furniture and other thrift-shop couture. The store has branched out to two other locations: 412 Metroplex (615-833-1319), and 2710 Old Lebanon Pike (615-872-0499).

For a truly amazing sight, visit the ***Upper Room Chapel and Museum*** (1908 Grand Ave.; 800-972-0433; upperroom.org). The stars of this establishment are an 8-by-17-foot wood carving of da Vinci's *The Last Supper* and an 8-by-20-foot stained-glass window with a Pentecost theme.

The museum features religious paintings and art objects dating back to the 1300s as well as religious artifacts from throughout the world. At Christmastime, the museum displays its collection of Ukrainian eggs and more than 100 nativity scenes. Open Mon through Thurs 8 a.m. to 4:30 p.m., Fri 8 a.m. to 12:30 p.m.; free, but donations are graciously accepted.

George Jones Museum

George Glenn Jones almost died before he got a chance to live. The family doctor dropped the baby shortly after delivery. The sturdy newborn survived with only a broken arm. But what a life the country music legend went on to live in that interval between the day he entered this world on September 12, 1930, and the day he left on April 26, 2013.

"George went to hell and back with many addictions and he beat them all," said his widow, Nancy Jones. To share the story of the man many consider the greatest voice in country music, the *George Jones Museum* (615-818-0128; georgejones .com) opened at 128 Second Ave. North on April 26, 2015.

A time line of George Jones's music invites visitors to put on headphones and listen to his songs over the years. A small theater with rocking chairs—a nod to his "I don't need no rocking chair" hit—allows guests to rock in comfort while watching Jones's video clips.

Other relics of the honky-tonk hero include his sequined suits and the infamous blue American Tourister overnight case that Jones called his "getaway bag," always kept packed and ready for a quick exit. A green John Deere lawnmower recalls the time family members hid Jones's car keys so he couldn't drive while drunk. Instead, Jones rode his mower to a nearby liquor store. Another exhibit dedicated to Jones's tumultuous marriage to county icon Tammy Wynette showcases her white satin and chiffon dress, which she left behind after their divorce.

A major turning point in Jones's troubled life occurred when he married Nancy Sepulvada in 1983. However, on April 18, 2013, the music was cut short when Jones was hospitalized with a fever and irregular blood pressure. He was 81 years old.

"I was with George the whole time," his wife said. Although she continued talking to him, she said Jones didn't open his eyes or talk for his final five days—until the last minute. "I was standing at the foot of his bed rubbing his feet," Nancy said. "Suddenly, he opened his eyes and said, 'Well, hello there. My name is George Jones, and I've been looking for you.' I know he was talking to God. And then he was gone."

Music City Marketplace (150 Fourth Ave. North, Ste. G250; 615-259-4747) is in the heart of downtown Nashville. The Marketplace shop offers items with a musical touch. Works from local artists adorn the walls and items are displayed in vintage instrument cases. The center is open Mon through Thurs 8 a.m. to 5 p.m. and Fri 8 a.m. to 4 p.m.

For sports fans, the *Tennessee Sports Hall of Fame* (615-242-4750; tshf .net) is a must stop. Located inside the Bridgestone Arena at 501 Broadway, the interactive facility chronicles the history of sports in Tennessee from the early 1800s to today. The Tennessee Sports Hall of Fame is open Tues through Sun

10 a.m. to 4 p.m. and later on days of Bridgestone Area events. Admission is $3 for adults and $2 for children.

With all the pickers in town, you should expect the Nashville area to have some excellent guitar shops. ***Artisan Guitars*** (615-595-2544, artisanguitars .com) proudly represents some of the world's finest acoustic guitar builders of this century. Known as luthiers, these talented builders are true artists. Owners Bill and Ellie Warmoth share a wealth of guitar information and can help a seasoned pro or a beginner find the perfect instrument for them. In today's world, it is surprising to find a store that still offers layaway. Artisan Guitars does. As the Warmouths explain, it is difficult to find the guitar of your dreams. And when you do, you might not have the money in your pocket to buy your treasure at that particular time. Artisan Guitars offers a 90-day layaway plan so that a special guitar doesn't get away. If all that doesn't tempt you to visit the shop, be aware that many well-known musicians like to frequent Artisan Guitars. In fact, the owners guarantee that they won't publicly mention any of those star customers. But I know that Brad Paisley likes to drop by the and play

Hot Chicken Comes Home to Roost

Perhaps one of the oddest food trends to hit an American city in recent years has been the explosion of hot chicken restaurants in Nashville. In fact, this particular variety of Southern food is so sizzling that a new eatery seems to open up every few months or so. It's fair to say that hot chicken has positively burst upon the scene here.

What is **hot chicken**, you may wonder? It is a unique brand of fried chicken that's highly seasoned, some would say to incendiary proportions. According to legend, Thornton J. Prince III came back from a night of catting around in the 1930s to find his girlfriend fixing him a Sunday dinner of fried chicken. To get revenge on her cheating lover, the gal dumped a hefty helping of hot spices on the chicken.

But the plot backfired. Prince loved the hot chicken so much that he refined the recipe and opened a restaurant. The chicken is cooked in cast-iron skillets, so the wait is seldom short, but loyal diners say it's worth it.

When we say this stuff is hot, trust us. It's positively flame-worthy. The chicken is served Southern-style, on a slice of white bread. The bread soaks up all the spicy chicken juices and is one of the best parts about eating a hot chicken dinner. The usual accompaniment to all this spicy fried deliciousness is a side of dill pickles, baked beans, and potato salad. It's all washed down with sweet tea.

Most hot children restaurants are little more than shacks with devoted proprietors who passionately guard their hot chicken recipes. Take a gander at some of the favorites in our places to eat listing at the end of this chapter.

around with the inventory. Artisan Guitars is located in the Track One building at 1201 Fourth Ave. South.

For assistance in planning a trip to Nashville, the **Nashville Convention and Visitors Corporation** (800-657-6910; visitmusiccity.com) features streaming headlines on their website and plenty of quick links to more than 50 area attractions, upcoming events, tours, and shopping. The main Visitor Center is located at 501 Broadway inside the glass tower at Bridgestone Arena.

Next to the Loveless Cafe, the Natchez Trace Shell gas station about 15 miles from downtown out West End Avenue (which becomes Highway 100), could really be called Last Chance Gas & Food. It's located at the entrance to the **Natchez Trace Parkway** at 8456 Hwy. 100, after which you won't find any food, gas, or lodging for your entire 450 mile trip to Natchez, Mississippi.

If you're going to travel the wonderful Natchez Trace for more than a couple of days, you'll probably want to stay overnight close to the trace, and a bed-and-breakfast inn is definitely your best choice. The trace itself is very noncommercial, with no buildings and no billboard or lodging signs, so it's a good idea to plan ahead and have reservations. The **Natchez Trace Bed & Breakfast Reservation Service** (800-377-2770; natcheztracetravel.com) is a good way to get access to and information on the nearly 40 inns close to the trace.

Just west of the entrance to the Natchez Trace at 8750 Hwy. 100, you'll find some of the best fresh produce in middle Tennessee. **McNeil's Fresh Produce Stand** (615-673-1016) is open Apr through Oct, and the open-air stand is known widely for carrying the best of whatever is in season. The corn is the best I've found in this area, and the locally grown vine-ripened tomatoes are huge and plump. It's a good place to load up on some healthy snacks before you hit the trace.

About 30 miles east of Nashville, the downtown square of **Lebanon** is antiques heaven. Within a 2-block area there are more than a dozen antiques stores and antiques malls. Most are open daily. There's plenty of parking, and there's always plenty of action in the downtown area.

The award-winning **Wilson County Fair** (945 E. Baddour Pkwy.; 615-443-2626; wilsoncountyfair.net), voted the state's best county fair several times, is held each August, and it truly is small-town Americana at its finest. Former vice president Al Gore showed animals here as a child, and thousands of kids prepare for the fair all year long. The carnival is colorful and fun, the exhibits are great, and the entertainment is top-notch.

The fair takes place at the James E. Ward Agricultural Center, where picturesque **Fiddlers Grove** (615-547-6111) is also located. The grove consists of more than 30 original and replicated log cabins moved to the fairgrounds,

The Loveless Cafe

Through the years, anyone who is (or was) anyone has eaten here. Country stars, national TV celebrities, and politicians from all over are spotted here almost on a daily basis. ABC-TV called the Loveless "the best country restaurant in America," and Martha Stewart told her audience once that the best breakfast she ever had was served at the Loveless Cafe. Breakfast is served all day. Bottled beer, house wine, and moonshine also are served.

Located on the grounds of the **Loveless Cafe**, the Loveless Barn was built to host celebrations and concerts. Since opening in 2009, the Loveless Barn has done just that. With two large lawns, covered porches, and walls that roll open to the outside, the Loveless Barn can handle large or small groups. The trademark neon sign still marks the spot on Highway 100 in the little community of Pasquo where the Loveless Cafe is located. Open 7 a.m. to 9 p.m. 7 days a week. Check it out at (615) 646-9700 or lovelesscafe.com. The website also features great Loveless recipes including the famous Bacon Apple Pie. That's right—this pie features a crispy bacon lattice top instead of the traditional pie dough lattice. And it is *go-oo-d*!

creating a compound of what a Wilson County community would have looked like in the 1800s.

There are such frontier staples as a jail, post office, blacksmith shop, and general store, and it's still growing year by year. Here is a low-key, out-of-the-way community where the early life of Tennessee is preserved and presented. It's a lot of fun, and the workers here are well versed in this particular era of the state's history. It's open during the fair and 10 a.m. to 3 p.m. Tues through Sat; Apr through Oct. Admission is free.

If you like wildflowers, make sure you visit the **Cedar Glade Wildflower Festival** (615-443-2769) each year in May at the Cedars of Lebanon State Park, just outside Lebanon. The 2-day event is structured to dazzle the experts and to create an interest in those just learning to appreciate one of nature's best gifts.

The country stars and the top bankers and businesspeople of the state might make their millions in Nashville, but when it comes to investing in their lifestyles and families, many come south to **Williamson County** (Williamson County Convention and Visitors Bureau: 615-791-7554; visitfranklin.com). It consistently has the state's highest per capita income and the lowest unemployment rate.

Lee Greenwood, Kenny Chesney, Tim McGraw, Brad Paisley, Faith Hill, Vince Gill, Amy Grant, Ted Danson, Mary Steenburgen, the Judds, and Tom T. Hall are among the inhabitants of the area. If you want to see them, though, you probably have a better chance hanging out at the local Kroger store than in front of their houses.

Franklin, the county seat, is 17 miles and "100 years" south of Nashville and is associated with old, restored homes and businesses, antiques shopping, and the Civil War. The entire downtown section is on the National Register of Historic Places.

It's got a funky name, and it's located in a surprising place. But the **Frothy Monkey** (125 Fifth Ave. South; 615-600-4756; frothymonkey.com) in Franklin serves some very good coffee as its dedicated patrons can attest. Housed in an old parsonage in downtown Franklin, the shop serves breakfast, lunch, and dinner (along with beer and wine) with late risers able to enjoy breakfast until 5 p.m. Open Mon through Thurs 6 a.m. to 9 p.m.; Fri 6 a.m. to 10 p.m.; Sat 7 a.m. to 10 p.m.; and Sun 8 a.m. to 9 p.m.

As locals themselves, the owners try to honor other local businesses. For example, all the milk used at the Frothy Monkey comes from the Hatcher Family Dairy. The sausage burger contains Allan Benton's meat. The trout comes from Bob White Springs from the small town of Only, Tennessee. The pasta is locally made from Al Fresco Pasta. Take time to read the menu. It's a joy and a difficult decision. The cider-glazed Viola Farms pork pot roast, sweet potato-pear gratin, mustard greens, and green tomato chow chow makes a good choice, as is the Bear Creek Farms Rada brisket, sweet potato herbed bread pudding, fried farm eggs, and buttered asparagus. Look for some familiar faces in the Frothy Monkey. Country music stars like Brad Paisley and other performers who live in Franklin have already discovered the charming critter.

The **Carter House** (615-791-1861; boft.org), south of downtown on Columbia Avenue, was caught in the middle of the fight aptly known as the **Battle of Franklin** on November 30, 1864. Bullet holes are still evident in the main structure and various outbuildings. One of the outbuildings has 203 bullet holes in it, making it the most battle-damaged building from the Civil War still standing anywhere.

The property is one of the 11 historic sites in the state owned and operated by the Association for the Preservation of Tennessee Antiquities. Open daily; admission is charged.

About 5 miles away, the **Carnton Mansion** (615-794-0903; boft.org) also played an important role in the Battle of Franklin. On the rear lines of the Confederate forces, the elegant estate witnessed a steady stream of dying and wounded during the battle. At one time the bodies of five slain Confederate generals were laid out on the back porch. Within view of that historic porch rests the only privately owned Confederate cemetery in the US. Open daily; admission is charged to the house; the cemetery is free.

A few blocks east of Franklin's town square, where the Confederate monument (circa 1899) rests, is the ***Hiram Masonic Lodge*** (615-790-1688). When the 3-story building was built in 1823, it was said to be the tallest structure in Tennessee. It was constructed to house the first Masonic Lodge in the state, which was chartered in 1803; later, in 1827, the first Protestant Episcopal Church in Tennessee was founded here.

The historic downtown area of Franklin is quickly becoming known as the newest "antiques capital of Tennessee." There are nearly three dozen antiques and craft stores within the downtown area, all within walking distance of one another. ***Franklin Antique Mall*** (615-790-8593) is the city's oldest and largest antiques mall. Used as a flour mill in the 1800s, the handmade-brick structure was the county's icehouse at the turn of the 20th century. Today it houses the goods of more than 60 different antiques dealers spread out over 12,000 square feet of space. At Second Avenue South and S. Margin Street at 2512 Second Ave. South; open daily.

On US 31 in Spring Hill is the ***Rippavilla Plantation*** (5700 Main St.; 931-486-9037; rippavilla.org). Built in 1852, the home has been restored and is the headquarters for the Tennessee Antebellum Trail organization and houses the ***Armies of Tennessee Civil War Museum***, which chronicles the effects of the war on the family, the plantation, and the community.

The Confederate army spent the night on the property before they moved north to join the Battle of Franklin, one of the last major battles of the Civil War. Legend has it that all five of the Confederate generals who were killed in that battle had slept at Rippavilla and had breakfast together before heading off to battle.

Today the beautifully restored home features many of the original family's heirlooms and furnishings and is open to the public Tues through Sat. There is an admission fee to enter the home, but you can walk the grounds and visit the welcome center for no charge.

Columbia is the center of commerce for Maury County. In addition to its reputation as the Antebellum Homes Capital of Tennessee, Columbia claims James K. Polk, one of the three presidents from the state, as a former resident. ***Polk's ancestral home*** (301 W. Seventh Ave.; 931-388-2354; jameskpolk.com) is open to the public. Built by his parents in 1816, this is the house where Polk began his legal and political career. There is plenty of one-of-a-kind memorabilia housed here, and the gift shop has more books written about Polk than you could have ever imagined.

A unique structure among Tennessee's antebellum homes is the ***Athenaeum Rectory*** (808 Athenaeum St.; 931-381-4822; historicathenaeum.com), built in 1837 in a Moorish-Gothic architectural design. In 1852, it became the home to the Columbia Athenaeum School for Young Ladies. Today, the building is owned by the Association for the Preservation of Tennessee Antiquities and is operated as a historic house museum.

Among things to look for as you tour the house is the chandelier in the reception room. It is made of seven metals and is original to the house. The front door side panels are flashed glass containing gold leaf from Europe, and the walnut and oak floors throughout are in a design known as wood carpeting.

Open for guided tours Thurs through Sat 10 a.m. to 4 p.m., Mon through Wed by appointment only.

The Polks were quite the building family here in Columbia. In addition to the James K. Polk Home and the Athenaeum Rectory, the family built three other historic structures—the Hamilton Place, St. John's Episcopal Church, and **Rattle and Snap Plantation** (931-379-1700; rattleandsnapplantation.com). All five were built within a 30-year period and only a few miles from one another. Special tours have been developed to visit all Polk structures.

The James K. Polk Home and Rattle and Snap Plantation are two of the 60-plus homes along the **Tennessee Antebellum Trail** (antebellumtrail.com). Within a 30-mile radius of Nashville lies the highest concentration of antebellum homes in the South today. Eight of the houses are open to the public. A splendid tour map that lists and describes each house is available at area attractions or by contacting the **Maury County Convention and Visitors Bureau** (888-852-1860; visitmaury.com) at 301 West Seventh St. in Columbia.

If you think you have stubborn friends, they are probably nothing compared with the critters that gather here each year during the first week of April! That's when the **Mule Day Festival & Parade** (931-381-9557; muleday.com) take place to celebrate Columbia's proud heritage as the mule-raising capital of the state. The parade features mules pulling just about everything down the highway, and the festival is loaded with arts and crafts booths, all kinds of food, a liars' contest, square dancing, and a mule show.

On Highway 50W about 8 miles from downtown Columbia, you'll find a good example of how industry and nature can live together. From 1937 to 1986, the **Monsanto** company had a plant here that produced elemental phosphorus. Through the years, as the company finished up strip mining an area of 5,345 acres, it planted trees and created lakes. Wildlife began moving in, and when the plant closed in 1986, the company worked with the Tennessee Wildlife Resources Agency to turn the entire area into a wildlife enhancement zone.

Out US 43 from Columbia is **Mount Pleasant**, a small community that calls itself the "Best-Kept Secret in Middle Tennessee." Their other slogan, which might be a bit more appropriate for this sleepy little burg, is "Stop, Shop, Eat, and Tour."

The town witnessed a great deal of troop movement during the Civil War, and after discovery of high-grade phosphate in 1896, the village of 400 residents became a boomtown of more than 2,000 when workers from 25 states and 10 countries came to toil in the local phosphate mines. By the early 1900s, there were more than a dozen companies operating here, and it was known as the "phosphate capital of the world."

Today the phosphate heritage and hundreds of other historical artifacts are preserved in the *Mt. Pleasant-Maury Phosphate Museum* (108 Public Sq.; 931-379-9511) downtown. Open most weekdays and Sat 10 a.m. to 4:30 p.m. Closed Sun. Admission is $2 per person or $5 for the entire family.

One mile from downtown Murfreesboro is an obelisk marking the geographic center of the state. The *Dimple of the Universe*, as it is called locally, is on Old Lascassas Pike. Turn left off Greenland Drive opposite the football fields at Middle Tennessee State University.

In the early days *Murfreesboro* was a little village known as *Cannonsburgh*. Today, *Cannonshurgh Pioneer Village* (312 S. Front St.; murfreesboro tn.gov; 615-890-0355) is a living museum depicting 125 years of southern life amid the hustle and bustle of the metropolitan area the city has become. Among its collections are a log house, blacksmith shop, general store, gristmill, one-room schoolhouse, and museum.

But the real star here is the *World's Largest Red Cedar Bucket*, manufactured locally by a bucket factory that toured the oddity as an advertising gimmick. It was built in 1887, is 6 feet tall and 24 feet around the top, and holds nearly 2,000 gallons of water. The museum here also holds what officials feel is the World's Largest Spinning Wheel. It stands 8 feet tall and was made by a local mortician.

Cannonsburgh is the site of the popular *Uncle Dave Macon Days* (833-615-7668; uncledavemacondays.com) early every July. There's plenty of music, food, games, and activities for the kids. There is a juried arts and crafts show and a special gospel music celebration on Sun morning. Cannonsburgh is open May through Nov, Tues through Sun. Grounds open year-round; admission is free.

More information on Murfreesboro, Smyrna, and the rest of Rutherford County can be found online at rutherfordchamber.org, or call the Tourism Council at (800) 716-7560.

One of the most interesting factory tours in the state is located north of Murfreesboro, just off US 41. The *Nissan Motor Manufacturing Corporation Truck/Auto Plant* offers tours on Tues and Thurs at 10 a.m. and 1 p.m. During the hour-long tram ride through the modern plant, you'll see men and women working side by side with hundreds of robots to produce more than 1,000 vehicles a day.

The complex covers about 800 acres and employs more than 6,000 local workers. Reservations are required (615-459-1444). Admission is free, and, of course, they don't give samples. No children under 10 are permitted on this tour. No cameras or recording devices are allowed.

Mr. Miller ran Christiana's only grocery store for 75 years, and in that funky old building today is *Miller's Grocery and Country Cafe* (7011 Main St.; 615-893-1878; millersgrocery.com). It's a "meat and three" during the week with live music from 5 to 8 p.m. on Fri and Sat. It's also the tiny town's only restaurant. Two meats and an array of veggies are available as a blue-plate lunch Tues through Sat 11 a.m. to 2 p.m., and the dinners are served Fri and Sat nights 5 to 8 p.m. A Sun buffet is served 11 a.m. to 2 p.m. There's a lot of old-time flavor in this old building: oilcloth-covered tables, wood floors, and all kinds of antiques and memorabilia that line the walls. Located about 8 miles from Murfreesboro and 7 miles south of I-24 off US 231. Head south, and when you see the Christiana signs, turn left onto Highway 269. Cross the railroad tracks, make an immediate left, and you're in the neighborhood.

The 16th century is celebrated at the *Tennessee Renaissance Festival* (615-395-9950; tnrenfest.com), held every weekend in May each year at *Castle Gwynn*, a wonderfully eclectic 20th-century castle at 2124 New Castle Rd. in Arrington. This is the time of King Henry VIII, and he's joined in the festivities by plenty of court jesters, street entertainers, musicians, Shakespearean actors, period games, combat chess, and full-armor jousts. Hundreds of craftspeople are open for business in the medieval marketplace, and there's a whole lot of great, unusual food and beverages. Located 25 miles south of Nashville on Highway 96, about halfway between I-24 and I-65 in Triune.

Southeastern Heartland

If you happen to be in *Manchester* during late October, be sure to visit the *Old Timers Day celebration* (931-728-7635; manchesteroldtimersday.com). The city fathers shut down the streets around the square for a Saturday and fill it with fun things to do, including a bluegrass music concert, arts and crafts, kiddie rides and games, and a whole lot of food.

Foothills Crafts (418 Woodbury Hwy.; 931-728-9236; foothillscraftsshop .com) in Manchester may be the ultimate quality crafts store. Run entirely by volunteer members of the Coffee County Crafts Association, the shop has an amazing array of handcrafted items for sale. It's a hard process to get your crafts represented here, but that process ensures that only the highest-quality items will be on display. Currently more than 200 different artisans are selling their work out of this old-time grocery store; it's open daily year-round.

On Highway 55, just before you reach Tullahoma, be on the lookout for the **Coca-Cola Bottling Company** plant. Next to it is the **Company Store** (1504 E. Carroll St.; 931-454-1030), a retail outlet open to the public. You'll be amazed at how many things are made with the Coke and Dr. Pepper logos on them. It's a virtual plethora of red-and-white merchandise, from clothes to antique reproductions to glasses. Open Mon through Sat 10 a.m. to 5 p.m.; closed Sun.

The **Tullahoma Fine Arts Center** and the **Regional Museum of Art** (931-455-1234; tullahomaartcenter.com) share space in the city's oldest brick house, at 401 Jackson St. The arts center features work of local and regional artists, including crafts as well as the fine arts. All items on display may be purchased. The Regional Museum of Art features traveling exhibits and the museum's private collection. Open Mon through Sat; admission is free.

When George Dickel first discovered tranquil Cascade Hollow outside Tullahoma, he knew he had found a gold mine. It was the water from a nearby spring that Dickel considered so valuable. The ancient limestone shelf of the plateau provided water that ran fresh and clear, without mineral deposits. That iron-free water was the perfect ingredient for smooth sippin' whisky. Dickel also made another important discovery—the batch of whisky he had made in the winter with that water was far smoother than the whisky he had produced in the summer. Dickel used the traditional Scottish spelling of "whisky" (as opposed to "whiskey") because he believed his product to be as high in quality as the best Scotch whiskies.

First produced in 1877, George Dickel whisky is still handcrafted. The **George Dickel Distillery** (1950 Cascade Hollow Rd.; 931-408-2410; georgedickel.com) offers tours of this isolated spot surrounded by true hill beauty. Visitors also can watch a George Dickel video in the visitor center, which is filled with antiques and photos. The **George Dickel General Store** is a nice place to shop and look. On-site is a US Post Office—the only working post office at any distillery in the US. Visitors can also see Oscar, a 1910 replica of the George Dickel Whisky delivery truck with the old-fashioned Dickel sign painted on the side.

If your taste in bed-and-breakfasts is more rustic and rural than froufrou and finery, here's a place for you. **Ledford Mill Bed & Breakfast** (1195 Shipman Creek Rd.; 931-455-2546) is located inside an 1884 gristmill and is on the National Register of Historic Places. John Spear purchased the inn during June 2002. The previous owners, who had turned the mill into a bed-and-breakfast, decided not to remove the equipment but instead created a bed-and-breakfast around all the milling apparatus.

In the Loft Room, the corn-cleaning machine separates the sleeping and sitting areas. The Creek Room has an entire wall of stone, an old-time tub, and a large private deck with a view of the falls and wooded hillside. The Falls Room, with a wall of Chattanooga shale, is the closest to the falls and has a large bathroom that showcases the main wheel—the "heart" of the mill. Plank flooring is used throughout.

Located in a "holler" at the spring-fed headwaters of Shipman's Creek, the mill sits over the water; that same spring water is what comes through the taps to drink.

Rooms run from $100 to $135, and the facilities are pretty well booked up in advance, so you'll probably need to do some planning if you want to stay here. Turn onto Ledford Mill Road at the Lowe's Superstore on US 41A, and go 3 miles to the mill.

Shelbyville, the Bedford County seat, is also the center of Tennessee's horse country. It plays host each year to the **Tennessee Walking Horse National Celebration** (931-684-5915; twhnc.com), an event during which the World Grand Champion is named. The Celebration Grounds are located on Madison Avenue, which is US 41A, east of downtown Shelbyville.

This special breed of horse, developed during 150 years of selective breeding, is promoted today as the world's greatest show and pleasure horse. The horse has an unusual rhythmic, gliding gait in which each hoof strikes the ground separately in an odd one-two-three-four beat.

The breed emerged from the plantations around here during the later part of the 19th century but today can be found across the country. The area around Shelbyville is still known for its farms, and most of the owners are happy to show off their facilities. Many have signs out welcoming you.

Nobody seems to know exactly how **Rover** got its name, but the most accepted story is that a bunch of bickering regulars at a local drinking establishment decided to name their community. After hours of arguing over a name, one of them piped out, "Why don't we just call it Rover—we all fight like dogs anyway." So be it.

Along Highway 269 in the northern corner of the county lies the quaint little village of **Bell Buckle**. The little downtown area, located along Railroad Square facing the active railroad, is a trip back in time. A covered wooden sidewalk leads you from one store to another. All the benches, rocking chairs, flowers, and store displays have a tendency to slow down pedestrian traffic a bit, but it gives you more time to look in the window or watch a train go by.

Ten little antiques and craft shops make up the downtown lineup. Margaret Britton Vaughn (friends call her Maggi), the state's official poet laureate, runs the **Bell Buckle Press** (105 Webb Rd.; 931-389-6878). Take time to drop in and chat with her for a few minutes; she's a true southern lady.

Featured prominently a few shops down is the **Bell Buckle Cafe** (16 Railroad Sq. East; 931-389-9693; bellbucklecafe.com). In addition to some great hickory-smoked barbecue and the world's greatest hand-squeezed lemonade, the cafe features live music three nights a week and is the site of a Sat afternoon live broadcast on WLIJ Radio 1580 AM from 1 to 3 p.m. You'll hear a lot of new and old country and bluegrass coming from the back room here. There are at least a couple shows each Friday and Saturday night. Food is served 7 days a week.

Phillips General Store (4 Railroad Sq.; 931-389-6547) has an amazing assortment of cool things. Of course, beauty is in the eye of the beholder, but this shop has it all. From architectural items to folk art to garden art, the place is heaven. Open daily.

The roads to Bell Buckle are lined with daffodils, and the city founders felt those flowers were a good reason for a party. **Daffodil Day** (931-389-9663; bellbucklechamber.com) is held on a Saturday in mid-March each year, and the town celebrates with a bake sale, Easter egg hunt, old-fashioned menu at the Bell Buckle Cafe, and people dressed up like it's the 1800s all over again.

For a bit of the true South, be here during June to help celebrate the **Moon Pie Festival**. That's when you'll get to join in the celebration of one of the area's finest traditions, Moon Pies and RC Cola. Yum yum! Contact the **Bell Buckle Chamber of Commerce** (931-389-9663; bellbucklechamber.com) for more information.

The village is also the home of **Webb School** (931-389-9322; thewebbschool.com), a preparatory school that has produced 10 Rhodes Scholars and the governors of three states. The Junior Room, the original wood-shingled one-room schoolhouse built in 1870, has been preserved as it was then, complete with potbellied stove and teaching paraphernalia. It's open for visitors daily and is free. The school hosts a well-respected arts and crafts festival the third weekend of each October.

The area west of Shelbyville on Highway 64 is loaded with horse stables and horse farms. A drive along this corridor into the city of **Lewisburg** definitely reminds you that you're smack-dab in the middle of Tennessee Horse Country. If you see training sessions taking place, chances are the owners won't mind if you stop and watch, but of course it's always polite to ask first.

If you'd like to learn a little history while you're in the Lewisburg area, drive south on US 31A from downtown and you'll run into the **Abner Houston** *home*, across from the Lone Oak Cemetery. The log cabin was the site of the first court of Marshall County in October 1836. It was moved to this site in 1957.

Deep in dry Moore County at 182 Lynchburg Hwy., you'll find a famous distillery known for its Tennessee sour mash whiskey. *Jack Daniel's Distillery* (931-759-6357; jackdaniels.com) put Lynchburg, a community of 360 residents, on the map. Mister Jack (as he is locally known) founded his business in 1866 and received the first federal license ever issued for a distillery.

If you want to take a tour, make sure you wear comfortable shoes: There's a lot of walking and hill climbing. This is true history and Americana at its finest.

One of the highlights of the tour is the visit to Daniel's office, left virtually the way it was when he died. Make sure you ask the guide to show you where Mister Jack lost his temper one day, eventually causing him to experience a slow, painful death.

Start your tour at the visitor center, located in the hollow. It's a huge stone building with a magnificent front porch; you can't miss it. Inside, you'll learn just about everything you'd ever want to know about Mister Jack, plus you'll see some great exhibits of rare bottles and jugs and a reproduction of his first-ever still. Tours leave every 15 minutes or so 9 a.m. to 4:30 p.m. daily and last for approximately 75 minutes.

There's a great deal of charm in the nearby village of *Lynchburg*, where Daniel lived his entire life. Today, surrounding the 1855 redbrick courthouse, the square is chock-full of gift shops, general stores, arts and crafts outlets, and stores selling Jack Daniel merchandise.

Used whiskey barrels, Jack Daniel memorabilia, and antique reproductions can be found at the *Lynchburg Hardware and General Store* (52

Claim to Fame for Miss Mary

Miss Mary Bobo, a close personal friend of Jack Daniel's and the proprietress of Miss Mary Bobo's Boarding House in Lynchburg for many years, holds the distinction of being the oldest woman to ever appear in the pages of *Playboy* magazine.

A Jack Daniel Distillery advertisement ran in the magazine in June 1980, congratulating Miss Mary on her 99th birthday. The ad ran a photo of her and encouraged everyone to send her a card. As a result of that ad, she received thousands of cards, 36 cakes, and numerous gifts.

Miss Mary ran her boarding business for another 3 years, dying in 1983—just shy of her 102nd birthday.

Mechanic St. South; 931-759-4200), on the east side of the square. Pop open a cold drink and listen to the locals discuss the latest news. Maybe you can challenge someone to a game of checkers. Jack Daniel's nephew Lem Motlow opened the store to earn a living during Prohibition. A full line of Jack Daniel's merchandise is available alongside historic general store and hardware items that are just for display.

The best-known place to eat in these parts is **Miss Mary Bobo's Boarding House** (931-759-7394; jackdaniels.com) in the southwest corner of downtown at 295 Main St. Miss Mary began serving meals in 1908 and served many of them to Mister Jack, who had lunch here quite often. Of course, both Mister Jack and Miss Mary are gone now, but the tradition lives on. Specializing in southern traditional foods, they serve their meals family style.

Each meal is different, and the usual offerings include your choice of two meats, six vegetables, bread, beverage, and a totally awesome dessert. Reservations are a must, since the popular eatery seats only 65 people. During most of the year, seatings are at 11 a.m. and 1 p.m., Mon through Sat. They are closed on Sun. During the slower periods, especially on Monday, there may be only one seating. It's best to be flexible when you call for reservations, and if you're looking for a Saturday seating, you'll probably have to call several months in advance. Meals for adults are $25; $9 for children (aged 3 to 10); 2 and under free.

If you're hungry for the best barbecue in the country, make plans to come to Lynchburg in late October. That's when the **Jack Daniel's World Championship Invitational Barbecue** (jackdaniels.com) takes place. Participation is by invitation and qualification only. In order to compete here, your team must have won a championship cook-off of 50 or more participants or be the designated champion of a state competition. There are also international teams involved. Of course, there are a lot of food booths for sampling, as well as games and music. Check the website for dates and times.

As you head west across the mountain from Monteagle on US 41A/64, you'll pass the beautiful **University of the South** in **Sewanee** (335 Tennessee Ave.; 931-598-1578; theology.sweanee.edu). Founded in the late 1850s, the 10,000-acre mountaintop campus is known for its shady lawns and Gothic sandstone buildings patterned after Oxford University in England.

Farther down the mountain you'll enter the village of **Cowan**, where you'll find the **Cowan Railroad Museum** (931-967-3078; cowanrailroadmuseum .org) along the still-busy railroad tracks at 108 Front St. The museum is housed in the large circa 1904 depot that once served as the busy passenger station.

People would come from all over the South to visit the Sewanee area and the **Monteagle Assembly**. They would disembark from the passenger train in

Cowan and take the Mountain Goat, a smaller train, up the mountain to their destinations. The Mountain Goat track, built in 1853, is no longer in use as a railroad track. It has been converted to a mountain bike trail.

Today the museum is full of railroad antiques and memorabilia of those early days. Outside there's a steam engine, a flatcar, and a caboose. Run by volunteers, the facility is open May through Oct on Thurs through Sat 10 a.m. to 4 p.m., and Sun 1 to 4 p.m.

Hang on, we're really going off the beaten path on this one. The **Cumberland Tunnel** is the longest and steepest railroad tunnel in the US. Built in 1852, it's 2,200 feet long, 21 feet high, and 15 feet wide. It's still used today and is listed on the National Register of Historic Places.

To get there is a somewhat tedious, albeit fun and adventurous trek. Across the track and the small park from the museum is Tennessee Avenue. Take it south to the first right possible and go over the tracks. Make an immediate left turn onto a gravel road next to the track. The tunnel is nearly 2 miles up that road. Go slowly, and if you have a low-rider, forget it. The road is bumpy, uneven, and when it rains, a bit muddy in spots, but it's worth the trip once you're there.

The gravel road crosses about 25 feet above the track, just 50 feet from the tunnel entrance. Before you come up, get a train schedule and plan on watching a few trains go through—it's quite fun. Pack a lunch, and between trains take a hike into the raw mountains that surround you. The working rail yard in Cowan has a pusher locomotive operating 24 hours a day to help trains climb up to the tunnel and then help them through it.

Remember when you could buy a house from Sears & Roebuck? The company sold a great many for several years, and a few are still standing, including the one at 518 W. Cumberland St. (US 41) here in Cowan. The house was ordered from the catalog in the early 1900s.

Do not pass through **Winchester** without first going to visit the **Old Jail Museum** (931-967-0524; winchester-tn.com). Built in 1897, the structure is now open only to those who really want to be here. After having served as the county jail for more than 75 years, the museum now preserves the various elements of the jail, including the cell area and maximum-security block. Six additional rooms have exhibits highlighting the county's history, from the frontier days through the Civil War to the present. The Old Jail Museum is located at 296 S. Bluff St., a few blocks from the Winchester Courthouse. Open mid-Mar through mid-Dec, Tues through Sat 10 a.m. to 4 p.m. Admission for adults, $1; children 50 cents.

In 1987 a group of Mennonite families migrated to mid-south Tennessee in search of farmland and with a desire to start a Mennonite church in an area that had none. Among those in the group was the Miller family, who saw the demand for homemade breads and pastries. The **Swiss Pantry** (10026 David Crockett Hwy.; 931-962-0567; swiss-pantry.com) had its beginning in the kitchen of Mrs. Miller, who sold her products to friends and neighbors. In 1989, Mrs. Miller was joined by her three sisters, and they moved the business into the present building, located along US 64 just west of Belvidere. Mrs. Miller's brother, Enos Miller, and his family purchased the store from the ladies in 1999 and now run the business.

Not only will you find 10 different types of fresh-baked breads but also rolls, cookies, pastries, homemade salad dressings and relishes, a large selection of fresh herbs and spices, more than 30 different cheeses, smoked bacon and sausages, nuts, snacks, dried fruits, homemade candies, and a selection of baking and cooking supplies. Outside, a small garden center has been established. They are open Mon through Sat, 9 a.m. to 5 p.m.

When you leave the Swiss Pantry, continue west on US 64 and head into Davy Crockett country. You'll be going by a roadside marker designating Kentuck, the homestead that he left in 1812 to go off to the Creek War. He and his first wife, Polly, and their children settled near here when he came back from the war. She died in 1815 and is buried in an old cemetery overlooking nearby Bean's Creek.

If you want further information on Davy Crockett's ties with this part of Tennessee, stop by **Falls Mill** (134 Falls Mill Rd.; 931-469-7161; fallsmill.com), near Belvidere, and talk with owner Janie Lovett. In addition to her duties at the mill she owns with her husband, John, she's active in the local historical association and seems to know everyone in the area.

The Lovetts bought the mill in 1984 and have been busy restoring it ever since. Built in 1873, the mill has operated as a cotton-spinning and wool-carding factory, a cotton gin, a woodworking shop, and a grist and flour mill through the years. Since 1970 it has also served as a sort of museum. But it wasn't until the Lovetts bought it that it started realizing its true potential.

Make sure you take a walk down to the river behind the mill to get a good view of the falls and the 32-foot overshot waterwheel, which is the largest still in operation in the country.

Grain is still ground and is available at the mill store, along with other local items. There's a weaving exhibit upstairs in the mill. An 1895 log cabin was moved here and reassembled and serves as a bed-and-breakfast for up to five persons. Rates are $125 plus tax per night for two people, $5 for each additional person. The mill and picnic grounds are open every day but Wed and Sun. Admission is $5 for adults, $4 for senior citizens, and $3 for children under 14.

Farther south on US 231 is *Fayetteville*, the seat of Lincoln County. The downtown area around the county courthouse is probably one of the busiest in the state. There's nary a building vacancy on the square, and it can be hard to find a parking spot at times.

Start your visit at the chamber of commerce welcome center (208 S. Elk Ave.; 931-433-1234; fayettevillelincolncountychamber.com), where you'll be able to pick up a walking tour map of the historic downtown area, use their restroom facilities, and obtain a welcome package containing coupons and free gifts. That's what I call southern hospitality. Find out for yourself.

While downtown, visit the *Lincoln County Museum* (521 Main Ave. South; 931-433-7182, ext. 130; flcmuseum.com). Located inside the old Borden Milk Plant, numerous displays and exhibits highlight the town's past. There's a great agricultural exhibit and an amazing display of arrowheads.

During the second weekend of November, the town features a Christmas celebration and festival. There are trolley rides, strolling musicians, a candlelight walking tour, and an old-fashioned high tea.

One block off the square at 114 Market St. West, you can have lunch or dinner at *Cahoots* (931-433-1173; cahootsmenu.com), located in an old firehouse and city jail. Sit out front or in back in one of the rugged limestone cells. Built in 1867, the building was the city's jailhouse until the 1970s. Menu items include burgers, chicken, a variety of sandwiches, and Mexican, seafood, steak, prime rib, chicken, and pasta dishes. Cahoots has a full-service bar. Open Tues through Thurs 10:30 a.m. to 8 p.m.; Fri and Sat 10:30 a.m. to 9 p.m.

Western Heartland

The bell that was cast in 1858 and hangs in the *Giles County Courthouse* on the public square in Pulaski still strikes on the hour, each hour, every day. The sound coming from the cupola is just one of the beautiful elements of this neoclassical building built in 1909. Outside, tall Corinthian columns mark the architecture. Inside, a balcony encircles the third floor and 16 caryatids (female figures) hold up the arched vault of the rotunda, with its stained-glass skylights. The courthouse is open Mon through Fri during business hours. Out in front of the courthouse, on the south side of the public square, is a statue of Sam Davis, the young Confederate scout who was captured and executed in Pulaski. He was caught behind enemy lines with damaging information in his possession, and instead of betraying the source of that information, he chose to be hanged. The *Sam Davis Memorial Museum* (931-424-4044) now stands on the spot where the "Boy Hero of the Confederacy" was executed on November 27, 1863. The museum contains Civil War memorabilia as well as the leg irons worn by Davis. Located on Sam Davis Avenue, the hours are sporadic, so call the chamber of commerce first if you want to visit.

The chamber of commerce publishes a driving tour guide map of Giles County's top antiques, crafts, and collectible shops. Pick up a copy at the chamber's office, 110 N. Second St. Contact them at (931) 363-3789, or visit gilescountychamber.com.

While there are few, if any, physical reminders, there's one part of local history most residents would like to forget—the Ku Klux Klan was founded in *Pulaski*. Resentment against the move toward black equality fueled the creation of white supremacist groups throughout the South. The most enduring of those, the KKK, was founded in 1866 by six Confederate officers.

onestop graveyard

The Old Graveyard Memorial Park in Pulaski is a city park, cemetery, and historic monument all rolled into one. It's a great example of how an old, neglected cemetery can once again be useful while preserving the respect due those buried there. It's a well-lit area where one can stroll and truly absorb the area's history. The monuments have all been restored, with inscriptions dating back to 1753. Located at the corner of Cemetery Street and US 31.

Historic *Lynnville*, population 297, has quite the history as a railroad town, and to help preserve that grand heritage, a reproduction of the circa 1877 depot was built in 1997 to house a local museum of railroad artifacts and vintage railroad equipment. The town's history as a railroad town is unique in that the city was originally located 1 mile away from where it is now.

After the Civil War the city fathers decided to move everything to make it more convenient to the railroad. Today the entire town of 59 buildings is listed on the National Register of Historic Places. Contributing to the quaint factor of the downtown business district are several craft and antiques shops and *Soda Pop Junction* (141 Mill St.; 931-527-0007), an old-fashioned soda shop inside the old Lynnville Pharmacy, built in 1860. You'll find much more than ice cream here, though. A few years ago, their hamburger was voted best in the state and their milkshakes, second best. "I think they cheated when they counted the votes for the shakes; we're definitely the best," kidded the owner. Open daily; hours vary.

The *Lynnville Railroad Museum* (931-478-0880) is open May through Oct, Thurs through Sun until 5 p.m. Lynnville is located on Highway 129, 7 miles from exit 27 off I-65.

Although his legacy is divided among several areas in the state, David (aka Davy) Crockett only helped in the organization of one of the counties in which

Treasures & More on Route 64

If some can get their kicks on Route 66, Tennesseans surely can see more on Route 64. Running from I-24 in the Heartland into the Memphis area, this US highway skirts the bottom of the state through 10 counties. Five of those counties have gotten together to create a map of the attractions, accommodations, and events that can be found along the route in their counties. Call (931) 967-6788 for a copy.

he lived, Lawrence County. He was working as a justice of the peace in the area in 1817 when it was ceded by the Chickasaw Indians to the US. He helped get things organized and was instrumental in getting Lawrenceburg named as the county seat of government.

In 1922, during the dedication of a large monument that still stands on the south side of the square in Lawrenceburg, officials gave Crockett the title of Father of Lawrence County.

Davy Crockett was truly a Tennessean. He was born in the eastern part of the state, ran a gristmill, was elected to Congress in 1821 from Lawrenceburg, and went off to fight in the Alamo from the west. Over his lifetime, Crockett was a pioneer, soldier, politician, and industrialist.

While serving as justice of the peace, Crockett established a diversified water-powered industry consisting of a powder mill, a gristmill, and a distillery. His entire complex and his financial security were washed away in a flood in 1821, causing him to move farther west a few years later.

Today, on the site along the river where Crockett lived and worked, Tennessee has created **David Crockett State Park** (931-762-9408; tnstateparks .com/parks/david-crockett). The 1,100-acre park has an interpretive center, which is staffed during the summer months and has exhibits depicting Crockett's life here and a replica of the gristmill he once owned. Other facilities in the park include a swimming pool, cabins, 107 campsites, and the **Crockett's Mill Restaurant** (931-762-9541), one of the best eateries in this part of the state. The park is located on US 64, just west of Lawrenceburg.

During the second full weekend of Aug, the park hosts **David Crockett Days**, a fun and educational festival featuring a bevy of frontier-type activities, from tomahawk throwing to long rifle gun making. There's a Crockett film festival, snake shows, and bluegrass music concerts. An arts and crafts festival takes place the first weekend in September each year, featuring a wide variety of exhibitors. Additional unusual events run throughout the year.

By the way, the county was named in honor of Captain James Lawrence, who commanded a ship in the War of 1812. Mortally wounded, it was he who shouted out the famous command: "Don't give up the ship."

The pace in the **Ethridge** area, just north of Lawrenceburg, is definitely life in the slow lane. More than 200 Amish families call this community their home. The Amish, known as the Plain Folk, have a reputation for being productive farmers and expert craftspeople. Many families sell their wares from their front porches.

The **Natchez Trace** is truly a road trip back in time. The 450-mile road has been a major highway between Nashville and Natchez, Mississippi, since the late 1700s. It is preserved today as a scenic 2-lane parkway with few intersections, no commercial activities of any kind, and numerous pull-offs at historic stands (resting areas usually placed one day's travel from the other). The parkway ends on Highway 100, across from the Loveless Motel and Cafe, in Davidson County.

One of the early travelers on the trace was **Meriwether Lewis**, the famed leader of the Lewis and Clark expedition. In 1809, he met a violent and mysterious death at **Grinder's Stand**. His grave is marked by a broken column, symbolic of his broken career. The monument is located near the intersection with Highway 20 here in Lewis County, east of Hohenwald.

The trace is overlooked by those in a hurry because the speed limit (50 mph or less) is monitored quite closely. Make sure you have a lot of gas before you set out. For a map and other details, call (800) 305-7417.

The village of **Hohenwald** is a junker's paradise. The downtown streets are lined with junk and secondhand clothing shops, and people come from

The Candy Bar Farm

Frank Mars, the founder of Mars Candy Company, may have made his millions elsewhere, but he came to the rolling hills of Tennessee in 1922 to build his dream mansion and farm. For his gem, he chose a site in Pulaski, south of Nashville on Route 31. Milky Way Farm (931-808-2281; milkywayfarm.org) is nestled among one of the stateliest stands of grand magnolias in the South, and the Tudor mansion has 21 bedrooms and 15 baths.

During its heyday, the Milky Way Farm consisted of 2,800 acres, 38 barns, numerous houses, the grand mansion, and its own railroad. The farm produced prizewinning cattle and horses, including a Kentucky Derby winner. The mansion is listed on the National Register of Historic Places. Tours of the Manor House, stables, and barns are available.

miles away to do their bargain hunting here. Used clothing is brought in from the Midwest and Northeast in bales and dumped on the floors of the shops. The bales are broken open at most of the shops each Wed, Sat, and Sun, the days to be there for the best selection. If you're knowledgeable about brands and clothing quality, some real bargains await you here. There are tales about people finding money and even diamond rings in the old clothes.

German immigrants created Hohenwald (which means "high forest") in 1878 as they developed a lumber industry in the area. With the help of the railroad, an organized colony of Swiss immigrants settled in 1894 and built New Switzerland, just south of Hohenwald, and the two towns later merged. A great deal of the German architecture is still evident throughout the community.

The **Lewis County Museum of Natural and Local History** (108 E. Main St.; 931-796-1550; lewiscountymuseum.com) houses one of the largest collections of exotic animal mounts in the US, including one example of each species of North American sheep. There are also skins of lions, Bengal tigers, and tundra grizzlies. The museum serves as the local history museum and has several displays on the county's past. Open Tues through Sat 10 a.m. to 4 p.m. Admission for adults is $5, for seniors $4, and for students $2.

Carol Buckley and her elephant, Tara, traveled and performed with circuses for years, and then Buckley decided Tara would be a lot happier away from show business and in an environment more natural and more fitting for elephants. She moved the two of them to Hickman County, where she set up the **Elephant Sanctuary** (931-796-6500), the country's first official elephant retirement home. "It's for the old, sick, and needy," she said at the time, "There are many elephants out there that need a place like this. I have a strong feeling that we're going to be the first of many such homes." Through donations, special events, and a lot of help from concerned friends, Buckley was able to raise the money to build the necessary facilities. Buckley stepped down from the Sanctuary in 2009 and founded Elephant Aid International. The sanctuary is not open to the public, but if you'd like to see residents who may be living here, visit elephants.com and you can watch them on the ELECAM.

The Elephant Discovery Center at (27 E. Main St.) in downtown Hohenwald offers interactive multimedia exhibits, a theater, outdoor classroom, and regularly scheduled programming about elephants. The center is open Tues through Sat from 9 a.m. to 4 p.m.

While many of the communities in the state have groups who sit around outside near the courthouse and spit and whittle their days away, you'll find the old-timers in **Centerville**, the county seat, playing checkers while they spit.

In Hickman County, nicknamed the Keg County, there's still a lot of moonshine made in these hills. If you're interested in sampling some, just put out the word. It has a way of finding you.

And speaking of tasty things, make sure you stop by **Breece's Cafe** (931-729-3481), on the square in Centerville. In business since the 1940s, it offers country cooking at its finest. A different plate lunch is offered each weekday, and they always have a selection of home-baked pies on hand. Ask for the blackberry; it's especially good. Open Tues through Sun 6 a.m. to 8 p.m. Breakfast is served anytime with country ham and red-eye gravy a favorite.

Head out Highway 100 toward Nashville, and as soon as you cross the Duck River, look to your right and you'll find the hottest spot in town for a catfish dinner. The **Fish Camp Restaurant** (931-729-4401), located next to two ponds, features Tennessee River catfish, and people come from all over to sample it. In addition to the fish, they have a full menu, including some great barbecue they smoke right on-site. No alcohol is served or allowed due to city regulations. Open Tues through Sun for lunch and dinner.

The strangest name of any community in the state is probably here in Hickman County. Out on Highway 50 south of Centerville is the small community of **Who'd A Thought It**. Story goes that a schoolhouse was being built out in the middle of nowhere, and a man pulled up in his buggy and asked what they were building. They told him, and he was last seen shaking his head and mumbling "Who'd a thought it" as he pulled away. Other interesting names in the county are Defeated Creek, Little Lot, Only, Pretty Creek, Ugly Creek, Spot, and Grinders Switch.

Up in Nunnelly, behind the Church of Christ where Highways 48 and 230 split, you'll find a monument marking the birthplace of **Beth Slater Whitson**, the writer of poems, songs, and short stories. Her best-known song lyrics were "Let Me Call You Sweetheart" and "Meet Me Tonight in Dreamland." She lived here from her birth in 1879 to 1913, when she moved to Nashville. She died there in 1930.

The coal miner's daughter owns **Hurricane Mills**, but no longer lives there. Lynn moved closer to Nashville after suffering a stroke in 2017. When country music's most-awarded female vocalist, Loretta Lynn, and her husband, Mooney, were house shopping back in 1966, she was searching for a big old "haunted looking" place. When she saw this century-old mansion, she knew this was her dream. She wanted it immediately, not knowing the entire town and old mill came with it. The **Loretta Lynn Ranch** (931-296-7700; lorettalynn ranch.net), on Highway 13 in Hurricane Mills, was her home as well as her museum and special place to welcome fans.

In 1975, a campground was developed, and since then numerous other attractions have been added to the ranch, including Loretta's personal museum, a replica of the coal mine her father worked in, a replica of her Butcher Holler house, a western store, and a gift shop.

Tours of her antebellum plantation mansion are given daily. Make sure you ask the guide about the haunted aspects of the building. Lynn once lived in a house behind the mansion. You can look out the windows of the mansion and see her former home. There is no charge to enter the ranch, but there is for the tours, museum, and other activities, including miniature golf and canoeing. There are dances every Sat night during the summer, and a few concerts during that time also. Located 7 miles north of I-40; open Mar through Oct with limited attractions open Nov through Feb.

Charlotte, the seat of Dickson County, looks much as it did in the mid-1800s. The circa 1834 courthouse is considered the oldest such building still in use in the state. Pre–Civil War buildings line the downtown square, and the old-timers still gather at the drugstore on the square to solve the world's problems.

But it could have been so different! The now quaint and quiet town was two votes short of becoming the capital of Tennessee. Only Nashville received more votes.

Northern Heartland

The 170,000-acre peninsula between **Kentucky Lake** and Lake Barkley owned and operated by the Tennessee Valley Authority is aptly called the **Land Between the Lakes** (800-525-7077; landbetweenthelakes.us), or LBL, as locals refer to it. About a third of it lies in Tennessee and the rest in Kentucky.

The area is an awesome display of nature. The Trace, the main north-south road, is 60 miles long, with southern entry just west of Dover off US 79. There's plenty to do here, and according to the rangers, most of the area is underutilized.

In addition to all the hiking trails and water activities, there are more than 100 miles of paved roads for biking. The **Homeplace** (931-232-6457; land betweenthelakes.us) is a 19th-century living history museum with 16 restored structures that were moved from other LBL locations and rebuilt at 4512 The Trace. Costumed personnel work the farm, and most will take time from their chores to talk history with you.

Homeplace employees eat here, with all food prepared over the open fires and in the kitchens of the restored buildings. While walking through the kitchens, talk with the cooks. They have some great stories to tell about their past cooking experiences. The Homeplace is open Mar through Nov.

There is a fee for many of the attractions, and there are several special events during the year that the free LBL newsletter available on the website covers in detail. Admission is $5 for ages 13 and up, $3 for ages 5 to 12, free for ages 4 and under.

Although it has to share honors with Kentucky, Montgomery County is the home of the famed 101st Airborne Division—Air Assault of the US Army. The **Fort Campbell Military Base** (204 State Line Rd.; 270-798-9322; military.com) covers more than 100,000 acres on the state line and is the county's largest employer.

The base is open, which means visitors are welcome as long as they pick up a pass at Gate 4 on US 41A. Located near the gate, the visitor center and the **Don F. Pratt Memorial Museum** (270-798-4986; fortcampbell.com). Named for Brigadier General Don Pratt, who was killed while leading the 101st Airborne's legendary glider assault into Normandy during World War II, the museum traces the history of the division from World War I through the present. Exhibits also depict the history of Fort Campbell and the land it occupies.

Probably the most interesting exhibit in the place is the replica of the fragile-looking glider that the members of the 101st Division used in France during the D-day invasion of 1944. More than 14,000 of the canvas-covered cargo gliders were built during the war, with such unlikely businesses as the Steinway Piano and Heinz Pickle companies contributing to the effort.

Across the street from the large indoor portion of the museum is a lot with a large collection of tanks, artillery field pieces, and airplanes. Open Tues through Sat 9:30 a.m. to 4:30 p.m.; free admission.

Clarksville is the state's fifth-largest city, with a population of about 104,000, but it probably has the largest selection of architectural marvels of any one city in the state. "Anyone interested in architecture will have a field day in Clarksville," maintains the curator of the **Customs House Museum & Cultural Center** (931-648-5780; customshousemuseum.org).

Any tour through the city should start at the Customs House, at the corner of Commerce and Second Streets at 200 S. Second St. Originally constructed as a US Post Office and Customs House in 1898, its eclectic architecture consists of Italianate ornamentation, an Asian-influenced slate roof, Romanesque arches, and Gothic copper eagles perched at each of the four corners.

Olympic star Wilma Rudolph was a Clarksville native. A bronze life-size statue of her is now on display inside the Customs House. It's a great tribute to the late, three-time Olympic gold medal champion.

Attached to the post office, the museum has a 53,000-square-foot cultural center complete with a 200-seat auditorium, several different art galleries, classrooms, exhibit halls, and the state's best artisan gift shops. If you can't find something here, maybe you're too picky.

Exhibits include one on the local tobacco industry and a salute to the local firefighters. This is one of the finest local museums in the state. Area tour maps can be picked up here. Open Tues through Sun with free admission on the second Sat of the month. Otherwise, admission is $7 for adults, $5 for seniors, $5 for teachers and students, $3 for children 6 to 18.

There are two self-guided tours of the city and county—a 2-mile (25-site) walking tour of the downtown architectural area and a 14-mile (50-site) driving tour.

Clarksville has a proud river heritage, and to celebrate the relationship between the city and the mighty Cumberland River, the city fathers have created the **Cumberland RiverWalk** (931-645-7476; visitclarksvilletn.com), a meandering riverfront promenade. Along the path you'll experience river overlooks, a playground, picnic areas, and a wharf. During the winter holidays, **Christmas on the Cumberland**, with dozens of colorful displays, takes place along the RiverWalk.

As The River Flows is the name of an exhibit in the **RiverCenter**, located along the RiverWalk. The center offers a great view of the river, and among its exhibits is a 12-panel chronological history of the Cumberland River and its significance to the development of Clarksville. The entire RiverWalk area is open daily.

McGregor Park, located along the RiverWalk, is home to the annual **Riverfest** (931-645-7476; clarksvilleriverfest.org), a 3-day arts, music, and food celebration in early September. There is a visual fine arts competition, which means you'll find some great, original regional art for sale. There are four stages with continuous musical performances and performing arts presentations. Plenty of food, ethnic culture, and youth activities can also be found. This is one of the more fun festivals in this part of the state!

Remember the Monkees' big hit "The Last Train To Clarksville"? Some say it was inspired by the **L&N Train Station** (931-553-2486; mchsociety.org) here in Clarksville at Commerce and Tenth Streets. Built in 1890, the once-busy depot is now open as a museum and art gallery. Open Tues, Thurs, and Sat 9 a.m. to 1 p.m.

There are several buildings high on the hill on the public square where advertising painted on their river-facing exterior walls years ago is still visible. Originally painted to be seen by river traffic, most of the ads have faded over the years. However, the ad on the circa 1842 Poston Building on the square can still be seen and appreciated. It was painted back when the Uneeda Biscuit Company was selling their product for a nickel a package.

For fun entertainment, the local professional theater group, the ***Roxy Regional Theatre*** (931-645-7699; roxyregionaltheatre.org), offers up 10 productions a year, all staged in the renovated Roxy Theater at 100 Franklin St. The theatre also hosts films, art exhibits, summer drama camp, and other events.

The ***Old-Time Fiddlers' Championships*** (931-647-7261; tnfiddlers .com) is a great time to visit for some authentic old-time music. It takes place in August at the Northeast High School and, with a large cash purse for the winners, attracts some great nationally known entertainers. Categories include Dobro, Bluegrass Banjo, Mandolin, Guitar, Open Fiddle, Blue Grass Bands, and Pee Wee Fiddle for ages 10 and under.

More information about Clarksville and Montgomery County can be found by calling (800) 530-2487 or at visitclarksvilletn.com.

Just outside Clarksville is ***Historic Collinsville*** (4711 Weakley Rd.; 931-245-4344; historiccollinsville.com), an authentically restored 19th-century log pioneer settlement that's a lot of fun to visit. It's a great glimpse into what it was like living in this area of the state 200 years ago. The buildings have all been saved, moved to the village, and lovingly restored by JoAnn and Glenn Weakley. There are now 16 buildings, including a dogtrot house and several outbuildings. Annual events range from a quilt show to a Civil War encampment. Admission is $7 for ages 7 and up, under 6 free. Open mid-Apr through Oct, Sat 10 a.m. to 5 p.m., Sun 1 to 5 p.m.; don't miss it.

Montgomery County's answer to California's Napa Valley can be found at the ***Beachaven Vineyards & Winery*** (1100 Dunlop Ln.; 931-645-8867; beachavenwinery.com), a few miles off I-24's exit 4. Co-owner Ed Cooke thinks his winery can offer as good a tasting tour as do his counterparts in California. "We offer the same thing, but we add southern hospitality," he said.

Beachaven's tasting concept is a great plus for those needing a little education before buying a wine. Cooke or one of the employees will be glad to give you a taste of all their varieties. Tours are given year-round for those who would like to see how the fruit of the vine becomes so divine. And these wines are really divine. Wine judges across the country think so, too. Look at all those ribbons awarded to the various products of Cooke and his family lining the walls. Their champagne is of "world renown," having been written up in the major wine books.

The most exciting (and aromatic) time to visit is in the fall while the crushing is taking place, but there is always something going on. During the summer, special concerts are presented in the vineyard's picnic area. The winery is open daily, Mon through Sat 9 a.m. to 6 p.m., Sun noon to 5 p.m.

The ***Dunbar Cave State Natural Area*** (931-648-5526; tnstateparks.com) is 110 scenic acres of true history and legend. The activities on this site range from when the local Native Americans inhabited the cave entrance 10,000 years ago to when country music legend and Grand Ole Opry star Roy Acuff owned the property and held weekly country music shows in the cave entrance.

A stately old bathhouse now serves as a visitor center and museum. If you want to take a cave tour, you have to call ahead and see when the group tours are being held. Even if you don't take the tour, the museum and the nature trails make this a fun place to visit. Fishing is permitted on the lake. Located just off US 79, 4 miles from I-24 (exit 4) at 401 Old Dunbar Cave Rd. Open 7 days a week; call for hours and events.

There have been ghosts and there have been legends, but the **Bell Witch of Adams** is probably the most documented story of the supernatural in all of American history. This witch is unique because of the large number of people who have had direct experience with it.

John Bell was a well-respected and influential member of the **Adams** community. He and his family lived on a 1,000-acre plantation along the Red River. The trouble started in 1817 when bumping and scratching sounds were first noticed in the house, but the Bells passed them off as being caused by the wind. The big problems started in 1818, when continuous gnawing sounds were heard on each member of the family's bedposts each night. When someone would get up to investigate, the sound would stop. The sound would go from room to room until everyone was awake. Then it would stop until the candles were blown out and everyone went back to bed, when it would start all over again.

Things grew from there. People came to town to witness the occurrences and weren't disappointed. Gen. Andrew Jackson came up to Adams from his Nashville home to investigate the matter but turned around when the wheels on his carriage mysteriously locked.

This has gone on through the decades. A few years ago, several reporters came to Adams with plans to stay in the Bell cave, where many of the experiences have occurred. They lasted a few hours before fleeing.

Today the **Bell Witch Cave** (615-696-3055; bellwitchcave.com) is open to those who think they are brave enough to possibly face the witch herself. Many have. Off US 41 at 403 Keysburg Rd., the cave is open May through Oct; but is closed during rainy periods due to possible flooding. Check for hours. Admission is $12 per person. No one under 18 is allowed without parental permission.

All the Bell buildings are gone now, except for a small, log slave building. It has been moved to the grounds of the old elementary schoolhouse and is open for viewing. You can't miss the graves of the Bell family at the Bellwood cemetery. There's a magnificent tower marking them—and a stone fence keeping the Bell Witch out.

The historic Red River is an easy river to experience by canoe. Where US 41 crosses the river in Adams, you'll find **Red River Valley** (615-696-2768; canoetheredriver.com), where you can both rent a canoe and get river information. Check the website for hours of operation.

Springfield is the county seat of Robertson County, and its past is told nicely in the restored circa 1915 US Post Office, now the **Robertson County History Museum** (124 Sixth Ave. West; 615-382-7173), just off Court Square. One of the exhibits points out a facet of the county that few people realize today: At one time it was home to 75 whiskey distilleries. That's a lot of booze, especially for the state that's considered the buckle of the Bible Belt.

Since 1820 the county has been known for its tobacco crops and is widely acknowledged as the dark-fired tobacco capital of the world. An exhibit chronicles those 180 years of agricultural significance. Open Wed through Fri 10 a.m. to 4 p.m., Sat by appointment. Admission is $4 for adults, $2 for seniors, $1 for students. A unique site.

The county courthouse on the Springfield square dates back to 1879. Along Main Street you'll find several interesting stores and shops located in the old distillery warehouses, dating back to the early 1900s.

Cross Plains was the first settlement in Robertson County when it was founded in 1779. Today there's a great deal of charm in the community of 1,353 people. The houses that line Main Street and the side streets are beautifully framed by big, mature trees, and there are plenty of friendly shops to keep you busy.

Pharmacist Dan Green is now caretaker of a bit of history in Cross Plains. He and his wife, Debbie, are the owners of **Thomas Drugs** (615-654-3877; thomasdrugs.com) and its historic black-and-chrome antique soda fountain. While Green tends to the business of the pharmacy, his soda jerk mixes up his own concoctions, from milkshakes to vanilla Cokes to ice-cream sundaes. Lunch is served Mon through Fri 10 a.m. to 2 p.m. and includes an array of fresh sandwiches and soups. Drinks and ice cream are served 8 a.m. to 6 p.m. Mon through Fri and 8 a.m. to noon on Sat.

In addition to the "regular" drugstore stuff, the store features antique reproduction toys and books, and local crafts including quilts and coverlets. You'll find it at the corner of Main and Cedar Streets at the four-way stop sign at 7802 Hwy. 25 East. Open Mon through Sat 8 a.m. to 6 p.m.; admission is free.

In the **White House** (615-672-0239; cityofwhitehouse.com), on Highway 76, 1 mile east of I-65 at exit 108, next to the firehouse, is one of the most distinctive library and museum buildings you'll find anywhere in the state. It's

The Catholics of Tennessee

The state's oldest Catholic church still in use is *St. Michael's*, located in the Flewellyn community near Cedar Hill. The church was built in 1842, and in the late 1890s a structure from the nearby Glen Raven Estate was moved and attached to the original church to make it larger. Today the white-clapboard church sits serenely among the trees in this rural area, surrounded by a cemetery.

St. Michael's is a mission church, which means it doesn't have a resident priest. A priest from Our Lady of Lourdes in nearby Springfield administers to the congregation of approximately 70 families and makes the drive out from town every Sunday morning to say the 8 a.m. Mass.

As you walk in the front door, look immediately to the right and you'll see a cutaway that shows what the original construction looks like behind the walls. Also of interest is the outdoor altar, built at the bottom of the cemetery. It was built with the stones from the original foundation of St. Michael's Academy for Boys, a long-defunct educational adjunct of the church.

To get to Flewellyn, take Highway 49 South from Springfield for 4 miles. At the Highway 49 Market, turn right (west) onto Highway 257. Go another 4 miles to Catholic Church Road, which is the first paved road to the left. Turn left and go another 4 miles until you reach the fork in the road; go right and you'll soon see the church at 3553 S. Carter Rd. It's locked up during the week, but you are invited to enjoy the grounds and the exterior and to join the congregation for Mass on Sunday. Call for their schedule at (615) 384-6200 or look on the website at ollsm.com.

a reproduction of the original White House Inn, which gave the area its name. The inn was a major stopover between Nashville and Louisville during the horse and buggy days.

The community library is on the first floor, the museum is on the second, and the chamber of commerce is out back in the bachelors' quarters. For a small community, they've done a splendid job in presenting a local history museum. Make sure you take a look at the firehouse next door, and don't miss the fun statue of a Dalmatian out front. Nice touch. Open Mon through Thurs 9 a.m. to 4 p.m. Enjoy this unique site.

Up in northern Sumner County, *Portland* (615-325-6776; citytofportlandtn.gov) has a long history and today has one of the longest-running commodity festivals in the state. Strawberries became an important crop for the area in the 1920s and soon became a major export item. Today the *Middle Tennessee Strawberry Festival* (middletennesseestrawberryfestival.net) is a salute to both the present and the past strawberry business. The free festival has been held each mid-May since 1941, and the weeklong roster of activities ends on a Saturday with a Rotary Pancake Breakfast, a parade, and the Lion's Club Bluegrass Festival.

There's plenty of food, crafts, entertainment, and of course strawberry delicacies. Check out the festival website for more details on the festival as well as a list of local farms where you can pick your own berries.

If you're into the quaintness of one-room schoolhouses, check out the **Cold Springs School** (hrhstn.org). Constructed in 1857, the building is now a museum of local history with a great deal of Civil War memorabilia. It was moved into Richland Park in Portland in 1975 and restored. Originally built in an area of the city that was a military training camp for Civil War soldiers, the little school was used as an infirmary during the war. It's run by the Highland Rim Historical Society. Tours are available from 2 p.m. to 4 p.m. Sun from June through Aug.

Another crop that is making a name for itself since the mid-1990s is the grape. That's when the **Sumner Crest Winery** (615-325-4086; sumnercrestwinery.com) was founded by two brothers at exit 117 off I-65 at 5306 S. Old Hwy. 52. Tours and tastings are available, and there's a nice little antiques gallery. Some of the wines they specialize in are Tennessee blackberry, Merlot, Cabernet, and Summer Queen.

Open daily at 9 a.m. and on Sun at noon. Closes at 5 p.m. on Sun, the rest of the week at 6 p.m. during the summer months, 5 p.m. during winter. During the summer, evening concerts are held on the grounds, plus some spiffy antique cars are on display, including a stunning 1957 Corvette.

The downtown commercial area of **Gallatin** is quite the historic area. With more than 25 restored buildings, many of which predate the Civil War, the area has been listed on the National Register of Historic Places. Occupying some of those buildings are antiques shops and restaurants.

A block off the main square area, you'll find the **Sumner County Museum** (183 W. Main St.; 615-451-3738; sumnercountymuseum.org), behind the historic Trousdale Place. The museum is the keeper of nearly a quarter million artifacts that tell the history of the county. Included in that collection are 475-million-year-old fossils and several displays featuring Native American and African American life in the area. Open seasonally and by appointment. Admission is $5 for adults, and $3 for children (ages 6 to 12). Children under 6 admitted free. Go back in time at this historic site.

Trousdale Place (183 W. Main St.; 615-452-5648; trousdaleplace.com) was home to Tennessee governor William Trousdale, who served the state from 1849 to 1851. The home has been restored and contains period antiques as well as a small Confederate library. Open by appointment. Admission is $5 per person. Trousdale Place is open free to the public four times a year in Apr, July, Sept, and Nov. Check the website for dates and time.

In *Castalian Springs*, what may be the largest log structure ever erected in Tennessee still stands. *Wynnewood* (210 Old Hwy. 25; 615-452-5463; historicwynnewood.org) was built in 1828 as a stagecoach inn and mineral springs resort, and by 1840 a row of cottages adjoining the inn had been built, as well as a horse racetrack.

The main house is 142 feet long with a dogtrot through the middle. Some of the logs, mostly oak and walnut, are 32 feet long. All the rooms have outside doors and are entered from a gallery that extends 110 feet across the back of the building. A stairway in the dogtrot goes to the second-story rooms.

Owned by the state, Wynnewood is located 45 miles northeast of Nashville, 8 miles east of Gallatin. It's open Wed through Sat 10 a.m. to 4 p.m., Sun 10 a.m. to 5 p.m., Apr through Oct. Admission is $10 for adults, $8 for seniors, $5 for children (ages 6 to 12), free for children under age 6.

About 100 yards east of the entrance to Wynnewood is a stone monument marking the location of a giant, 9-foot-diameter sycamore tree in which Thomas Sharp Spencer lived during the winter of 1778–79. Spencer, the first white settler in middle Tennessee, called the tree home while he was building a cabin nearby.

Also located along Highway 25, about 5 miles from Gallatin is *Cragfont Museum House* (200 Cragfont Rd.; 615-452-7070; cragfrpmt/met), one of the finest examples of federal architecture in the state. Built between 1798 and 1802 by General James Winchester of Revolutionary War fame, the limestone house has been restored and is open to the public. Open Apr 15 to Nov 1, Tues through Sat, 10 a.m. to 4 p.m.; Sun 1 p.m. to 4 p.m.; closed Mon. Admission is $5 for adults, $4 for seniors, and $3 for children (ages 6 to 12).

More information on Gallatin and the rest of Sumner County can be found at sumnertn.org. You can also contact *Sumner County Tourism* (615-230-8474 or 888-301-7866; visitsumnertn.com).

Places to Stay in the Heartland

CLARKSVILLE

Lylewood Inn Bed & Breakfast
110 Camp Lylewood Rd.
(931) 627-2116
Lylewoodinn.com

Riverview Inn
50 College St.
(877) 48-RIVER
theriverviewinn.com

DICKSON

East Hills Bed & Breakfast
100 E. Hills Ter.
(615) 441-9428
easthillsbb.com

LAWRENCEBURG

David Crockett State Park
1400 W. Gaines St.
(931) 762-9408 or
(877) 804-2681
tnstateparks.com

Richland Inn
2125 N. Locust Ave.
(931) 762-0061
richlandinnlawrenceburg
.com

MANCHESTER

Mint Julep Manor
3141 Murfreesboro Hwy.
(615) 585-7702

Tims Ford State Park
570 Tims Ford Dr.
(931) 965-3536
Tnstateparks.com

MURFREESBORO

Carriage Lane Inn
337 E. Burton St.
(615) 890-3630
carriagelaneinn.com

Childress House B&B
225 N. Academy St.
(615) 268-8063
childresstn.com

NASHVILLE

Bobby Hotel
230 Fourth Ave. North
(615) 782-7100
bobbyhotel.com

Daisy Hill Bed and Breakfast
2816 Blair Blvd.
(615) 297-9795
daisyhillbedandbreakfast
.com

Fiddler's Inn Opryland
2410 Music Valley Dr.
(615) 885-1440
fiddlersinnopryland.com

404 Hotel
404 Twelfth Ave. South
(615) 242-7404
the404hotel.com

Gaylord Opryland Resort & Convention Center
2800 Opryland Dr.
(615) 889-1000
Marriott.com

Hermitage Hotel
231 Sixth Ave. North
(615) 244-3121
thehermitagehotel.com

Hotel Preston
733 Briley Pkwy.
(615) 361-5900
hotelpreston.com

Millennium Maxwell House Hotel Nashville
2025 Rosa L. Parks Blvd.
(615) 259-4343
millenniumhotels.com

Nashville KOA
2626 Music Valley Dr.
(615) 889-0282
koa.com

Noelle
200 Fourth Ave. North
(615) 649-5000
noelle-nashville

Thompson Nashville
401 Eleventh Ave. South
(615) 262-6000
thompsonhotels.com

Timothy Demonbreun House
746 Benton Ave.
(615) 383-0426
tdhouse.com

Union Station Hotel
1001 Broadway
(615) 726-1001
unionstationhotelnashville
.com

TULLAHOMA

Grand Lux Inn
212 E. Lincoln St.
(931) 461-9995
thegrandluxinn.com

Ledford Mill Bed & Breakfast
1195 Shipman's Creek Rd.
(931) 455-2546

Places to Eat in the Heartland

ADAMS

Adams Station
7716 US 41
(616) 696-1110
adams-station.business.site

Moss's Restaurant
7617 US 41
(615) 669- 1224
mossrestaurant.com

Thomas Drugs
On corner of Main and
Cedar Streets
(615) 654-3877
thomasdrugs.net

ASHLAND CITY

Cody's Diner
113 Cumberland St.
(615) 415-3368

Riverview Restaurant
110 Old River Rd.
(615) 792-7358
riverviewrestaurant
andmarina.com

Sidelines Grill
232 Hutton Pl.
(615) 792-6800

BELL BUCKLE

Bell Buckle Cafe
16 Railroad Sq. East.
(931) 389-9693
bellbucklecafe.com

**Bell Buckle Coffee Shop
& Book Swap**
2 Railroad Sq.
(931) 813-3333
bellbucklecoffeeshop.com

**Southern Charm Gift
Shop & Tea Room**
29 Railroad Sq.
(931) 389-0003
bellbucklesoutherncharm
.com

CENTERVILLE

Breece's Cafe
111 S. Public Sq.
(931) 729-3481

Fish Camp Restaurant
406 Hwy. 100
(931) 729-4401

Muddy Duck
200 E. Public Sq.
(931) 729-8330
the-muddy-duck-coffee
.business.site

Papa Kayjoe's Bar B Que
119 W. Ward St.
(931) 729-2131

CHRISTIANA

**Miller's Grocery and
Country Cafe**
7011 Main St.
(615) 893-1878
millersgrocery.com

FAYETTEVILLE

Cahoots
114 Market St. West
(931) 433-1173
Cahootsmenu.com

**Marvin's Family
Restaurant**
4130 Thornton Taylor
Pkwy.
(931) 433-3101
marvinsfamilyrestaurant
.com

FRANKLIN

BrickTop's
1576 W. McEwen Dr.
(615) 771-8760
bricktops.com

Cork & Cow
108 Fourth Ave. South
(615) 538-6021
corkandcow.com

55 South
403 Main St.
(615) 538-6001
eat55.com

Gray's on Main
332 Main St.
(615) 435-3603
graysonmain.com

**Puckett's Grocery
& Restaurant**
120 Fourth Ave. South
(615) 794-5527
puckettsgro.com

Red Pony
408 Main St.
(615) 595-7669
redponyrestaurant.com

LYNCHBURG

Barrel House BBQ
105 Mechanic St.
(931) 759-5760
barrelhousebbqtn.com

BBQ Caboose
217 Main St.
(931) 759-5180

**Miss Mary Bobo's
Boarding House**
295 Main St.
jackdaniels.com

NASHVILLE

Acme Feed & Seed
101 Broadway
(615) 915-0888
acmefeedandseed.com

The Bluebird Cafe
4104 Hillsboro Pike
(615) 383-1461
bluebirdcafe.com

Bongo Java Coffeehouse
2007 Belmont Blvd.
(615) 385-5282
bongojava.com

Capitol Grille
231 Sixth Ave. North
(615) 345-7116
capitolgrillenashville.com

Cock of the Walk
2624 Music Valley Dr.
(615) 889-1930
cockofthewalkrestaurant
.com

Etch
303 Demonbreun St.
(615) 522-0685
etchrestaurant.com

Farm House
210 Almond St.
(615) 522-0688
thefarmhousetn.com

Fido
1821 21st Ave. South
(615) 777-3436
bongojava.com

Gray & Dudley
221 Second Ave. North
(615) 610-6460
grayanddudley.com

Hattie B's Hot Chicken
112 Nineteenth St. South
(615) 678-4794
hattieb.com

Jack's Bar-B-Que
416 Broadway
(615) 254-5715
jacksbarbque.com

Loveless Cafe
8400 Hwy. 100
(615) 646-9700
lovelesscafe.com

Monell's
1235 Sixth Ave. North
(615) 248-4747
monellstn.com

Moto
1120 McGavock St.
(615) 736-5305
mstreetnashville.com

Nashville Farmers' Market
900 Rosa L. Parks Blvd.
(615) 880-2001
nashvillefarmersmarket.org

Nashville Palace
2611 McGavock Pike
(615) 899-1540
Nashville-palace.com or
musicvalleyattractions.com

Prince's Hot Chicken Shack
5814 Nolensville Pike
(615) 810-9388
princeshotchicken.com

NORMANDY

River Bistro
4 Front St.
(931) 857-3900

The Western Plains

History on the Plains

Nathan Bedford Forrest, the notorious hard-riding Confederate cavalry officer known for his unexpected and often offbeat tactics, pulled off one of the Civil War's most interesting victories along the Tennessee River here in the fall of 1864. It was probably the first time in military history that a cavalry force attacked and defeated a naval force. High atop **Pilot Knob,** the highest point in this part of the state, Forrest secretly assembled his troops. He had his eye on the Union army's massive supply depot, directly across the river.

At the time the depot had more than 30 vessels, most fully loaded and waiting to head out to Union forces. Stacks of supplies lined the wharf. Forrest attacked and caught the Yanks off guard. Within minutes all 30 vessels and the various warehouse buildings were on fire, and within 2 hours everything was destroyed. By nightfall Forrest's troops had vanished into the dense woods.

The land surrounding Pilot Knob is now known as the *Nathan Bedford Forrest State Park*. Atop the hill is a monument to Forrest. Also at the top is the *Tennessee River*

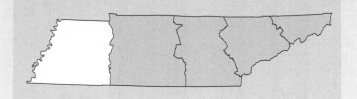

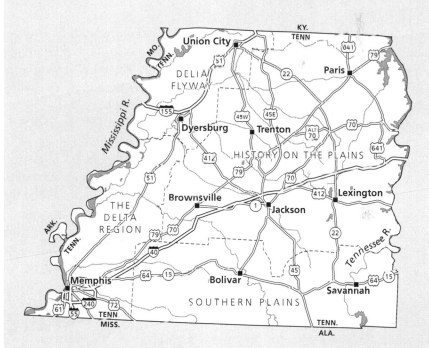

lotsoffish,too

With more than 2,300 miles of shoreline, Kentucky Lake is the second-largest man-made lake in the world.

Folklife Center (731-584-6356; tnstate parks.com), "designed to explore the relationship between the river and the people who use it."

Most of the exhibits incorporate segments of oral histories taken from the locals who "lived the life." Separate accounts recall the early industries and the music, religion, and community events of the area.

The most colorful audio presentation highlights the days when folks would gather at the river to welcome the big showboats to their landing. The biggest exhibit is *Old Betsy*, an entire workboat from the early musseling industry along the river. The most visual representation of early river life is from the Brownie camera of Maggie Sayre. She lived on a houseboat for more than 50 years and photographed everyday life around her.

Most rural areas throughout the South have their own version of the liars' bench and the spit and whittle club. The view from the porch or from under the tree may be different from town to town, but the plot is the same. A story is told, then retold, then exaggerated to the point where it becomes a modern-day myth. A typical riverfront liars' bench has been reconstructed here at the center, with a breathtaking view of the Tennessee River far below. Walk up, push a button, and sit down and relax. The series of taped stories (from original spit and whittlers) will keep you in stitches.

The center is open every day 8 a.m. to 4:30 p.m. Admission is free. As you enter the park, the visitor center is to your right. Inside are several exhibits, including artwork and tanks containing local fish. Check here to see if the folklife center is open; if not, ask and they will probably send someone up with you. The historical park area offers camping, hiking trails, and picnic areas. Both areas are at the end of Route 191, about 10 miles out of Camden.

It has been found that the Tennessee River and Kentucky Lake provide the perfect environment in which to grow freshwater pearls. It is warm year-round, unpolluted, and high in lime content.

That's what the late John Latendresse and his wife Chessie discovered when they were perfecting the process of growing freshwater pearls that are today worn by the likes of Hillary Rodham Clinton and Tipper Gore. The farm is now owned by Robert G. Keast, owner of Birdsong Resort, Marina, and Campground.

The *Tennessee River Freshwater Pearl Farm and Museum* (255 Marina Rd.; 731-584-7880; tennesseeriverpearls.com) is located in the Birdsong Resort and Marina, along the river just outside Camden. There are pontoon boat tours of the operation and a jewelry shop inside the marina that features the cultured pearls. The story behind the procedure—how river mussels are implanted with pieces of shell and how those pieces grow into pearls inside the mussels through a "secret process"—is explained by the experts.

Talented country music star **Patsy Cline** was killed on March 5, 1963, when her airplane crashed about 2.5 miles northwest of Camden. Today there's a small monument marking the spot, way off the main road, down a gravel path. The monument was set up to honor Cline and those killed with her: Cowboy Copas, Hawkshaw Hawkins, and Randy Hughes. There's also a gazebo with newspaper articles describing the careers of the stars and the monument itself.

The monument is located deep in the woods 12 miles north of I-40, off US 641. Just north of US 70, turn west on Mt. Carmel Road at the Shell gas station; go 3 miles, then turn right onto a gravel road. Be careful and don't go too far—there's a big dropoff at the end of the path. Country music fans, call (731) 584-8395 or visit bentoncountycamden.com.

There's no place better than an organized wildlife refuge to observe that area's wildlife population, and the **Tennessee National Wildlife Refuge** (731-642-2091) is no exception. Nature trails, paved roads, and observation points are plentiful in this 80-mile-long stretch along the Tennessee River. The area is an important resting and feeding place for migrating waterfowl each winter.

Beginning about mid-October, up to 100,000 Canada geese and 250,000 ducks start their annual fall trek to the refuge, where they will spend the winter safe and warm—and well fed. The major attraction here for the animals is the farming program, which provides them with a great deal of food all winter long.

In addition to the waterfowl, the refuge is home for more than 200 species of birds, a fact that brings in serious birders from all over the country. Maps,

AUTHOR'S TOP TEN PICKS

Buford Pusser Home & Museum	Sun Studio
Danny Thomas Grave & Gardens	Tennessee River Folklife Center
Dixie Gun Works and Old Car Museum	Tennessee River Freshwater Pearl Farm and Museum
Graceland	Trenton Teapot Collection
Mindfield Outdoor Sculpture	West Tennessee Strawberry Festival

brochures, and specific wildlife information are available. Open Mon through Fri year-round. Don't miss this refuge.

For more information on Camden, Holladay, and the rest of Benton County, call (731) 584-8395 or log on to bentoncountycamden.com.

In nearby **Paris** the self-proclaimed **world's biggest fish fry** (paris chamber.com) is held each April. Since the early 1950s, the city has hosted the event at the fairgrounds and has achieved a well-deserved reputation for the quality of its catfish dinners and the traditional Tennessee way of preparing them.

Each year more than 5 tons of catfish are cooked in black pots containing more than 250 gallons of vegetable oil. The 4-day event also includes a rodeo, a carnival, a 2-hour parade, and a fishing rodeo.

Here it is, a sugar heaven if ever we tasted one! With more than 100 varieties of freshly made candies, **Sally Lane's Candy Farm** (731-642-5801; sally lanes.com) is a stop well worth making in the Paris area. Founded in 1958, the store has customers who regularly drive up to a couple of hours to get here. In addition, people in 48 states use mail order to receive their treats, which range from hand-dipped chocolates to hard candies to the famous Kentucky Lake Frog—a chocolate, caramel, and pecan concoction. Make sure you try the divinity; it's made from scratch and is totally awesome, as are most of the goodies. It's the store's pink and green mints, though, that put them on the map. "We literally make tons of mints each year," said candy makers and store owners Bobby and Shelby Freeman and Pan and Rick Rockwell. The candy is sold locally at 2215 Gum Springs Rd.

And what would Paris be without the **Eiffel Tower**? There's a 65-foot scale model of the famous structure standing at the entrance of Memorial Park on Volunteer Drive, east of downtown between Highway 69A and US 79.

The **E. W. Grove–Henry County High School** was the first privately funded public high school in the state. Known locally as the school "that came out of a bottle," the building was funded from the proceeds of "Grove's Tasteless Chill Tonic." Today the tower building houses the Henry County Board of Education and is located on Grove Boulevard, at the highest elevation in West Tennessee. Turn off Veterans Drive onto Dunlap Road, just north of US 79. Turn right onto Grove Boulevard and go to the top of the hill.

If you'd like to get a closer look at some of the historic structures in West Tennessee's oldest incorporated community, an audiotaped walking tour is available. CDs and maps can be had at the chamber of commerce, W. G. Rhea Library, and the Paris–Henry County Heritage Center at no charge. The chamber is located at 2508 E. Wood St. Call them at (731) 642-3431 or visit paristnchamber.com.

OTHER ATTRACTIONS WORTH SEEING

Britton Lane Battlefield
Jackson
(731) 935-2209
brittonlane1862.madison.tn.us

C.H. Nash Museum
Chucalissa Archaeological Site
Memphis
(901) 785-3160
memphis.edu/chucalissa

Fire Museum of Memphis
Memphis
(901) 320-5650
firemuseum.com

Memphis Botanic Garden
Memphis
(901) 576-4100
memphisbotanicgarden.com

Oaklawn Gardens
Germantown
(901) 757-7375

Gordon Browning's first driver's license is on display at the *Gordon Browning Museum* (640 N. Main St.; 731-352-3510; tn-roots/com/Gordon Browning) in the old post office building in downtown *McKenzie* in Carroll County. What makes that license so special is that it is Tennessee's first driver's license.

Browning got it because he happened to be governor of the state in 1938, when licenses were first required. In all, Browning served three terms as governor. He was also a US congressman and a chancery court judge, and he served in both world wars. By the looks of the quantity of the memorabilia on display, he never threw anything away. A flag that he brought back from World War I is on display, as are various other patriotic mementos.

The museum is a great small-town collection dedicated to the life of the county's favorite son. It gives a good perspective on the values that he and the curator of the museum deemed important.

The museum is open Mon, Tues, Thurs, and Fri 9 a.m. to 4 p.m. Admission is free.

Actress *Dixie Carter* was born and raised in *McLemoresville*, population 311. Even though she left town and became a successful star, she would come back home each year for several weeks to enjoy Tennessee and her family and friends. She died April 10, 2010. Her house is just off the little business section, and just about anyone around can point it out to you.

When bare-knuckled pugilism was popular and legal in America during the first half of the 19th century, one area of Gibson County was well known for its unique version of prizefighting sans gloves. *Skullbone* and the surrounding *Kingdom of Skullbonia* hosted a type of fighting that became known as skullboning. All bare-knuckled punches had to be delivered to the head. Hits below the collar were not permitted and were considered fouls. To "play," fighters would stand opposite each other and take turns trading blows. Each round lasted until one fell to the ground. The match lasted until one was satisfied that he had had enough. After bare-knuckled fighting became illegal in America and communities went "underground" for the excitement, matches in Skullbone continued to be held in the open. When adoption of standard rules for prizefighting occurred in 1866, non-gloved activities died out just about everywhere except Skullbone, where it continued well into the 20th century.

Today just about all that remains of Skullbone is the former general store, built in 1848. The store closed in March 2019, but the outside of the building is quite a landmark. With its map of the Kingdom of Skullbonia painted on one side and various soft drink signs and paintings on the front, it makes it impossible for any stranger to drive by without stopping to investigate. Across the street a stacked row of directional road and mileage signs points the way to worldly centers such as Singapore 9,981 miles; Anchorage 3,320 miles; and Shades Bridge 1 mile. Skullbone isn't on most maps, but it's located on Highway 105 about 3 miles from Bradford.

It's amazing that just 3 miles away from the skullbone capital of the world one can find the **Doodle Soup Capital** of that same world. What is Doodle Soup? It's a spicy, cold-weather dish. It's actually more of a sauce or gravy than it is a real soup. One of the most popular methods of eating it is by pouring it over a plateful of cracker crumbs or homemade biscuits and letting it soak in for a while before eating.

Here is one of the "official" recipes. Be forewarned: There has been a battle going on for years as to which of the myriad recipes floating around should be considered official. Take a large broiler chicken. Melt butter and run it all over the chicken. Put in broiler pan, split-side down; salt to taste. Put in oven at 375 degrees; let cook until brown and tender; take chicken out of the drippings that were cooked in the pan. Add 11 cups of water, 1 cup vinegar, plenty of hot peppers, and 3 tablespoons of cornstarch so it won't be just like water and will stay on the biscuits. Let cook until it gets as hot as you want. Taste it along. Although Doodle Soup is a local tradition, most locals haven't eaten it, saying it sounds too greasy.

At the **Trenton Teapot Museum** (309 College St.) in **Trenton**, you'll find the world's largest collection of 18th- and 19th-century night-light teapots (*veilleuses-théières*). A New York doctor, originally from Trenton, was going to give his multimillion-dollar collection of 525 pieces to the Metropolitan Museum of Art in New York City, but his brother convinced him to give them to his hometown instead.

TOP ANNUAL EVENTS

JANUARY

Elvis Presley Birthday Celebration
Memphis
(800) 238-2000
graceland.com

APRIL

Teapot Festival
Trenton
(731) 855-2013
teapotcollection.com

MAY

Memphis in May International Festival
Memphis
(901) 525-4611
memphisinmay.org

Tennessee Iris Festival
Dresden
(731) 364-2270
tennesseeirisfestival.net

West Tennessee Strawberry Festival
Humboldt
(731) 784-1842
strawberryfestivaltn.com

JUNE

Shannon Street MusicFest
Jackson
(731) 427-7573

JULY

Savannah Bluegrass Festival
Savannah
(800) 552-3866

SEPTEMBER

Saltillo River Day
Saltillo
(731) 925-8181
Tourhardincounty.org

Originally displayed in the trophy cases at the local high school, the unique Trenton Teapot Collection found a permanent home when a new city building was built. The teapots now line the walls of the city building's chambers. If you get there during regular business hours between 9 a.m. and 5 p.m., you're welcome to walk around and study this one-of-a-kind collection. Admission is free.

The teapot website offers great photos of the collection and has information about the well-attended annual *Teapot Festival* (731-855-2013; teapot collection.com).

No one seems to know why it was done in the first place more than 10 years ago, but there are no 30 mph signs in Trenton. They are all 31 mph signs. "I have no idea, but I think it's kind of cool. We get a lot of publicity out of it, like in *Tennessee Off the Beaten Path*," laughed one city official when asked about the signs.

Up US 45W from Trenton is *Rutherford*, where a former *David Crockett Cabin* (731-665-7166; goahead.org) is open to the public. David (as residents prefer him to be called) moved to the area in 1823. His original cabin, built

5 miles east of town along the Obion River, was dismantled and stored with the intent of rebuilding it at a later date near where his mother is buried. But before it could be rebuilt, some of the logs were used in fires by campers.

Some of the logs were saved, though, and are now a part of the reproduction of that original cabin. On display are tools, furniture, and utensils from the period, as are letters that Crockett wrote home during his years in Congress. The grave of Rebecca Hawkins Crockett, Davy's mother, is next to the log home.

The cabin is open Tues through Sat 9 a.m. to 5 p.m., Sun 1 to 4:30 p.m. from Memorial Day to Labor Day. It's located on the city's grammar school property on US 45N at 219 N. Trenton St. Open daily; admission is $2 for adults, $1 for children, and $5 for a family.

For more information on Trenton, Rutherford, and the rest of Gibson County, contact the chamber of commerce at (731) 855-0973 or gibsoncountytn.com.

Farther up US 45W you'll find an amazing colony of **white squirrels**, one of only a few such colonies in the world. As you enter **Kenton**, a town of about 1,500 residents, you'll be greeted by a big sign proclaiming KENTON: HOME OF THE WHITE SQUIRRELS. Although the exact number is hard to pinpoint, as most white squirrels look alike, the city's official stance is that about 200 of the critters live here. The squirrels are fed by just about everybody, and there's a $50 fine if you kill one.

A wildlife biologist explains that the animals are actually "albino gray squirrels who have survived for so many years because the people have taken such good care of them." They have inbred for so long that the normally recessive albino trait has become predominant.

Exactly how the first such squirrels came to the area about 120 years ago is the subject of a great many speculations. The most common theory is that during the early 1870s a band of gypsies spent the night on a local farm. The next morning, in appreciation of the farmer's kindness, the leader of the gypsies presented two white squirrels to the farmer. Thus it began.

The best time to see the flock (bevy? herd?) of white squirrels is in the morning and evening, when they are most apt to be scurrying from tree to tree. Stop by the city hall, which also informally serves as a white squirrel visitor information bureau.

Across Gibson County from Kenton is **Humboldt**, home of the **West Tennessee Strawberry Festival** each May. It features a big parade, which is promoted as the longest nonmotorized parade in the nation; a street dance; a checkers tournament; a strawberry recipe contest; and a carnival with all sorts of family and kiddie amusement rides, plus any kind of strawberry-flavored food you can think of.

A museum for a strawberry festival? Yep, this may be the only one of its kind. The **West Tennessee Historical/Strawberry Festival Museum** (1200 Main St.; 731-420-1316; humboldttnmuseum.weebly.com) is on the first floor of the 1912 restored neoclassical building that once served as city hall. The museum salutes local Humboldt history as well as the history of the popular festival, from its beginning in 1934 to its latest event. Open Mon through Wed 2 p.m. to 4 p.m. or by appointment.

The **West Tennessee Regional Arts Center** (731-784-1787; wtrac.tn.org) is on the upper floors, over the strawberry exhibits. It represents works of regional artists throughout Tennessee as well as surrounding states, including Red Grooms, Paul Harmon, Carroll Cloar, and Gilbert Gaul. The valuable collection was owned by a local doctor who donated it in honor of his parents and for the aesthetic education of students of all ages.

The arts center is open Mon through Fri 9 a.m. to 4:30 p.m. Open Sat and Sun only during special events. Admission is free.

Crockett County was established in 1871 and named in honor of the famed Tennessee frontiersman Davy Crockett. The county seat of the 14,000 residents of the county is Alamo, where the *Crockett Times* newspaper at 46 W. Main St. has been published for more almost 150 years. Get more info at (731) 696-4558.

Crockett had already been killed when the county was formed, so when it came to finding a name for it, locals thought naming an entire county for the man would be an appropriate tribute. Cageville was renamed Alamo and became the county's center.

Crockett never lived in the county, and there is no record that he ever visited here, but the people are proud of their living monument to one of the state's best-known sons.

Carl Perkins, Elvis Presley, Roy Orbison, and all the other rockabilly stars are honored in Jackson's **International Rockabilly Hall of Fame** (105 N. Church St.; 731-427-6262; rockabillyhall.org). The history of the genre is told on tape and film by the stars themselves. One of the most unusual objects on display might be the heart paddles and defibrillator said to have been used on Elvis before he was pronounced dead on August 16, 1977.

The founder of the facility, Henry Harrison, once told me that Jackson is the only place in the world where this facility should be located. "West Tennessee is the birthplace of rockabilly. It all started here and spread through the world. The roots are right here," he said, adding that the attraction is "located halfway between Graceland [in Memphis] and the Grand Ole Opry [in Nashville]." Harrison died April 22, 2019. He was 82 years old.

Tennessee's Only Archeofest

A unique two-day festival takes place each fall deep in the heart of Pinson Mounds State Archaeological Park. **Archeofest** is a celebration of Native American culture and archaeology and features Native American dancers, haywagon tours, storytelling, Native American foods and crafts, wildlife programs, flint knapping, and artifact identification. And it's all free. Pinson Mounds is a 1,086-acre prehistoric Indian ceremonial center containing the second-highest mound in the US. The fest takes place the third weekend of September. Located off US 45, south of I-40, southeast of Jackson. Call (731) 988-5614.

A huge 28-foot-by-66-foot mural outside the Rockabilly Hall of Fame features Carl Perkins and his band members, brothers Jay and Clayton Perkins, and other rockabilly artists. Look closely and you can see Paul McCartney in the painting. The Beatle was a great fan of Carl Perkins, and Harrison said McCartney was honored to be included.

The museum is open Tues through Thurs 10 a.m. to 3 p.m.; Fri and Sat 10 a.m. to 2 p.m. A live band and line dancing classes are offered some evenings. Visit their website for a great video on the history of rockabilly music.

Right off Courthouse Square, the **West Tennessee Farmers' Market** (91 New Market St.; 731-425-8308) features fresh-from-the-garden produce and flowers during the growing season. Located at New Market Street and North College, the covered market is open daily except Sun and Mon and features various activities and festivals during the year.

Jackson's original **Greyhound Bus Terminal** (731-427-1573) is still in operation and as beautiful as ever in its 1920s art deco glory. Several movies have been filmed here, and it's a popular spot for still photographers from all over the mid-South at 407 E. Main St across from city hall at North Cumberland.

A few blocks from downtown Jackson, on the left side of S. Royal Street just after you cross the railroad tracks, is the site of the city's first modern waterworks at 604 S. Royal St. During its construction in the mid-1880s, one of the area's most prolific underground mineral rivers was discovered. By the early 1900s, thousands were visiting and drinking water from this artesian well, searching for a cure for their stomach, liver, and kidney ailments. Today the powerful **Electro Chalybeate Well** still bubbles forth inside a gazebo built adjacent to the city's restored art deco water plant. A small park separates the well from the railroad tracks. For information or directions contact the chamber of commerce at (731) 423-2200 or visit online at jacksontn.com.

On the other side of the tracks is a local railroad museum, created inside the restored century-old depot. The city purchased the depot from the railroad, which had not used it for 20 years and had plans to tear it down. Restoration was completed in 1994, and it was opened as a museum in late 1995. Inside are exhibits, photos, a model railroad, and other memorabilia that tell the story of the five different railroads that serviced Jackson through the years. Known locally as the *N.C. & St. L Railroad Depot* (582 S. Royal St.; 731-425-8223; jacksonrecandparks.com), the museum is open Mon through Sat 10 a.m. to 3 p.m. Admission is free.

A very pleasant place to stay while you're in this area is the *Highland Place Bed and Breakfast* (519 N. Highland Ave.; 731-427-1472 or 877-614-6305). Innkeepers Cindy and Bill Pflaum have created quite an elegant home that is convenient to downtown Jackson. It's a traditional colonial revival mansion, circa 1911, with 10-foot-wide hallways, towering ceilings, an elegant center stairway, and a warm, very studious-feeling cherry-paneled library. Old French Country pine furniture and comfortable couches dominate the huge living room. The modern 4 guest rooms have private baths, Internet access, and a wide choice of books, and CDs. No smoking or pets. Rooms run $125 to $175 per night, full breakfast included.

"Come all you rounders if you want to hear a story about a brave engineer." That's the beginning of the tale of Casey Jones, an engineer who became a legend after being killed in a much-publicized train crash. The *Casey Jones Home and Railroad Museum* (731-668-1223 or 800-748-9588; caseyjones .com) tells the story of that fateful night. Casey was at the throttle of "Old 382" when it approached a stalled train on the same track near Vaughn, Mississippi, on April 30, 1900. The fireman jumped and yelled to Casey to do the same, but instead he stayed on and valiantly tried to stop the train. He didn't succeed, but he slowed it down enough so that he was the only casualty of the wreck. The engineer immediately became a folk hero, and his story has been recounted for more than a century in story and song.

Casey was living in Jackson at the time of his death. His home has since been moved and now serves as the centerpiece of the museum, located in Jackson's *Casey Jones Village* on the US 45 Bypass, just off I-40 at 30 Casey Jones Lane. Open daily Mon through Fri 10 a.m. to 4:30 p.m., Sat 9 a.m. to 5 p.m., Sun 1 p.m. to 5 p.m. year-round; admission is $6.50 for adults, $5.50 for seniors, $4.50 for children ages 6 to 12, and free for children ages 5 and under.

In addition to the museum, the village contains specialty shops and *Brooks Shaw's Old Country Store and Restaurant*, a country restaurant complete with an 1890s-style soda fountain and a large gift shop.

Walking into Brooks Shaw's Old Country Store is literally a step back in time to the 1890s. Brooks Shaw was an American picker before his time who would be right at home on the popular TV show. The walls are adorned with antiques. More antiques hang from the ceiling. It takes time just to stand and admire everything that is there. Shaw traveled around the back roads of West Tennessee in the early 1960s to collect his treasures. He found them in dilapidated barns, in antique shops all over the South, wherever his fancy took him. Shaw family outings often turned into treasure hunts for some little gem. It started as a relaxing hobby, turned into a passion, and resulted in one of the South's largest private antique collections. Opened in 1965 as an antique museum, the Old County Store evolved into an always-packed Dixie Café restaurant serving southern favorites.

When I first saw the dilapidated **Providence House** that the Shaw family had moved to Casey Jones Village, I wondered how in the world they could salvage it. Well, they certainly have. Providence House has seen a wealth of history and is now set for even more. Until 2010, this home stood in Trenton, Tennessee, 30 miles north of Casey Jones Village. Townspeople climbed to its roof in 1862 to witness the Civil War Battle of Trenton.

But in recent years, the house was fighting a losing battle of its own and seemed doomed for demolition. Then Clark Shaw and his wife Juanita stepped in. The couple had the house moved behind the Old Country Store and Restaurant and beautifully renovated. Now it can be used for special events and will be pivotal in living history reenactments. The house is also a favorite photo site for visitors.

The Shaws then added still another special spot. More than a century old, the **Village Chapel** has been relocated to Casey Jones Village from Haywood County. Formerly known as the Brown's Creek Primitive Baptist Church, the church now has a steeple, complete with an antique bell and is open to the public as a place of prayer and contemplation. The restaurant has become quite famous for its three daily all-you-can-eat buffets. The breakfast buffet plus drinks costs $7.99 Mon through Thurs, $9.99 on Fri, Sat, and Sun. The luncheon buffet plus drinks is $11.99 Mon through Thurs, $11.99 on Fri and Sat, and $14.99 on Sun; the dinner selection plus drinks is $11.99 Mon through Thurs, $14.99 on Fri, Sat, and Sun.

Outside, in addition to the Casey Jones Museum, there's a train store, a well-shaded and well-run miniature golf course, the Casey Jones Village Amphitheatre, and a bunch of shops, including a tourist information center. Live bluegrass music is often offered free.

Covering 48,000 acres, the **Natchez Trace State Resort Park and Forest** (731-968-3742; tnstateparks.com) is Tennessee's largest state-run facility. It

Rusty's TV and Movie Car Museum

Growing up in the 1980s, Rusty Robinson says he was as enamored of the vehicles roaring across movie screens as other viewers might have been of the actors. "The car was a big a part of the show to me," he said. "I think a lot of other people feel the same way."

Robinson must be right. **Rusty's TV and Movie Car Museum** (323 Hollywood Dr.; 731-267-5881; rustystvandmoviecars.com) in Jackson draws people from around the world. "People from other countries love David Hasselhoff," he said. "They always want to see Kitt, the car David Hasselhoff drove in *Knight Rider*."

Robinson has been collecting automobiles since he was a teen. One of his first prized possessions was a General Lee, a red '69 Dodge Charger driven by the Duke cousins, Bo and Luke, in the television series *The Dukes of Hazzard*. Over the years his collection grew, and folks started stopping by his home to see their favorite vehicles. That's when Robinson decided he had better open a museum.

"I've gotten to meet all kinds of different people at the museum," he said, noting that group tours are welcome and parking is free and easy. "You'd be surprised how many people of all ages like to see these cars."

Robinson has about 30 vehicles in his museum and he usually serves as the guide, sharing little tidbits about each car. Celebrity cars (or replicas) include a *Ghostbusters* ambulance, *Death Race* Mustang, *Death Proof* killer car 1970 Chevy Nova, *Blues Brothers* Bluesmobile, *Batman* Batcycle, *Herbie the Love Bug*, Scooby Doo's Mystery Machine, *The Fast and the Furious*, *Back to the Future*, and the 1976 AMC Pacer from *Wayne's World*.

One of the museum's newest vehicles is the original red 1978 Chevy Monte Carlo driven by Jesse in the *Breaking Bad* series. For his "dream" vehicle, Robinson yearns for the 1967 Shelby Mustang GT500 gunned by Nicholas Cage in the movie *Gone in 60 Seconds*.

"That one sold for half a million the last time it sold so I know it is out of my price range," Robinson said. "But I can watch the movie and dream about it."

is cared for by three state agencies. The Division of State Parks cares for the people, the Tennessee Division of Forestry cares for the trees, and the Tennessee Wildlife Resources Agency cares for the animals.

The massive park, with its lakes, trails, and heavily forested areas, is a success story for one of President Franklin D. Roosevelt's New Deal programs. When the US Department of Agriculture acquired the land in the early 1930s, the area was some of the most heavily abused and eroded land in the state. The area's occupants were relocated, and a "Land-Use Area" project was set up to demonstrate how wasteland could again be made productive through proper conservation practices.

This is an interesting place to explore, with its three lakes, miles of hiking and equestrian trails, and plenty of off-the-beaten-path solitude.

There are three active churches within the park's borders. One of them, **Mt. Comfort Missionary Baptist Church**, was founded in 1846 by the great-grandfather of Gene Autry, the singing cowboy. Tombstones in the adjacent cemetery date back to 1830. In all, there are 25 cemeteries in the park. All are marked and allow visitors.

There are plenty of lodging opportunities here. The **Pin Oak Lodge** (567 Pin Oak Lodge Rd.; 800-250-8616), located next to the 700-acre Pin Oak Lake, offers 47 modern rooms. Nearby are 10 2-bedroom cabins, offering great views of the lake. There are also 17 rustic cabins, 5 camping cabins, an RV camp-ground with full hookups, and plenty of rustic camping throughout the park.

On May 5, 1999, a windstorm leveled 7,200 acres of trees, but Mother Nature is slowly reforesting the area. The roads were cleared, but the forest areas are being left alone to reforest themselves.

Each April, coon hunters gather at the Decatur County fairgrounds just south of Parsons on Highway 69 to take part in an event that is billed as the **world's largest coon hunt**. Depending on the year and the weather, about 600 hunters from 35 states come here to hunt for the state's "official" animal, the raccoon.

This is basically a competition for dogs, so no guns are allowed and no coons are hurt. The hunter with the dog who does the best "tracking and tree-ing" goes away as the winner. Since coons are nocturnal, most of the action on this weekend takes place at night. A country band plays until 3 a.m., and the local Jaycees keep their concession stands open around the clock for the entire weekend.

The event is considered to be the biggest independent fund-raiser for St. Jude Children's Research Hospitalin Memphis. More than $100,000 is raised and donated each year. Over $4.5 million dollars have been donated from this event in more than 40 years.

Down the road apiece, where Highway 100 meets US 412, is the little river-side community of **Perryville**. In town, up on the very top of Pentecostal Hill, the **Tennessee River Antiques-Flea Market** (545 Pentecostal Campground Rd.; 731-847-9383) does business year-round every Fri through Sun. The old church camp that now features more than 50 dealers within the 12,000-square-foot building. There's a big collection of antiques in here as well, including a lot of glassware. What a collector's heaven this is. You'll find some great stuff, and the best part, it's off the beaten path. Follow Pentecostal Camp Road to the top.

Southern Plains

The ***Shiloh National Military Park and Cemetery*** (1055 Pittsburg Landing Rd.; 731-689-5696; nps.gov/shil), 12 miles south of Savannah on Highway 22, is a grim reminder of how bloody the Civil War really was.

On April 6 and 7, 1862, the North and South fought the first major battle in the western theater of the war here, just a few miles north of the Mississippi state line. More than 23,000 soldiers died, about one-fourth of the total forces that fought. The casualties in this one battle exceeded the total American casualties from the nation's three preceding wars: the Revolutionary War, the War of 1812, and the Mexican War.

Known as Bloody Shiloh, the battle went down in the history books as one of the most gruesome in all American warfare. The park was established in 1894 and includes the battlefield and environs. A 9-mile self-guided auto tour highlights the battle and explains the various monuments that have been erected. The visitor center has a library and a museum complete with relics and maps and a movie explaining the battle. Open daily, year-round 8 a.m. to 5 p.m. for the Visitor Center and Interpretive Center. Grounds are open daily from sunrise to sunset. Don't miss this historic site.

For a month prior to Shiloh, the Union forces, under the leadership of Gen. Ulysses S. Grant, used the grounds of ***Cherry Mansion*** (265 W. Main St.; 731-925-8181), in nearby Savannah, as Union headquarters. Tents were set up in the yard, and Grant slept in the house and dined with the Cherry family. He was eating breakfast on April 6 when he got word of the battle of Shiloh.

Built in 1830, the house is the oldest structure in Savannah and is currently a private residence. There's a monument to General Grant 1 block east of the mansion.

The ***Tennessee River Museum*** (731-925-8181; tennesseerivermuseum .org) in Savannah is a tribute both to the Tennessee River—from Paducah, Kentucky, to Muscle Shoals, Alabama—and to the influences it has had on the people who lived and worked along it. Several exhibit areas include displays on the early steamboats that plied the river, paleontology, archaeology, the Civil War, and a great collection of locally made musical instruments. Several gunboats are on display. Officials say their ceremonial Shiloh Effigy Pipe is world famous. Located in the old post office building at 495 Main St., the museum is open daily year-round, Mon through Sat 9 a.m. to 5 p.m., Sun 1 p.m. to 5 p.m. Admission is $3 for adults, free for children.

Both ***Saltillo*** and ***Cerro Gordo*** were named for Mexican communities by soldiers returning to their Tennessee farmlands following the Mexican War. Homes throughout the area date back to the 1840s and include an eclectic assortment of architecture, from early farmhouse to Greek Revival. Several cemeteries predate the Civil War. A brochure listing 17 points of interest in Saltillo is available from city hall.

The signs along US 64 outside **Adamsville** proclaim the community to be the **biggest little town in Tennessee**. A lot of that obvious pride may come from the fact that the town was home to one of America's most celebrated lawmen, Buford Pusser.

Pusser, who died in an auto accident in 1974, is immortalized in the **Buford Pusser Home & Museum** (342 Pusser St.; 731-632-4080; buford pussermuseum.com). He was sheriff of McNairy County from 1964 to 1970 and had the reputation of a no-nonsense, hard-nosed lawman. The exploits of this 6-foot, 6-inch tall, 250-pound "legend" were the basis of the three *Walking Tall* movies.

Today in the quiet residential area that he called home, his brick ranch house is overflowing with artifacts of his life. Following his death, his mother allowed nothing to be removed. Opened officially in 1988 as a museum, the facility is owned and operated by the city. Everything from his credit cards to his toothbrush to the roll of $100 bills he had in his pocket when he was killed are on display. An advertisement from a mattress company rests on his bed. "Big Buford Bedding, designed to honor a man who walked tall in Tennessee."

The years he spent as sheriff were hard ones on this "soft-spoken country gentleman." He was shot eight times, knifed seven times, and gunned down in an ambush that killed his wife. Many residents believe the flaming auto crash that took his life was no accident.

According to the museum's hostess, Pusser was constantly on guard and often remarked that he was "on borrowed time." His home is a reflection of that attitude. He had a special entrance built on the lower level, where his underground bedroom and living quarters were. He slept with his head against the earthen wall to help protect himself against the continuous threats.

In addition to his personal belongings, numerous scrapbooks of newspaper clippings, a videotape of television interviews, and a copy of his 1956 high school yearbook are on display. Admission to the museum is $10 for adults, $8 for seniors, $3 for children ages 7 to 17. For extra fun, plan your visit for the last weekend in May. That's when the **Buford Pusser Festival** takes place, with live music and a carnival.

Up Highway 224 near Leapwood, the **Coon Creek Science Center** (2983 Hardins Graveyard Rd.; 901-636-2362; cooncreek.ontheinter.net) reveals that this whole area was under a sea about 70 million years ago. The center, opened in 1989, is owned and operated by the Memphis Museum System, although it is more than 100 miles from that city.

When emptied, the warm, shallow ocean left behind an abundance of unusual and significant geological treasures. The marine shells found here in the bottomlands are not actually fossils but the real things, since they have not undergone the process of mineralization and have not turned to stone. The clay of the area has preserved the shells in their original form.

Known as the Coon Creek fossil formation, the entire area attracts geologists from all over the world. The center has been established to preserve the area and to provide an educational facility for the study of the earth sciences.

little-knownfacts abouttennessee

One of the toughest-fought elections in the state took place in 1933 during the election to determine which bird should be the Tennessee State Bird. More than 72,000 votes were registered, with the mockingbird edging out the robin by 450 votes.

Various educational exhibits and programs have been established and are available for groups of 15 or more. If you're not in a specific group and want to see the place, the center sponsors several "family days" during the year when individuals can sign up for a program.

The hog is king at **Pappy Johns Original Barbecue** (731-645-4353; pappy-johns-original barbecue.business.site) on US 45 South a few miles outside Selmer at 3597 US 45. Here you've got to be hungry for pork or chicken, because that's all they have. No burgers, no fries. Open daily, a good deal of the business here is takeout, but if you enjoy eating near the hickory pits where the cooking is done, there are tables inside.

Hardeman County's first courthouse, now known as the **Little Court House Museum** (731-518-7148), was built in 1824, making it one of the oldest original courthouses in western Tennessee. Located at 215 E. Market St. in Bolivar, the restored structure now houses the county museum.

The original part of the existing building was a 2-story log structure that served as the courthouse. In 1827 the building was purchased and moved to its current site, where additions were made to the log structure. It was converted into a family residence in 1849 and more additions were made, turning it into a large federal-style home.

The building itself is worth the stop, but some of the items inside highlighting this county's past are fascinating in themselves. Open every second and fourth Sat 10 a.m. to 2 p.m. or by appointment. Admission is $5 for adults and $2 for children.

Another historic structure in Bolivar is **The Pillars** (522 S. Washington St.; 731-518-7148), former home of John Houston Bills, one of the original settlers of West Tennessee. Built prior to 1826, the building saw the likes of James K. Polk, Davy Crockett, Gen. Ulysses S. Grant, and Sam Houston. Open by appointment or chance; admission is $5 per person.

Over on US 64 at 16030 US 64 in Somerville, you'll find a real gem. The **Tennessee Pewter Company** (901-465-2609; tnpewter.com) is the only commercial producer of a full line of pewter products in the South. Pewtersmith Kathleen Armour Walker works to create new items while preserving traditional pieces. Pewter was widely used from the Middle Ages to the 19th century until glass and porcelain began to be mass produced. After that, pewter was used more for heirlooms and decorative items. An alloy of tin, copper, and antimony, pewter is completely lead free and never tarnishes. No more silver cleaning with pewter.

The small community of Grand Junction, located near the point where Highway 57 is joined by Highway 368, is known throughout the world as the home of the **National Field Trial Championships**. Held nearby at the 18,600-acre Ames Plantation since 1896, the annual February event is often called the Super Bowl of Bird Dogs.

The competition lasts 8 to 10 days, with the winning dog earning the title of World Champion Bird Dog. Hunting mostly for quail, the dogs and handlers are followed by a large gallery of spectators on horseback. Ames Plantation, located 4.3 miles off Highway 18 just north of Highway 57 at 4275 Buford Ellington Rd., is not only synonymous with the quest for canine excellence, it also plays an integral part in the University of Tennessee's livestock and agriculture program. The facility is one of the 11 branch experimental stations in the university's system. Built in 1847, the magnificent **Ames Manor House & Plantation** (901-878-1067; amesplantation.org) is open for tours on the fourth Thurs afternoon of each month, Mar through Oct, 12:30 to 4 p.m., with a $2 admission charged. Adjacent to the manor house is a small collection of original log cabins that have been moved here to create a small farmstead, which is open daily.

Across the street from Dunn's is the **Field Trial Hall of Fame** and **National Wildlife Heritage Center** (731-764-2058; birddogfoundation.com). It was created by the Bird Dog Foundation; the dedication plaque reads: DEDICATED TO PRESERVING THE PAST, PROTECTING THE FUTURE FOR SPORTING DOG FANCIERS THE WORLD OVER.

Films, paintings of some of the most famous bird dogs of the past hundred years, artifacts, literature, photography, and other memorabilia are featured here and help tell the story of the talents of well-trained bird dogs. If you're not familiar with any of this, don't worry; the folks working here are more than eager to share their love of the sport and of the dogs with you. Closed Mon; admission is free.

Heading toward Memphis on Highway 57, you'll find *LaGrange*, a quaint little village that has been able to avoid the commercialization that the others have fallen to along this busy highway corridor. In addition to a couple of antiques shops, the streets are lined with a plethora of well-kept little white cottages with green shutters and trim. Settled in 1819 on the site of an Indian trading post, the town was named for General Lafayette's ancestral home in France. Translated to mean "beautiful village," it was occupied by Union forces from 1862 to 1865. It was an antebellum center of wealth, education, and culture, having had two colleges, four academies, two newspapers, and 3,000 residents in 1862.

The best way to get into Memphis from this part of the state is to continue west on Highway 57. If you do that, you'll go through *Collierville*, a neat little community with a historic town square and a countless number of antiques shops and unique eateries. Along the square, which serves as a gathering place for the locals, the *Fair on the Square* takes place in May each year, and a free *Sunset Concert Series* is held every Thurs evening during June and July. For more information on this sleepy little suburban community, call the chamber of commerce at (901) 853-1949 or go to colliervillechamber.com.

The Delta Region

With a population of about 650,000, *Memphis* rests along the Mississippi River and is one of the river's largest inland ports. Among many other things, the city is famous for its impact on the development of popular American music as well as the blues. For a good overview of the area call (888) 633-9099 or visit memphistravel.com.

The history of music in the Memphis area revolves around the King of Rock 'n' Roll, *Elvis Presley*. Although he died in 1977, Elvis is even more popular today than when he was alive, and his estate is worth much more now (between $200 and $400 million) than it was when he died ($4.9 million) because of his home (Graceland Mansion), souvenir and tourist shops, and museums. Estate revenues were topping $15 million annually by the late 1980s, more than the singer made in any one year of his career.

Graceland Mansion (3734 Elvis Presley Blvd.; 901-332-3322 or 800-238-2000; graceland.com) is one of the many unique places in the state where the beaten path catches up with the unbeaten one. There's nothing like this anywhere else in the world, and it shouldn't be missed. Elvis and members of his family are buried here in the Meditation Garden, and tours of the mansion

Graceland—Where Elvis Lives

"Welcome to my world," Elvis sings as our shuttle crosses the street to enter the musical gates of **Graceland** in Memphis. The former home of Elvis is a strange bubble in time.

It is not near as grand as many visitors think it would be. Rock stars and other entertainers have far more elaborate homes today. It is a tribute that Elvis chose to live in his hometown—and he is still a powerful source of income for Memphis area residents.

The last time Elvis walked through the Graceland doors, it was 1977. Times have changed, a Graceland guide points out. Fashions have changed.

Graceland hasn't.

It is a blend of the '50s, '60s and '70s. It is a poor boy's idea of luxury, a gift he promised his parents they would have one day.

Legend goes that when Elvis Presley was a youngster, he told his parents he would grow up to make a lot of money and buy them the finest house in town. He would take care of them and end his parents' years of poverty and struggle, Elvis vowed. At age 22, Elvis did just that. Elvis bought Graceland in 1957 for $102,500 in cash after topping his record-breaking music success with the film "Loving You."

Built in 1939 and named for its former owner's great-aunt, Grace Toof, Graceland was the American Dream come true for Elvis and his family. Although he hired an interior decorator, Elvis used his own tastes instead. What you see is what he was.

The tour starts off across the street at Elvis Presley's Memphis, a $45 million, 200,000-square-foot entertainment complex. It is five times the size of the previous complex which opened in 1982. Shuttle buses take visitors from the new complex across the street to Graceland.

Before you even head to the mansion, you can spend hours at Elvis Presley's Memphis. Attractions include the Elvis Presley Automobile Museum which features more than 20 of Elvis's automobile and motorized vehicles and has a small theater area showing Elvis movie clips on cars and racing.

On display is the iconic 1955 pink Cadillac that Elvis bought for his mother Gladys, even though she didn't have a driver's license. A sleek 1973 Stutz Blackhawk in the museum was the last car Elvis was driving when he drove through the gates of Graceland for the last time on August 16, 1977. A photo shows Elvis waving to fans. He died later that day.

The cornerstone of the new complex is "Elvis: The Entertainer" featuring hundreds of artifacts of Elvis's life and career from his childhood in Tupelo, Mississippi, his Sun Studio recordings, US Army service, Hollywood career, Las Vegas years, and much more.

Elvis Presley's Memphis also offers souvenir shops, coffee bar, ice cream shop, and two themed restaurants named for Elvis's parents. Gladys' Diner serves sandwiches, pizza, salads, and Elvis's favorite grilled peanut butter and banana sandwiches. Vernon's Smokehouse has authentic Memphis BBQ.

Although it's a major tourism mecca, the Graceland company allows nothing to be sold or advertised on the grounds of the mansion. All tickets, souvenirs, film, food, and other items are sold only in the visitor center across the street. Once you cross Elvis Presley Boulevard and enter the mansion grounds, you see Elvis's home the way he enjoyed it—as a sanctuary.

First on the tour is the formal part of Graceland—the foyer, dining room, living room, and music room. Not too glitzy, but rather cool and elegant. Just off the dining room is the kitchen—the heart of the home. The kitchen reflects Elvis's last remodeling in the '70s—dark wood cabinets and paneling, appliances in stainless steel or in classic harvest gold and avocado green.

One of the most infamous rooms is the nicknamed "Jungle Room." This room has prompted the most labels of poor taste that Elvis picked up along the way. In actuality, the room is fairly representative of the '60s, except it has a full-wall stone waterfall at one end. Here, Elvis recorded his 1976 album, *From Elvis Presley Boulevard, Memphis, Tennessee*, and over half of his last album, *Moody Blue*. In that last year, Elvis had RCA bring their equipment to him rather than going to a Nashville studio as usual.

In the backyard, visitors pass by the pasture where Elvis kept horses. An addition Elvis made to Graceland now houses his awards and mementos, along with telling the story of Elvis's life and career. The tour continues back outside, past the swimming pool to the racquetball building. It features a two-level lounge and racquetball court on the ground floor. Elvis was in this building just hours before his death.

At the last tour stop, visitors walk quietly through the Meditation Garden. Consisting of a curving brick wall with stained glass windows, a fountain and a semicircle of Greek-inspired columns, Elvis used the area as a private retreat through the years. It is now where he is buried.

are run daily year-round, except for Christmas, Thanksgiving, and New Year's Day. Guests are welcome to visit Meditation Garden daily for free from 7:30 a.m. to 8:30 a.m.

You'll get a chance to walk the grounds, see Elvis's Jungle Room, his mother's bedroom, the trophy building, and tour his private jet, the *Lisa Marie,* named for his daughter. You'll also have the opportunity to add to his estate at a variety of merchandise shops across the street from the mansion. It would be a good idea to make reservations, because the lines can get very long, especially during the summer months. Admission is charged.

Each year in mid-August Memphis hosts **Elvis Week**, an annual gathering of friends and fans from around the world celebrating Elvis's life and music career during the week surrounding the anniversary of his death on August 16,

1977. During Elvis Week, visitors experience concerts, tribute artists, movies, tours, Elvis insiders' conferences, and the famous Candlelight Vigil on the lawn of Graceland.

A beautiful place to spend the night while in Memphis is the new 450-room, $92 million resort, *The Guest House at Graceland* (3600 Elvis Presley Blvd.; 901-443-3000, guesthousegraceland.com). Located just steps from Graceland Mansion, the Guest House has five dining options, a 464-seat theater, outdoor pool, gift shop, and conference center. The Chapel in the Woods can be booked for weddings.

Inspired by Elvis's personal style and his iconic home, the Guest House shows free Elvis movies most nights in the theater and serves peanut butter and banana sandwiches with milk for a complimentary nightly snack for guests. Live music is featured many nights in the lobby, and the place is hopping during Elvis Week.

Sun Studio (706 Union Ave.; 800-441-6249; sunstudio.com), where Elvis recorded a song for his mother for $4, is open to the public. Founded by disc jockey Sam Phillips, Sun was the first studio to record such musicians as Presley, Jerry Lee Lewis, Carl Perkins, and Johnny Cash. The studio is located just a few blocks from Baptist Hospital, where Elvis was pronounced dead. The studio is open 7 days a week from 10 a.m. to 6 p.m., with 45-minute guided tours scheduled every hour on the half hour. Admission is $14 for adults, $12 for students, and free for children ages 5 to 11. Children under 5 are not permitted. The website has a wealth of information and some really great sounds recorded, of course, in Sun Studio.

A great way to travel between Graceland, Sun Studio, and the Rock 'n' Soul Museum is a free shuttle. You can pick up the shuttle at any of the three locations, but it might be best to park your car in the free lot behind Sun Studio and catch the shuttle there.

Beale Street, in downtown Memphis, is considered the spiritual home of the other type of music the city is famous for, the blues. During its heyday in the twenties and thirties, there wasn't a tougher, more swinging street in America. The zoot suit originated here, and Machine Gun Kelly peddled bootleg on the streets. Always a mecca for musicians, the street's nightclubs were frequented by the country's best blues artists, including the man known as the Father of the Blues, the legendary William Christopher (W. C.) Handy.

Today the street is once again a hot nightspot with numerous clubs, restaurants, and shops. And the best part is that the sound of the blues has not been forgotten. Several clubs now offer traditional blues and jazz, including the *Rum Boogie Cafe* (182 Beale St.; 901-528-0150; rumboogie.com) and *B. B. King's Blues Club* (143 Beale St.; 901-524-5464; bbkings.com/memphis).

Sun Studio: Birthplace of Rock 'N' Roll

When 18-year-old Elvis Presley walked into **Sun Studio** for the first time, he was asked who he sounded like. His reply, "I don't sound like nobody."

When he sang, "That's all right, momma," listeners agreed. Sun Studio became known as the birthplace of rock 'n' roll. "It was phenomenal," said studio tour guide Jason Freeman. "You're walking on hallowed ground when you come in here."

On July 5, 1954, Presley recorded his first single, "That's All Right," at Sun Studio. Sun Studio has changed little through the years. It has the same acoustic ceiling, the original lights, and the old floor that so many legends once trod—Presley, Jerry Lee Lewis, B.B. King, Rufus Thomas, Howlin' Wolf, Johnny Cash, Carl Perkins, and Roy Orbison, among others.

Radio engineer Sam Phillips started Sun Label in 1952 and shared his tiny office with his secretary Marion Keisker. Legend has it that Keisker is the one who was working when a young Presley plopped down $4 to make his first recording.

On a hot summer day in 1953, a shy Presley stopped by the studio to make a recording of "My Happiness." Local lore says the recording was intended as a birthday present for his mother. More likely, Freeman said, the teen was hoping to be discovered. He was yearning for stardom. And that's exactly what he found— more than anyone could ever dream.

So impressed was Keisker that she kept a backup tape of Presley's singing. In the studio log, Keisker noted Presley was a "good ballad singer." The story goes that Keisker pestered Phillips until he gave a listen to the unpolished Presley tape. The rest was history.

In the small studio, you can peek into the control room and stand behind the same kind of microphone Presley used. Playing in the background on an old Ampex tape deck are bits of songs recorded at Sun. Old instruments are scattered around the room. A guitar with a dollar bill stuffed between the strings is how Cash produced the "chuffing" sound to imitate trains on his recordings.

Ringo Starr has been quoted as saying, "If it hadn't been for what happened at Sun Studio, there wouldn't have been a Beatles."

There also might not have been an Elvis.

At the time, Presley was delivering electrical appliances for Crown Electric. "He probably stopped by here while he was out delivering or maybe after work," Freeman said. "Crown Electric was less than a mile from here so it was easy for Elvis to come by."

Without Sun Studio, would Presley have made that first recording? Would someone have noticed his talent and given him a chance? "That's something we'll never know," Freeman concluded. "What happened at Sun Studio was history."

Virtually unchanged through the years is **Schwab's** dry goods store (163 Beale St.; 901-523-9782; a-schwab.com), where a sign still hangs in the window proclaiming if you can't find it here, you're better off without it. The clerks still offer old-time service.

The Schwab family has created a museum, and having been on Beale Street since 1876, they have been able to collect quite a few memories of the "good ole days" to display. Upstairs, the store sells all sorts of items, from dream books to straw sailors to crystal balls to size 74 men's pants. Forty-four kinds of suspenders are kept in stock.

The **Memphis Rock 'n' Soul Museum** (191 Beale St.; 901-205-2533; memphisrocknsoul.org) is a true treasure and an intimate salute to the early soul music that permeated Memphis culture. The museum features the Smithsonian Institution's *Rock 'n' Soul: Social Crossroads* exhibit. Seven different galleries within the museum present a chronology of the hearts and souls that created the Memphis sound.

Those who helped create the Memphis Sound include Elvis Presley, Otis Redding, B. B. King, and Jerry Lee Lewis. The city's recording studios produced more than 120 top-20 hits. Many musicologists call Memphis the Holy Ground of American Music. In fact, when the Smithsonian began putting this exhibit together, an official of the National Museum of American History was quoted as saying: "In our quest to identify an American popular music, all roads led to Memphis."

The exhibits feature artifacts, pictures, and, of course, music. With each admission purchased, you get an audio gallery guide with more than 300 minutes of information, more than 100 songs, and interviews of dozens of soul music pioneers. The audio guide lets visitors move at their own pace through the galleries featuring three audiovisual programs, more than 30 instruments, 40 costumes, and other musical treasures.

The museum is open daily, 9:30 a.m. to 7 p.m. Admission is $13 for adults and $10 for ages 5 to 17.

Two white marble lions guard the entrance. A large bronze bell gongs every 90 seconds. With its 50-foot pagoda, tinkling waterfall, goldfish pond, bamboo stands, and strutting pheasants, the home of the giant pandas at the **Memphis Zoo** (2000 Prentiss Place; 901-276-9453; memphiszoo.org) seems like China's Forbidden City. The 3-acre, $16-million China exhibit immerses visitors in the history, culture, and wildlife of China.

The Memphis Zoo has come a long way from its simple beginnings with a bear named Natch. The black bear was a mascot for the Memphis baseball season. After the baseball season ended, Natch was chained to a tree in Overton Park. Col. Robert Galloway took pity on him and began lobbying for funds in 1904 to build Natch a real home. In 1906, the Memphis Zoo opened with 23 simple cages and a row of concrete bear dens. In the 1990s, zoo officials and local folks organized a tremendous fund-raising drive to turn the facility into a world-class zoo. Open all year, the zoo spans 70 acres and is home to over 4,500 animals representing more than 500 species.

A new taste treat awaits at ***Dyers Burgers*** (901-527-3937; dyersonbeale .com) featuring deep-fried hamburgers, and the grease they are cooked in has not been changed since 1912. It has been strained, but the same basic grease has been used all these years, and officials say it has never been allowed to cool and has never been solidified. When the restaurant was moved to 205 Beale St. from another part of town, the truck with the hot grease was given a police escort to make sure they could make it before the grease got cold. Open daily.

For a listing of all the clubs, restaurants, and shops on Beale Street, as well as a listing of concerts and events, visit bealestreet.com.

If it's history you came to Memphis for, take the short trip out to Mud Island, in the Mississippi River across from downtown. The city has developed this area to display its rich river heritage. The ***River Walk*** is a 5-block-long scale model of the entire Lower Mississippi's 1,000 miles from Cairo, Illinois, to the Gulf of Mexico. Every twist, turn, and split that the river makes is shown on the model. Each step equals 1 mile along the mini-river, where each bridge and town is also depicted. Markers along the way point out interesting facts and figures. Water flows down the model into a 1-acre Gulf of Mexico.

A visit to the ***Peabody Hotel*** (149 Union St.; 901-529-4000; peabody memphis.com) in downtown is a must. Built in 1925, the grand hotel has been restored and carries on a tradition started back in the mid-thirties. Each morning at 11 o'clock, five ducks are transported by elevator from their penthouse facilities to the lobby of the hotel.

As the doors slowly open, a red carpet is unrolled from the big fountain to the elevator as the "King Cotton March" is played over the sound system.

With an official Duck Master in control, the ducks waddle to the fountain, where they will spend the day. At 5 p.m. the action is reversed, and the ducks go back to their duck palace on the roof. During the day, if you visit the roof home of the ducks, you'll find a sign on their door proclaiming: GONE TO WORK IN THE LOBBY. BE BACK AT 5 P.M.

To get a prestigious gig like this, a duck first has to be lucky enough to be recruited from a duck farm in Arkansas. Mostly three-year-olds get the job. The lucky duck gets sent to Memphis, where he spends two weeks in training, learning from the veterans already working there. Once he becomes a part of

A SAMPLING OF HISTORIC AFRICAN AMERICAN SITES & ATTRACTIONS

Beck Cultural Exchange Center
1927 Dandridge Ave., Knoxville
(865) 524-8461
beckcenter.net
Archives, research, and museum for the city's African American citizens

Bessie Smith Cultural Center
200 E. Martin Luther King Blvd., Chattanooga
(423) 266-8658
bessiesmithcc.org
Portrays history and culture of Bessie Smith and the city's African Americans and their contributions to society

Bethlehem Cemetery
878 Henning-Bethlehem Rd., Henning
(731) 738-2240
Alex Haley's family burial plot; where Chicken George is buried

Fisk University Historic District
1000 17th Ave. North
Nashville
(615) 329-8500
Founded in 1887 as "free school" for blacks; area consists of vintage buildings, theaters, galleries

Highlander Research Foundation
1959 Highlander Way, New Market
(865) 933-3443
highlandercenter.org
An important training center for the modern civil rights movement; graduates include Dr. Martin Luther King Jr. and Rosa Parks

Meharry Medical College
1005 Dr. D. B. Todd Blvd.
Nashville
(615) 327-6000
mmc.edu
First medical education program in US for African Americans

National Civil Rights Museum
450 Mulberry St., Memphis
(901) 521-9699
civilrightsmuseum.org
Housed in Lorraine Motel, where Martin Luther King Jr. was assassinated

W. C. Handy Home & Museum
352 Beale St., Memphis
(901) 527-3427
wchandymemphis.org
Where W.C. Handy penned his many famous songs' memorabilia and artifacts

the first team, he'll work for about three months before being returned to the farm.

The penthouse is open to visitors, but that's not all you'll find up there. You'll also find a very impressive view of the river and downtown Memphis. Lots to see!

I hope the irony isn't lost that Peabody's famous ducks live just across town from the ***Ducks Unlimited National Headquarters*** (One Waterfowl Way; 901-758-3825; ducks.org). Founded in 1937, the international organization's mission statement reads: "To fulfill the annual life cycle needs of North America's waterfowl by protecting, enhancing, restoring, and managing important wetlands and associated uplands." The headquarters is open for tours Mon through Fri 8 a.m. to 5 p.m. Along the way, you'll see exhibits of DU memorabilia and displays of wetland ecosystems.

Metalsmithing, everything from delicate gold jewelry to massive wrought-iron fencing, is the subject of one of the area's most unusual museums. In downtown Memphis on a bluff overlooking the Mississippi River, the **Metal Museum** (901-774-6380; metalmuseum.org) was opened to the public in 1979 as a memorial to metalsmithing.

Changing exhibits form the basis of the museum, but its permanent collection contains a variety of items from jewelry to handmade nails to large outdoor sculptures to ancient iron locks. In the museum's smithy (anyplace where metal is worked) work is done daily by resident artists and members of museum classes. On the third weekend of October each year, Repair Days are held. People from all over the South bring in their broken metal items to be fixed. On average, 200 metalsmiths are available during that time to repair "broken, bent, or otherwise mutilated metalwork."

Make sure you pay attention to the front gates as you enter. Known as the Anniversary Gates, the tall metal gates contain nearly 200 specially designed rosettes, each made by a different metal craftsman. Each was submitted as part of the museum's tenth anniversary project and placed in an S scroll on the gate. Designs range from the traditional to contemporary, abstract, and whimsical. This is a great piece of unique art, and in no way should you visit Memphis without seeing it.

The grounds immediately surrounding the museum are also unique. Talk about artistic yard art! Wonderful metal sculptures and doodads are placed throughout. In the gazebo, you can see the Mississippi River from high above.

The museum grounds, at 374 Metal Museum Dr. (formerly known as West California), are a part of what was once known as the Marine Hospital, with the oldest of the three large brick buildings dating from 1870. That building was used in the extensive Memphis research that led to a cure for the yellow fever epidemics that once swept the area. The museum's main exhibit building was constructed as a Works Progress Administration (WPA) project in 1932 and once served as a nurses' dormitory for the hospital complex. Admission is charged.

At **Huey's** restaurant and bar (77 S. Second St.; 901-527-2700; hueyburger .com) you are encouraged to use your straw to shoot frill picks into the ceiling! Name another eatery that permits that. The menu consists mostly of burgers, salads, pitas, and other sandwiches. Make sure you bring your Sharpie—you're also allowed to write on the walls. Opens daily at 11 a.m. and closes well after midnight; located across from the Peabody Hotel.

Museum Honors Civil Rights Leader

In this motel room, he ate his last meal and shared a telephone conversation with his mother. Then he stepped onto the upper balcony, waved to a minister down below, and responded to a question about his favorite church hymn—"Precious Lord."

Suddenly the peaceful scene exploded. Shots fired from across the street ripped through his throat, hitting him with such force that his shoes were knocked off his feet. Dr. Martin Luther King Jr. crumpled to the concrete as pandemonium broke loose.

On April 4, 1968, King was gunned down at the Lorraine Motel in Memphis. Almost 40 years later, the motel where he died and the rooming house where his assassin allegedly fired the fatal shots are now the **National Civil Rights Museum** (901-521-9699; civilrightsmuseum.org) at 450 Mulberry St. A wreath was put on the railing shortly after the assassination and one has been maintained ever since as a reminder of the place Dr. King last stood. The room where he spent his last night alive has been reconstructed and preserved.

The museum is particularly effective because it is not a replica of an historic site. It's the actual place. The doors of the National Civil Rights Museum opened in 1991, and the facility has been expanded over the years to include the boarding house where James Earl Ray allegedly fired the fatal shot.

Shortly after the murder, when people began flocking to the spot where the 39-year-old King died to silently pay their respects, Lorraine Motel owner Walter Bailey knew he must protect a piece of history. When people began to plan for a civil rights museum, the logical location was the site where the great civil rights leader was slain.

The main exhibits in the museum are vignettes capturing the essence of key events during the civil rights movement, from struggles in the courts to struggles in the streets. Exhibits include Little Rock, the Montgomery Bus Boycott, Student Sit-Ins, Freedom Rides, the Letter from Birmingham Jail, March from Selma to Montgomery, and the People of Memphis.

In 1968, racial tension was simmering just below the surface in Memphis. It needed only one spark to erupt into violence. That was provided by a city sanitation workers strike in February. That is what brought Dr. King to Memphis.

The civil rights leader had come to lead a march supporting the striking sanitation workers. When King was in Memphis, he always stayed in the Lorraine Motel, owned by an African American and one of the nicest places in town where African Americans could stay.

The morning of April 4 dawned damp and cool. King slept late in Room 306. Around noon, King and the Rev. Ralph Abernathy shared a lunch sent up—catfish, hush puppies, and potatoes. Room 307 was used by King's entourage and for meetings. It was from Room 307 that King stepped onto the balcony.

Across the street at the new addition, visitors can examine investigative materials and a video presentation about Ray. Prosecutors said Ray fired the fatal shot from the bathroom of the rooming house. Visitors can see a reproduction of the bathroom as it was when the shooting happened. Witnesses said that moments after the shooting, they saw Ray running from the building carrying a bundle.

Ray fled abroad and moved from city to city. On June 8, he was finally apprehended at London's Heathrow Airport. Ray reportedly put his head in his hands and wept when authorities confronted him. The FBI quickly identified Ray as the primary suspect. Authorities found Ray's fingerprints on the rifle, a scope, and a pair of binoculars He pleaded guilty in March 1969 and was given a 99-year prison sentence. Ray later recanted his guilty plea. He died at age 70 in prison in 1998 of liver failure.

Soul music was practically invented in Memphis, mostly in a small neighborhood just south of downtown known today as ***Soulsville, USA***. Stax Records and Hi Records were both located in this area in the late 1950s, and this is where the greatest soul singers of all time were born, lived, or recorded. Aretha Franklin was born in the neighborhood, and the likes of Al Green, Ann Peebles, Rufus Thomas, Maurice White, Isaac Hayes, and Booker T. and the MGs spent countless hours here.

The center of attraction was the Stax Records studio, where the hottest soul records of all time were recorded between 1959 and 1975. During that 15-year period, Stax released 300 LPs and more than 800 singles. An incredible 167 singles made it to the top 100 Pop Chart, and 243 made it to the Top 100 on the R&B charts.

The ***Stax Museum of American Soul Music*** (926 E. McLemore Ave.; 901-942-7685; staxmuseum.com) is now on the same corner where Stax Records once stood. Run by a nonprofit group for inner-city youth, the museum showcases an amazing collection of more than 2,000 artifacts, photos, and exhibits. Along with a running historical commentary and the legendary Stax Sound, the museum also spotlights the music of Muscle Shoals, Motown, Hi, and Atlantic Records.

The "real-cool" exhibits include Isaac Hayes's 1972 gold-trimmed, peacock blue "Superfly" Cadillac, Phalon Jones's saxophone recovered from the lake where the airplane of Otis Redding and the Bar-Kays crashed, and Albert King's famous purple "Flying V" guitar.

It's open daily year-round Tues through Sun 10 a.m. to 5 p.m. Closed Mon. Admission is $13 for adults, $12 for seniors; and $10 for children ages 9 to 12. Children 8 and under and museum members get in free. The gift shop has a super selection of music to buy. A good website to surf for additional Memphis music attractions and links is memphislocal.com.

Bringing Salt Cave to Memphis

Lean back, close your eyes. Breathe the salty air. Hear the whisper of the wind. Imagine the surf rolling in to caress the shore. Seems like a leisurely day on some faraway beach. But it's not. It's a re-created therapeutic salt cave right in Memphis.

"It's maybe the closest you can get to the ocean without actually going there," said Karen Moss at *Better Bodies Yoga* (692 W. Brookhaven Cir.; 901-618-2878; better bodiesyoga.com) in Memphis. "Our salt room is a magical place."

To start with the history first, halotherapy—derived from the Greek word "halos" which means "salt"—is an alternative medicine which makes use of salt. Halotherapy has its origins from the salt mines of Europe and Russia where salt miners were found to rarely suffer from respiratory ailments or lung diseases.

People with respiratory problems quickly began heading to salt mines for treatment. Then, about 25 years ago, Russian medical experts discovered a way to duplicate the dry salt microclimate of a salt mine. The result was indoor reproductions of salt mines. Although halotherapy is relatively new to America, the concept has quickly caught on and people who use them attest to the health benefits.

Moss said she knows first-hand of the benefits of salt caves. "I suffer from allergies, sinusitis, headaches, and skin rashes all year long, and have had two sinus surgeries in the past," Moss said. "I felt that taking so many antibiotics was not good for my immune system, and started seeking more natural ways to deal with my chronic symptoms."

Most salt caves have walls lined with pink Himalayan salt and floors covered with pink Himalayan salt pebbles. Some have a halogenerator which grinds pharmaceutical grade sodium chloride into a mist and filtrates it through a vent in the room with a pleasant whooshing sound. Recliners, heated beds, twinkle lights in the ceiling, soothing music, and different colored lights for chromotherapy (light therapy) also are often used in salt caves. A usual therapy might last 45 minutes to an hour.

Moss also said that her salt cave and yoga studio are a loving legacy to her parents who both died of cancer. "I believe my parents would have enjoyed and benefited from being in the salt caves since they also suffered from allergies and stress," she said. "I started a free yoga program in memory of my parents for individuals who have cancer, are survivors, and for their support person. We still offer those free classes on Saturday afternoons."

The *National Civil Rights Museum* (450 Mulberry St.; 901-521-9699; civilrightsmuseum.org) is the nation's first museum dedicated to documenting the complete history of the American civil rights movement. Constructed around the Lorraine Motel, where Dr. Martin Luther King Jr. was assassinated on April 4, 1968, the center features an interpretive education center, audiovisual displays, interactive exhibits, and civil rights memorabilia. Large exhibits portray several memorable moments in the movement, including the arrest of Rosa Parks for not moving to the back of the bus when requested, the sanitation workers' strike in Memphis, and the assassination of Dr. King.

King used to stay in Room 307 at the motel when he came to Memphis, and it was outside that room on the balcony that he was shot. Visitors can now look into that room and be immersed in the assassination story. It's quite moving, and if you see nothing else, this is the one exhibit you shouldn't miss. The museum is open daily year-round 9 a.m. to 5 p.m. Closed Tues. Admission is $17 for adults, $15 for seniors and students, $14 for ages 5 to 17.

Danny Thomas, entertainer, humanitarian, and founder of **St. Jude Children's Research Hospital** (901-578-2042; stjude.org), is buried in a memorial garden in front of the hospital, next to a beautiful pavilion that features his life, his career, and his love for his fellow man. There are videos of his *Make Room for Daddy* television series and a wall full of photos of Thomas posed with other legendary stars. In addition, there are hundreds of personal items and most of the trophies and awards he won during his illustrious career. Located in downtown Memphis at 332 N. Lauderdale, the pavilion and gardens are open 7 days a week from 8 a.m. The pavilion closes at 4 p.m., the memorial garden at 5 p.m. Admission is free.

The **Crystal Shrine Grotto** (5668 Poplar Ave.; 901-302-9980), inside the **Memorial Park Cemetery**, is a must-stop if you're looking for the unusual in unusual locations. A unique cave was constructed by cemetery founder Clovis Hinds and Mexican artist Dionicio Rodriquez during the period of 1935–38. The cave and exterior environs were built of concrete in imitation of rocks, boulders, and trees. The entranceway appears to be through a tree trunk.

Natural rock and quartz crystal collected from the Ozarks form the background for nine different scenes from the life of Christ. Because of those scenes, the local kids often call the cavern the Jesus Cave. It's beautiful and quite an unusual work of naturalistic art. The shrine is open daily 6 a.m. to 10 p.m., just off I-240 east of downtown.

In **Mason**, just across the Tipton County line at 342 Hwy. 70, is **Bozo's Hot Pit Bar-B-Que** (901-294-3400; bozoshotpitbar-b-q.com). Look for one of those tiled cafe buildings that dotted America's landscape in the 1950s, and you'll find Bozo's.

Founded in 1923 by Bozo Williams, the restaurant stayed in the family until 2001, when Hayne Ozier purchased it from Bozo's great-grandson. Famous for its pork shoulder barbecue sandwiches and plates, Bozo's has a full menu that has not changed since shortly after World War II. Save room for a piece of Ms. Perry's famous pie. Having never advertised, the restaurant's 100 seats are filled by longtime customers and newcomers who have heard about the place from

andthebelltolls

The bell on top of the gingerbread-enhanced Carpenter Gothic Cottage, inside the Elmwood Cemetery, tolls for each interment today, just as it has since 1870. The 80-acre, circa 1852 cemetery is now the eternal home to two governors, four US senators, 22 mayors, soldiers from all US wars, including 19 Confederate generals, and an array of jazz singers, madams, suffragists, and beer drinkers. Purchase a map or rent an audio car-tour tape at the cottage and take a tour of this beautiful parklike facility. It's located at 824 S. Dudley St. Call (901) 774-3212, or visit elmwoodcemetery.org.

a friend. On weekends about 50 percent of the business comes from Memphis, 35 miles away. Bozo's is open Tues through Thurs 10:30 a.m. to 8 p.m., Fri and Sat 10:30 a.m. to 9 p.m. and offers the same menu items all day.

Farther north on US 51 in Tipton County is **Covington**, where you'll find an eclectic architectural area known as the **South Main Historic District** (901-476-7163; covingtontn.com). In all, there are more than 50 different structures reflecting "architectural styles that were sought by the emerging, affluent members of society in the late 19th and early 20th century," reads the historic marker. Among the styles represented: American four-square, prairie bungalow, colonial revival, and Queen Anne.

The restored **Ruffin Theater** (113 W. Pleasant Ave.; 901-610-6076; ruffin.theater) is part of the historic district. Built in the art deco style in 1937, it now serves as a performing arts center for the community.

Over in **Brownsville**, West Tennessee's most unusual outdoor sculpture is located 3 blocks from the courthouse on W. Main Street. Reaching heights of 75 feet, **Mindfield** is a work in progress by local artist and welder Billy Tripp, who lives in his welding shop behind the sculpture. The huge, eclectic steel structure symbolizes life and the process of growing up, and it's up to all who see it to interpret it for themselves. He adds to it constantly and says he will do so for as long as he physically can.

Nestled among the old structures in Brownsville College Hill historic district is the **Haywood County Museum** at 127 N. Grand Ave. The center houses the **Morton Felsenthal Lincoln Collection**. Now the property of the city, the large collection of books and memorabilia concerning the 16th US president is an all-encompassing exhibit.

A walking tour of the historic homes in this area is available; brochures can be obtained at the Brownsville-Haywood County Chamber of Commerce (731-772-2193) at 121 W. Main St.

The blues music heritage is alive and well and in good hands around here. The annual **Hatchie Fall Fest** (731-772-2193; hatchiefallfest.com) is held in late September or early October and features live music, a baking contest, cornhole contest, and various children's activities. The **West Tennessee Delta Heritage Center** (121 Sunny Hill Cove; 731-779-9000; westtnheritage.com), at exit 56 off I-40, is probably the state's coolest visitor center. Not only can you obtain information for the entire Western Plains area of Tennessee here, but there's also a museum with four major exhibit areas, a gift shop offering the work of regional artisans, an ATM, the Sleepy John Estes house, and an outside area, where concerts are held to promote the arts and musical heritage of the area.

The four exhibit areas are the Tennessee Room, which showcases West Tennessee towns and attractions; the **West Tennessee Music Museum**, highlighting such area talent as Tina Turner, Eddy Arnold, T. J. Shepherd, and Carl Perkins; the Scenic Hatchie River Museum, explaining the entire river watershed and ecosystem; and the Cotton Museum, which shows how cotton has affected the lives of West Tennesseans and its economic impact upon the area.

The house where **Sleepy John Estes** last strummed his guitar is part of the center. This is where the blues legend was living when he died in 1977. There are photos and memorabilia, and blues music fills the house. Open Apr to Sept, Mon through Sat 9 a.m. to 6 p.m., Sun 10 a.m. to 5 p.m.; Oct to Mar, Mon through Sat 9 a.m. to 5 p.m., Sun 1 p.m. to 5 p.m.

Up Highway 19 from Brownsville, in the small community of **Nutbush**, Anna Mae Bullock was born on November 26, 1939, to sharecropper parents. She was a young girl surrounded by cotton fields and plenty of dreams. With a few lucky breaks and an immense amount of talent, this young lady moved away, got married, and became Tina Turner, Queen of Rock 'n' Roll.

She immortalized her hometown in her 1973 hit, "Nutbush City Limits," and she was inducted into the Rock and Roll Hall of Fame in 1991. The sharecropper's shack in which she was born has long since disappeared, but the farm where that shack stood is still there. A sign now marks the farm, located on Highway 19 adjacent to the cotton gin.

After two years of restoration, the Tina Turner Museum opened September 26, 2014, in the historic blacks-only one-room schoolhouse she attended as a child. Inside the former Flagg Grove

onthebeatenpath

Interstate highways—you know, those concrete ribbons that cross the state and all look the same? Well, there are 1,074 miles of them in Tennessee, and although they can save time, they certainly aren't the way to go if you want to see more than cows and billboards. Want to avoid truck traffic? Stay off the interstates! In 2012, more than 12.5 million semitrucks and commercial vehicles stopped at the state's five interstate weigh stations.

School, visitors can see Turner's stage outfits, gold and platinum records, photos, and other memorabilia. The school was located in Nutbush until it was moved to the West Tennessee Delta Heritage Center. Admission is free.

Henning, the boyhood home of the late author Alex Haley, is a picturesque town of Victorian homes and turn-of-the-20th-century storefronts. The town probably would have progressed quietly like many small towns had it not been for native son Haley.

His 1976 Pulitzer prize-winning novel, **Roots**, and the subsequent TV miniseries, based on the family stories his grandmother and aunt told him, brought international fame to Henning, where Haley's family home is now the *Alex Haley House Museum and Interpretive Center* (731-738-2240; alexhaley.com).

Those stories inspired Haley to research his family members who were brought to America as slaves, and the book came as a result. He recalls sitting on the front porch of his boyhood home and listening for hours to the stories.

Haley's museum by description is a "tribute to Kunta Kinte's worldwide family." Built in 1918 by a Kunta Kinte descendant, the house has been restored and serves not only as a tribute to Haley but also as a good example of rural small-town life in West Tennessee. It is also the first African American state historic site and the only writer's home open to the public in Tennessee.

Following his death on February 10, 1992, Haley was buried in the front yard of the house, and his grave site is available for viewing at any time.

The center showcases a new exhibit gallery that has a large model of a slave ship, Haley's iconic eyeglasses, his childhood violin, genealogical charts, a video interview with Haley, a replica of the Haley home front porch where family stories were passed down, and more. Located at 200 S. Church St. at Haley Avenue, the museum is open Tues through Sat 10 a.m. to 5 p.m. Admission charged.

In a bright red caboose in downtown Henning on Main Street, adjacent to the city hall, the area's historical society has its records and artifacts on display in its heritage museum. If you'd like to visit, go into city hall and someone will come out and unlock the doors for you. Open hours are scarce and sporadic. To be sure not to miss it, call first at (731) 738-5055.

North of Henning, just off US 51 is *Ripley*, the seat of Lauderdale County. Believe it or not, this place has a wonderful array of interesting buildings, including two magnificent structures created by the Works Progress Administration in the 1930s. On Court Square is the *Lauderdale County Courthouse*, which is listed on the National Register of Historic Places. The center of the lobby has a colorful map, made of tile, of the county.

At 117 E. Jackson St. is the Ripley post office. In the lobby of this WPA structure, which is listed on the National Historical Register of Post Offices, is a beautiful oil mural, worth a stop even if you don't need stamps. Phone them at (731) 635-9691. The bell in use when the First Presbyterian Church (130 N. Jefferson St.; 731-635-9751) opened in 1892 is still in service today and is made of the silver dollars donated to the bell fund.

Farther north on US 51 is **Halls**. Among its interesting structures is its public library, housed in an original 1930s-era art deco building at 110 N. Church St., formerly a Sinclair service station. Call for hours open: (731) 836-5302.

believe**itor**not!

Remember the 1986 Hands Across America effort to help raise awareness and money for the homeless? Americans joined hands from New York to Los Angeles, and the halfway point was at the intersection of Cleveland Street and US 51 in Ripley, Tennessee.

More than 20,000 bales of what the locals call White Gold are processed each fall at the Halls (cotton) Gin Company. Located at 1279 Industrial Rd., this modern, computerized gin is adjacent to the Halls Dyersburg Army Airbase, where an exceptional air show takes place each year.

While in Halls, stop by and meet Murray Hudson, who owns and operates **Hudson's Antiquarian Maps, Globes, Books & Prints** (109 S. Church St.; 800 748-9946; antiquemapsandglobes.com). It's a collector's paradise where you'll find maps, globes, and books. It's kinda cool to see all those globes when you first walk in, and Murray, a former English teacher, certainly looks the part of a map and globe collector!

Here's one for the "engineers" who are looking for off-the-beaten-path mechanical wonders. Outside Dyersburg is the world's only surviving "swing span, pony Pratt through truss bridge." Known for the town from which it came, the **Lenox Bridge**, as it is now called, was built in 1917 and moved and restored in 1985. The bridge was positioned for land travel. When a ship would need to go through, it would blow its whistle to alert the bridge tender, who would come down, walk out to the center pier, and crank the bridge open by hand. The bridge would turn away from both riverbanks and line up out of the way of the ship in the middle of the river, parallel with the shores, supported only in the center.

The bridge is 150 feet in length and 14 feet wide, and the pier is 18 feet in diameter. Jere Kirk, whose grandfather helped with the construction of the original bridge, bought and refurbished it. It is now on display over a body of water in the Lakewood subdivision. Take Highway 78 north out of Dyersburg. From I-155, go 2.7 miles and turn left on Highway 182 South. Go 1 mile and turn left into Lakewood. Stay right; the bridge is on your right, just past the lake.

Delta Flyway

The $10 million ***Discovery Park of America*** (830 Everett Blvd.; 731-885-5455; discoveryparkofamerica.com) in Union City is a 50-acre complex offering education and entertainment. The complex has more than 70,000 square feet of exhibits focused on nature, science, technology, history, and art. The focal point of the new park is Discovery Center, a 100,000-square-foot building with 10 exhibit galleries—Children's Exploration, Energy, Enlightenment, Military, Native Americans, Natural History, Regional History, Science/Space/Technology, and Transportation.

You can feel a theater simulation of the 1811–12 earthquakes that shaped the land in this region. Marvel at a planetary tour in the starship theater. Glimpse underwater life of ***Reelfoot Lake*** in a 20,000-gallon aquarium. Zoom down a 30-foot slide that is part of a 60-foot replica of a human body.

On the grounds of Discovery Park is a 100-year-old church as well as a train station with a locomotive and various cars. Visitors also can see a replica of the Liberty Bell, along with log cabins, farm buildings and equipment, and family items that illustrate rural life in the 1800s.

A water feature flows north to south, bisecting the site. Starting at a circa 1800s gristmill, the feature include waterfalls and bridges, plus a heap of lovely landscaping. Japanese, European, and American gardens allow visitors to enjoy nature and learn about plants and flowers from around the world.

Gun collectors worldwide probably already know about this city's ***Dixie Gun Works and Old Car Museum*** (1412 W. Reelfoot Ave.; 731-885-0561; dixiegunworks.com), while noncollectors across town may have never heard of it. Founded by the late Turner Kirkland in the early 1950s, the business is now considered the world's largest supplier of antique guns and parts. The firm sells about 80,000 guns a year, including antique reproductions.

At any given time a walk through the Dixie Gun Works' showroom is like walking through an antique firearms museum, except that you can buy most of the guns you see here. Usually, more than 1,500 guns are on display. Kirkland's other passion, antique automobiles, is also in evidence. Adjacent to the gun showroom is an auto museum with 36 old cars, including a 1908 Maxwell.

A small log cabin gunshop is a part of this attraction. Originally built in this area around 1850, the shop contains two rifling machines and more than 1,000 gun-making tools. The complex is located on the Highway 51S Union City Bypass. The museum is open Mon through Fri 8 a.m. to 5 p.m., Sun 8 a.m. to noon. Admission is charged for this interesting museum.

Adjacent to the county courthouse, in the center of Union City, is the ***Flame of Freedom***, an eternal flame dedicated to "all veterans of Obion

County in all wars and conflicts, past, present, and future." It was dedicated in 1971. Along the railroad tracks on South Depot Street next to the municipal building, Kiwanis Park offers a nice place to rest for a spell. Make note of the Confederate monument in the park. It's one of the few in the South that looks north. There's a band shell, fountains, playground equipment, and plenty of huge shade trees.

At the end of Edwards Street is the first monument erected in honor of the unknown Confederate soldier. It was dedicated on October 21, 1869.

If it's architecture you like, don't overlook the **First Christian Church** at W. Lee and S. Second Streets. The circa 1912 domed church is the third to be built on the site. The bell that is on display on the church lawn was the first bell of the brick church built on this site after the 1862 destruction of the 1857 frame church by Union forces. Check out the beautiful stained-glass windows of the church.

The **Masquerade Theatre Company**, a community theater group in Union City, raised the money to buy and has now restored the beautiful circa 1927 **Capitol Theater**, at 118 S. First St. Through the years, it was used as a film house, a stage for traveling legitimate theater, and a vaudeville stage. The theater group will produce several shows a year in the 364-seat venue now named **Masquerade Theatre** (ucmasqueradetheatre.com) and will host a bevy of local entertainment events such as recitals. If you're hungry for what a lot of people around here consider the best cheeseburger in the world, stop by **P.V.'s Hut** (209 E. Florida Ave.; 731-885-5737). It's open Tues through Sat 11 a.m. to 7 p.m.

Following World War II, housing was in demand throughout the US, as a result many all-steel prefabricated homes were built. They were quick to put up and reasonably inexpensive for the returning servicemen. Only one remains in Obion County. It's at 1020 Church St. and has been maintained quite nicely through the years.

A couple streets over in the oldest residential neighborhood in town, the home of Lexie Parks still stands at 822 E. Main. The house contains the first elevator in town— and the ghost of the wealthy Mr. Parks. He was killed in the house by his butler, who was never convicted of the crime. Residents who have lived here since have documented Parks and his congenial hauntings as he walks through the house. It seems he is upset that the butler got away with the murder.

Additional information about Union City and Obion County can be had by contacting the chamber of commerce at (731) 885-0211 or obioncounty.org.

Reelfoot Lake is the result of a true quirk of nature. The worst earthquake ever measured in American history took place in this area in 1812. On February

The "Real Legend" of Reelfoot

Once upon a time in the early 1800s, there ruled a mighty Chickasaw chieftain whose only son had a deformed foot. The son ran with a rolling motion, so the tribe nick-named him Kaolin, meaning "Reelfoot." When the son became chief and was to be married, he found he had no feelings for any maidens in his tribe.

He went searching for a wondrous beauty and found her among the Choctaws. She was the daughter of the chief. Reelfoot immediately fell under the spell of the prin-cess and asked her father to allow a marriage.

The old chief replied: "It is true that my daughter is enchanting, and she will only be given in wedlock to a Choctaw chieftain. I will not ever permit her to join a tribe which is so unfortunate as to have a clubfooted chieftain." Reelfoot was more determined than ever, but the Great Spirit had a few words for him. "An Indian must not take his wife from a neighboring tribe, and if you disobey and take the princess, I will cause the earth to rock and the waters to swallow up your village and bury your people in a watery grave."

Reelfoot chose not to believe the Great Spirit, and within months he had captured the princess and brought her back to West Tennessee. As the marriage rites took place, the earth began to roll, and Reelfoot cried out for mercy on his people. The Great Spirit answered, "I will show you and your people mercy, but you will have to pay for your disobedience. I will form a lake where I stamp my foot, and you and your people will forever watch over the lake, for I will rest your souls in the cypress."

The 1812 earthquake continued, the lands dropped, and the Mississippi River filled the new basin. Cypress trees became abundant, and Reelfoot Lake was formed.

7 the quake hit, and the lands of northwest Tennessee near the Mississippi River dropped as much as 20 feet.

For 15 minutes, the river's water flowed backward to fill this major void, which had been a swampy forestland. Now the area is a 13,000-acre shallow lake, an average of 5.2 feet deep, with the remains of the forest just under the surface, which makes boating quite an adventure. The water is a dark green color, with visibility never more than a few inches. The area surrounding the lake is now a state park, and a journey through here is truly a trek into unspoiled nature. The combination of shaggy cypress trees, some of them cen-turies old, and water lilies is most unusual for this state.

Reelfoot Lake is the winter home to more than 100 American bald eagles. The birds, with wingspans of 6 to 8 feet, come here from their northern sum-mer homes to spend the winter in a warmer, ice-free environment. The park provides numerous eagle programs, including bus tours of the area, during winter.

The park's museum offers the chance to experience an earthquake firsthand. The 1812 quake has been reproduced, to a lesser degree, and allows guests to feel and hear what took place during those 15 minutes. You can also sit in a stump jumper; learn about its creators, the Calhoun family; see Native American artifacts; and read firsthand accounts of the creation of the lake. The museum is also the loading site for the lake's sightseeing cruises. The museum is open daily 8 a.m. to 4:30 p.m. Call (731) 253-9652.

Deep Swamp Canoe Trips are offered by the museum every Mar and Apr on Sat and Sun at noon. Cost is $20 if a state park canoe is used. Private canoes are no charge. Reservations required. Call (731) 253-9652. Join park naturalists for canoe trips into the old-growth cypress forest of Reelfoot Lake. As the canoe glides around huge cypress trees, watch for a variety of birds, including a nesting pair of bald eagles. Canoe participants are advised to bring snacks, drinks, change of clothes, camera, and binoculars in a waterproof floatable container.

The park has camping sites, a camp store, and hiking trails. Guided "swamp tromps" are offered during the year. The entrance to the park is located off Highway 21.

A fantastic place to stay while you're in this area is the *Blue Bank Resort* (813 Lake Dr.; 877-258-3226; bluebankresort.com), on Highway 21 a few miles east of Tiptonville. Located on the water's edge, the rooms are rustic in style but are new and offer great views of the lake. The water practically comes up to your door! Rates start at $149 per night, per room. Special hunting and fishing packages, which include lodging, boat, motor, bait, and ice, are available and can save you quite a bit of money.

The *Blue Bank Fish House & Grill* (813 Lake Dr.; 877-258-3226; bluebankresort.com/fishhouse-restaurant). The restaurant opens early each morning with a hearty breakfast and has steaks, quail, frog legs, crappie, country ham, ribs, and chicken for dinner.

wildlifegalore

Reelfoot Lake is an oasis for wildlife because of its shallow, pristine waters, marshlands, and dense stands of bald cypress trees. In addition to the 100-plus American bald eagles that winter there each year, more than 60,000 geese and a quarter million ducks visit the area annually. There are also 54 species of fish in the lake, and there have been 53 mammal species spotted in the area. Who counts these things anyway? What a job!

Places to Stay in the Western Plains

BUCHANAN

Paris Landing/Kentucky Lake KOA Holiday
6290 E. Antioch Rd.
(731) 642-6895
koa.com/campgrounds/paris-landing

CAMDEN

Birdsong Resort and Marina
255 Marina Rd.
(731) 584-7880
birdsong.com

COUNCE

Little Andy's Sportsman's Lodge
7255 Hwy. 57
(731) 689-3750
littleandysmotel.net

Pickwick Landing Inn & Conference Center
120 Playground Loop
(800) 250-8615
Tnstateparks.com

JACKSON

Highland Place Bed and Breakfast
519 N. Highland Ave.
(731) 427-1472
highlandplace.com

MEDINA

Peaceful Oaks Bed Breakfast and Barn
636 Barnes Rd.
(731) 697-4252
peacefuloaksbandb.com

MEMPHIS

ARRIVE Memphis
477 S. Main St.
(901) 701-7575
arrivehotels.com

Big Cypress Lodge
1 Bass Pro Dr.
(901) 620-4600
big-cypress.com

Graceland RV Park & Campground
3691 Elvis Presley Blvd.
(901) 396-7125
graceland.com

Guest House at Graceland
3600 Elvis Presley Blvd.
(901) 443-3000
guesthousegraceland.com

Hostel Memphis
1000 Cooper St.
(901) 270-6980
hostelmemphis.com

Hu Hotel
79 Madison Ave.
(833) 585-0030
huhotelmemphis.com

James Lee House
690 Adams Ave.
(901) 359-6750
jamesleehouse.com

Madison Hotel Memphis
79 Madison Ave.
(901) 333-1200
madisonhotelmemphis.com

Peabody Hotel Memphis
149 Union Ave.
(901) 529-4000
peabodymemphis.com

River Inn of Harbor Town
50 Harbor Town Sq.
(901) 260-3333
riverinnmemphis.com

PARIS

Home Sweet Home Bed and Breakfast
108 N. College St.
(731) 642-8135

PICKWICK DAM

Pickwick Landing State Park Inn
Highway 57
(800) 250-8615

SPRINGVILLE

Mammy & Pappy's Bed & Breakfast
7615 Elkhorn Rd.
(731) 642-8129
mammy-pappysbb.com

Pleasant View Resort
289 Pleasant View Resort Rd.
(731) 593-5511
pleasantviewresort.us

TIPTONVILLE

Blue Bank Resort
Highway 21
813 Lake Dr.
(877) 258-3226
bluebankresort.com

Blue Basin Cove Lodge
100 Blue Basin Rd.
(731) 253-9064
bluebasincovelodge.com

WILDERSVILLE

Pin Oak Lodge and Restaurant
567 Pin Oak Lodge Rd.
(731) 968-8176
Tnstateparks.com

Places to Eat in the Western Plains

DECATURVILLE

Little Josh's Restaurant
4238 US 412
(731) 847-9005

Ramey's Bar B Que
14 Holley St
(731) 847-7714

HORNBEAK

Blue Bank Fish House & Grill
813 Lake Dr.
(877) 258-3226
bluebankresort.com

DD's Diner
203 W. Main St.
(731) 907-1010

Pier Restaurant
600 E. Lakeview Dr.
(731) 538-2803

JACKSON

Brooksie's Barn
561 Oil Well Rd.
(731) 664-2276
brooksiesbarn.com

Casey Jones Village
56 Casey Jones Ln.
(800) 748-9588
caseyjones.com

Chandelier
575 S. Royal St.
(731) 554-2221
chandelierjackson.com

Old Town Spaghetti Store
550 Carriage House Dr.
(731) 668-4937
oldtownspaghettistore.com

Rafferty's
162 Old Hickory Blvd.
(731) 664-8118
raffertys.com

Redbones Grill & Bar
584 Carriage House Dr.
(731) 660-3838
redbonesgrillandbar.com

MASON

Bozo's Hot Pit Bar-B-Que
342 Hwy. 70
(901) 294-3400
Bozoshotpitbar-b-q.com

MEMPHIS

Andrew Michael
712 W. Brookhaven Cir.
(901) 347-3569
Andrewmichaelitalian
kitchen.com

Arcade Restaurant
540 S. Main St.
(901) 526-5757
arcaderestaurant.com

Automatic Slim's
83 S. Second St.
(901) 525-7948
automaticslimsmemphis
.com

Charles Vergo's Rendezvous
52 S. Second St.
(901) 523-2746
hogsfly.com

Chez Phillippe
149 Union Ave.
(901) 529-4188
peabodymemphis.com

Dyers Burgers
205 Beale St.
(901) 527-3937
dyersonbeale.com

Flight Restaurant and Wine Bar
39 S. Main St.
(901) 521-8005
flightmemphis.com

Gus's World Famous Fried Chicken
310 S. Front St.
(901) 527-4877
gusfriedchicken.com

Huey's
77 S. Second St.
(901) 527-2700
hueyburger.com

Iris
2146 Monroe Ave.
(901) 590-2828
restaurantiris.com

Maciel's
45 S. Main St.
(901) 526-0037
macielsdowntown.com

McEwen's
120 Monroe Ave.
(901) 527-7085
Mcewensmemphis.com

Paulette's Restaurant
50 Harbor Town Sq.
(901) 260-3300
Paulettes.net

Seasons 52
6085 Poplar Ave.
(901) 682-9952
seasons52.com

Soul Fish Café
4720 Poplar Ave.
(901) 590-0323
soulfishcafe.com

PARIS

Prater's Taters
1055 Minerals Wells Ave.
(731) 642-7224
praterstaters.com

SAVANNAH

Dae Break Café
990 Pickwick St.
(731) 438-3461

Hickory Pit
555 Main St.
(731) 925-2268

Mollie Monday's
275 Eureka St.
(731) 925-9334

SELMER

Pappy Johns Original Barbecue
On US 45 South
(731) 645-4353
Pappy-johns-original-barbecue.business.site

Rockabilly Café
103 S. Front St.
(731) 645-6070

TIPTONVILLE

Boyette's Dining Room
10 Boyette Rd.
(731) 253-7307

Sherry's Kuntry Kupboard
350 Carl Perkins Pkwy.
(731) 623-4184

Index